By the hard work of others, w
to the most beautiful things th ... ugged
out of darkness and into the light.
Everyone is invited to experience the light
of every age and every people.
So, let us walk hand in hand with those from every age.
Let us turn from this brief and transient time
and offer our minds and hearts to the past,
which is long and eternal.

—Seneca, *On the Shortness of Life*

THE CLASSICS CAVE
Sugar Land

THE CLASSICS CAVE
the earliest light for a brighter life
www.theclassicscave.com

ARE YOU looking for the best books ever? Or new ways to read and benefit from them? Let The Classics Cave be your guide!

THE CLASSICS CAVE is an educational organization centered on the classics of antiquity, with an emphasis on Greece and Rome.

OUR MISSION is to shine the light of the past into the present for a brighter life today.

OUR GOAL is practice—the application of ancient wisdom and ways to our contemporary lives.

WE develop and provide online materials, organize and do outreach, and produce and distribute a variety of print and other media intended to entertain and educate, cultivate and motivate.

VISIT The Classics Cave online (www.theclassicscave.com) to support our mission and to access a growing catalogue of engaging books, useful goods, and other helpful materials for educators and all others interested in benefiting from ancient literature.

SUPPORT The Classics Cave by telling others about our work and by leaving a positive review online. Thanks!

IN PRAISE & RECOGNITION OF THE ANCIENT GREEKS

"All the branches of [Greek] learning . . . contain also liberal instruction that is better adapted to the use of truth, and some most excellent precepts of morality."
—Augustine of Hippo, *On Christian Doctrine*

"Philosophy . . . is the clear image of truth, a divine gift to the Greeks." —Clement of Alexandria, *Stromata*

"In Greek philosophy we watch problems come to light that have by no means lost their relevance for us, we find answers suggested that are not without value. . . . Greek philosophy remains one of the glories of the European achievement."
—Frederick Copleston, *A History of Philosophy*

"Of all peoples the Greeks have best dreamed the dream of life."
—Johann Wolfgang von Goethe, *Maxims and Reflections*

"The only literature, to which I would allow a place in the ordinary curriculum, are those of the Greeks and Romans . . . While, in studying the great writers of antiquity, we are not only learning to understand the ancient mind, but laying in a stock of wise thought and observation . . . the treasure which they accumulated of what may be called the wisdom of life. . . . All that is left to us of the ancient historians, orators, philosophers, and even dramatists, are replete with remarks and maxims of singular good sense and penetration, applicable to both political and to private life."
—John Stuart Mill, *Address at the University of St. Andrews*

"To know himself a man must know the capabilities and performances of the human spirit. The value of the humanities—of *Altertumswissenschaft*, the science of antiquity—is that it affords for this purpose an unsurpassed source of light and stimulus. Whoever seeks help for knowing himself from knowing the capabilities and performances of the human spirit, will nowhere find a more fruitful object of study than the achievements of Greece in literature and the arts."

—Matthew Arnold, *The Higher Schools & Universities in Germany*

"To whatever heights you ascend in literature the Greeks are always there. Literature is one of the greatest forces in the world and always has been and always will be so. It comes to us with open hand, offering us knowledge, spiritual inspiration, the vast world created by human imagination, laughter and tears, happiness, sympathy, enjoyment, forgetfulness. Over a large part of this spacious kingdom of the mind rule Greece and Rome."

—Senator Henry Cabot Lodge, from *Value of the Classics*

"That is why the Greeks maintain a hold on education. With a clearness of thought and expression, . . . they offer us many things—unsurpassed achievements in art and literature, the example of a rich, complete life, the spectacle of reason incarnate, reason in religion, politics, philosophy, history, letters, life. They knew less than we, but they had more of the spirit which begets knowledge."

—Richard W. Livingstone, *A Defense of Classical Education*

"Our whole civilization is rooted in the history of these peoples [Greece and Rome], and without knowledge of them cannot be properly understood. The small city communities of Greece created intellectual life in Europe. In their literature we find models of thought and expression, and meet the subtle and powerful personalities who originated for Europe all forms of poetry, history and philosophy, and even physical science itself, no less than the ideal of freedom and the conception of a self-governing democracy; while the student is introduced to the great problems of thought and life at their springs, before he follows them through the wider but more confused currents of the modern world."

—British dignitaries, *selection from a signed public letter*

ARETĒ

—Excellence or Virtue—

ARETĒ

—*Excellence or Virtue*—

What the Ancient Greeks Thought and Said about *Aretē*

in their own words

Homer, Hesiod, Tyrtaeus, Sappho, Solon, Xenophanes, Simonides, Theognis, Pythagoras, Pindar, Bacchylides, Aeschylus, Sophocles, Euripides, Aristophanes, Herodotus, Thucydides, Socrates, Antisthenes, Xenophon, Plato, Diogenes, Isocrates, Demosthenes, Aristotle, Epicurus, Zeno, Crates, Diodorus Siculus, Epictetus, Dio Chrysostom, Plutarch, Diogenes Laertius, Lucian of Samosata, Galen, Athenaeus of Naucratis, Plotinus, Julian, Procopius, and Others

selected, introduced, and edited by
The Classics Cave

CAVE BONFIRE SERIES
the best of the ancient Greeks for now

THE CLASSICS CAVE
Sugar Land

Aretē: Excellence or Virtue
What the Ancient Greeks Thought and Said about Aretē

Copyright © 2021 by Tim J. Young

Library of Congress Catalogue-in-Publication Data available on request.

ISBN 978-1-943915-15-6

Published in the United States by
The Classics Cave
P.O. Box 19038
Sugar Land, TX 77496
contact@theclassicscave.com
www.theclassicscave.com

The Classics Cave is an educational organization centered on the classics of antiquity, with an emphasis on Greece and Rome. Our mission is to shine the light of the past into the present for a brighter life today. Our goal is practice—the application of ancient wisdom to our contemporary ways and lives. We develop and provide online materials, organize and do outreach, and produce and distribute a variety of print and other media intended to entertain and educate, cultivate and motivate.

Visit The Classics Cave online (www.theclassicscave.com) to support our mission and to access a growing catalogue of engaging books, useful goods, and other helpful materials for educators and all others interested in benefiting from ancient literature.

CONTENTS

The Classics Cave Catalogue

CAVE BONFIRE SERIES
INTRODUCTION
The best of the Ancient Greeks for now

Just as we see the bee settling on all the flowers and sipping the best from each, so also those who strive for education and culture . . . should collect useful knowledge from every source.　　　　　　　　　　　　　　—Isocrates, *To Demonicus*

Those who make it their business to collect whatever is beneficial from every writing are like rivers that grow larger by taking in the flow of streams from every side. The poet's saying about "adding little to little" is true not only for the accumulation of money but also for gathering together every kind of knowledge.
　　　　　　　—Basil the Great, *How to Benefit from Reading Greek Literature*

S IMILAR TO PREHISTORIC people gathering nuts and berries, we modern humans like to collect ideas. Typically, we do so from individuals. What was the Buddha's position on suffering? How did Jesus speak about love? What did Isaac Newton postulate about gravity? What did Edmund Burke say about revolutions? Otherwise, we take an idea and trace its history, studying what people from one or different lands have thought and said about it over time. We analyze and synthesize, drawing our own secondary conclusions that pass themselves off for the original.

This is all greatly beneficial, of course. But what if we listen to people speak *in their own words*?

This is what The Classics Cave does in the Cave *Bonfire* Series. We let people speak for themselves. Specifically, the series presents what the ancient Greeks thought, said, and wrote about any number of topics. What did they say about the nature of reality? The purpose of life? Human flourishing? Love, friendship, and the family? Desire and pleasure? Freedom? Education? Economics and political organization? Whatever they said about these topics and many more, we want to know.

The purpose of the Cave *Bonfire* Series is to get the job done. And like a great bonfire constructed of sticks and logs, some hefty and some not as much, each volume presents what the Greeks thought and said about a topic *in their own words*. Beginning with Homer and Hesiod, the earliest Greek literature we have from the late 700s BC, and ending with those writing toward the collapse of the ancient world some one thousand years later, the Cave *Bonfire* Series blazes before the reader with the light of each source, the brightest or best of what the ancient Greeks had to say.

You may wonder, Why should we care about what the ancient Greeks thought or had to say?* The reasons are many, beginning with the fact that they stand as the font or source of many contemporary interests, ideas, behaviors, and institutions. Shifting metaphors, if the Greeks were us humans when we first spoke in writing, then their words were our very first words—at least one set.** As any parent knows, there's something special about a child's first words, something that indicates whom he or she will grow up to be in terms of inclinations, interests, and loves. As others have noted, "The child becomes the father of the man." Who and what was that child? And what were his or her first words? The Cave *Bonfire* Series collects these words and presents them in such a way so that we understand their general context and significance.***

But more. What the ancient Greeks have to say is entertaining. And inspirational. Not only that but as many have recognized for centuries, Greek ideas have a special power to cultivate and educate the human mind and heart. There's wisdom there! And so, guidance. We can take what the Greeks had to say and better move forward today with the light they provide—this in another part of the Cave *Bonfire* Series found in a section offering "Principles" or a "Plan of Life," along with "Points of Wisdom" and "Ways of Practice." The latter "Ways" consist of workbook or journal-like prompts and exercises intended to motivate the reader to feel, think, and act in beneficial ways according to the former "Points."

Finally, in a section called "Other Matters of Interest Related to [the Idea or Topic]," the reader will find additional information about the idea or topic, further resources, a glossary of relevant Greek terms, suggestions for further reading, and so on.

So let's go! Let's see what the Greeks have to say about *aretē* (excellence or virtue). We'll come away richer for having done so. And if we are lucky, our riches just may turn into wisdom, practice, and a better life—if only a little!****

---

* For more on why we should care, see *The Value of the Classics: What the Ancient Greeks, Romans, and Others through History Have Thought and Said about the Classics* (Sugar Land: The Classics Cave, 2021). ** Other sets include those of ancient China, India, and the Near East, as well as the literature, both oral and written, of the earliest Australians, Africans, Americans, and other Europeans. ***For more, see the Cave's *First Words* series at www.theclassicscave.com and on various social media platforms. **** Of course, the latter is up to us—*what we do* with what we read. (Be sure, though, that we at the Cave are cheering everyone on!)

INTRODUCTION

B E BEST." SO ran the motto of an initiative—that of a former First Lady of the United States—to help children flourish. The program's mission was to "encourag[e] children to BE BEST in their individual paths, . . . teaching them the importance of social, emotional, and physical health." One of its three pillars was well-being, an objective that implied the effort to bring one's being—one's very existence and essence—into a condition of wellness, of wholeness, of fullness, so that one would be flourishing as a human being, thriving.

The underlying point of the Be Best initiative is anything but new. It is what all parents and elders, teachers, mentors and coaches have wanted for children from time immemorial. We are told, for instance, in Homer's *Iliad* (late eighth century BC) that "Old Peleus ordered his son Achilles to always be the best and to stand out among other men." Similarly, Lycian Glaucus (also in the *Iliad*) explains to his battle opponent Diomedes, "My father sent me to Troy and insistently ordered me to always be the best and to stand out among other men."[1] We hear echoes of this encouragement, perhaps, in Led Zeppelin's 1969 song, "Good Times Bad Times," in which Robert Plant sings, "In the days of my youth, I was told what it means to be a man. And now I've reached that age, I've tried to do all those things the best I can."

From Homer on, the ancient imperative was, "Be *the* best." Articulated in a more contemporary, subjective form, it is, "Be *your* best." Expressed either way, whether with the objective "the" or the more subjective "your," there was and is the recognition of a measure or standard of how to be and act—a goal, something to achieve, something to rise to, something to fulfill. To contract the two, the objective and the subjective, we might say, "Be best."[2]

Greek Words and Possible Definitions of *Aretē*

The Greek word for "best" is *aristos*, a word found in the English word "aristocracy" (the rule of the best, the noblest) and in the name of Aristotle (one of ancient Greece's outstanding philosophers). *Aristos* itself is a word that originally meant "most fitting," from the suffix -*isto*-, signifying the superlative, and the root *ar*-, "to fit together," —as when an expert builder joins two walls together well or a shipwright the parts of a ship or a poet the elements of a poem. In the ancient world, therefore, to be *aristos* was to be the most fitting kind of thing. As for humans, it was to be the "noblest, bravest, most virtuous, and most excellent" kind of human being.

Related to *aristos* is the Greek word *aretaō*, a word that means "to be fit or proper, to thrive, prosper, flourish." What sort of things do so (*aretaō*)? Good deeds thrive (we are told by Homer). Fields flourish with grain (we see elsewhere in Greek literature). And humans prosper and thrive and flourish (as we also observe in the same).

This—the meaning of *aristos* and *aretaō* for humans—brings us to *aretē*, the subject of this book.

Simply put, *aretē* is "bestness" —to give, perhaps, an odd form of the word. It is what one is if one carries out the command of the fathers of Achilles and Glaucus to "be the best." It is a state or condition of thriving, flourishing, or prospering. In short, *aretē* is "excellence," an English word that itself may be traced back to earlier forms that mean something as concrete as a "hill" rising from the flatlands, and thus the adjectives "towering" and "lofty," to more abstract meanings such as "superior," "outstanding," and "prominent."

Liddell & Scott's *Greek-English Lexicon* offers the following senses of *aretē* (with italics in the original). Generally, *aretē* means "*goodness, excellence*, of any kind, especially of *manly* qualities, *manhood, valor, prowess*." Related to skill or the making of things (*technē*), it is "*excellence* in any art." In a "moral sense," and relative to "character," it carries the connotation of "*goodness, virtue*," and "*merit*."

As we will see, the word *aretē* has had a very full and varying life among the ancient Greeks—in their feelings, thoughts, speech, and writing. It is a term that has shifted meaning depending on, among other aspects, its subject (what or who is *aretē*), its context (when, where, and how *aretē* occurs), and who is thinking and writing about *aretē* (poets, for example, or playwrights, orators, historians, satirists, or philosophers). Aside from the more general definitions of "excellence" and "virtue," *aretē* has signaled "valor" and "merit" and "success." At times it has had a moral meaning, denoting "goodness," and at other times it has not.

In the final analysis, however, all understandings of *aretē* seem to come back to its relationship with *aristos*, with "best," in that whatever is *aretē* is somehow "best" (though not necessarily *the* best), whether relative to others or to itself. There is excellence (bestness) in battle (often given as "valor" in English), in governing city-states (this turns up as "merit"), in farming and household organization ("success"), and in one's internal life relative to one's character or ongoing dispositions ("virtue"). But all these words—valor, merit, success, and virtue, not to mention others such as "fertile," the excellence of soil,—are just interpretive masks for *aretē*. Behind the masks we find *excellence*. And that which is excellent is, in some sense, best.

As for the title of this book, *Aretē: Excellence or Virtue*, the explanation is straightforward. The term "excellence" covers all forms of "bestness," including the more specific "virtue," whereas "virtue" applies to humans and human life alone, connoting things like wisdom, courage, moderation, and justice. More on this point in a moment under "The Organization of *Aretē*."

Ongoing Greek Inspiration and Influence

However we define *aretē*, one point is certain. Ancient Greek thinking and writing about *aretē* and the pursuit and practice of the excellent or virtuous life has influenced and inspired others down to the present moment.

We see this inspiration and influence in the ancient world upon most Roman authors, both Latin and Greek-writing, authors such as Cicero, Seneca, Epictetus, Plotinus, and Boethius, toward the very end of the Classical Age. It is there in Hebrew (Jewish) literature in the Greek translation of the Old Testament (the Septuagint—in the prophets Isaiah, Habakkuk, and Zachariah, and the Wisdom of Solomon[3]), and in the first century AD writings of Philo of Alexandria.

The same is true for early Christian literature. It shows up in the Christian (Greek) New Testament in the letters of Peter and Paul, and it is present in the writings of the Christian Fathers, including St. Basil of Caesarea in the East and St. Augustine in the West.

During the Middle Ages, its presence may be noted among Jewish, Christian, and Muslim writers. We see it in the "Eight Chapters" of Maimonides; in the "projected encyclopedia of human activity," commissioned by the Byzantine emperor Constantine Porphyrogenitus, a work that included a section "On virtue and vice"; in the *Summa Theologica* of St. Thomas Aquinas; and in Al-Farabi's *On the Perfect State* or *The Virtuous City*.

Moving on in time, the thought of the ancient Greeks continued its inspiration and influence past the Middle Ages into the early modern period and beyond. To give a handful of examples, we see it in the *Institutes of Christian Religion* of John Calvin, the *Ethics* of Baruch Spinoza, *The Theory of Moral Sentiments* of Adam Smith, the writings and speeches of the American founders, the *Doctrine of Virtue* of Immanuel Kant, and in the short essay "On Virtue and Happiness" of John Stuart Mill, not to mention later writers.

Today, though there are a few other prominent ethical approaches that appear to be in competition with the ancient understanding of *aretē*, the inspiration and influence of the ancients is also evident. In fact, in the past half century, there has been a revival of ancient *aretē* in what has been called "virtue ethics." Let's take a few moments to observe some recent ideas about *aretē* alongside other views.

Contemporary Ideas about Ethics and *Aretē*

It is usual to read, as we do in the article on "Virtue Ethics" in the *Stanford Encyclopedia of Philosophy*, that "virtue ethics is . . . one of [the] major approaches in normative ethics."[4] Glancing at a recent anthology of ethical writing, *Ethical Theory*, we note that the others are consequentialism, deontology, contractarianism, and feminist ethics. What, in a nutshell, does each one of the alternative approaches to ethics hold? And who are significant thinkers in each? Let's take a brief look before turning to contemporary virtue ethics.

As its name indicates, *consequentialism* generally argues that the value of an act is based on its consequences, that is, the results that follow from acting in one way or another. (The root word of "consequence"—*sequence*—signifies "that which follows.") Answering the question, "What should I do?" the consequentialist response is always, "It depends on what'll happen when you do X, Y, or Z." The straightforward goal in acting is to get the best "what'll happen" or results—a goal that inevitably begs the question, "What *is* the best?" Depending on the consequentialist you're talking to, the best or the good may vary. According to utilitarianism, the most extensively elaborated form of consequentialism, the best or good is "happiness," which is founded on the thoughtful acquisition of pleasure and the equally as thoughtful avoidance of pain. Alternative forms of consequentialism may zero in on other bests or goods such as beauty, tranquility, or even, because of consequentialism's interaction with virtue ethics, the promotion of virtue. Well-known consequentialists are Jeremy Bentham, John Stuart Mill, and, from the ancient world, Epicurus.

Deontology (a word derived from the Greek words *deon*, that which is binding, needful, right, proper, and *logos*, an account, study of) generally holds that the value of an act derives from the obligatory nature—or not—of the act itself rather than any results that may or may not follow from it. In reply to the question, "What should I do?" the deontologist response is always, "You should do what you *ought* to do," with a strong emphasis on the "should" or "ought" of doing, an imperative saturated with notions of obligation and duty, and oftentimes encapsulated in a rule (such as Kant's "Categorical Imperative"). Of course, such notions raise many questions, and so deontology is not as straightforward as it may seem at first glance. Who has the obligation? In what sense? Toward whom? How did these obligations arise in the first place? To these we must add, thanks to deontology's dialogue with virtue ethics, the question of virtue's role in carrying out what one ought to do. And so on—to give only the simplest of questions. Well-known deontologists are Immanuel Kant and, from the ancient world, most of the Stoics, including Zeno of Citium and Epictetus.[5]

Contractarianism is related to social contract theory, the idea that we humans live by various agreements (contracts) that limit what we may or may not do (particularly relative to what we desire and how we may satisfy our desires, with what freedom), as well as prescribe what we must do (relative to others and the state). To give an example, the ancient Greek philosopher Epicurus espouses a contractarian view of justice when he states, "There is no such thing as justice in itself. Rather, justice is an agreement neither to harm nor be harmed that is made when men gather together from time to time in various places."[6] Therefore, to the question, "What should I do?" the contractarian would respond, "Whatever we've agreed to do." Aside from Epicurus and others in the ancient world, who seem to have explored or espoused some form of the theory, other well-known contractarians are Thomas Hobbes, John Locke, Jean-Jacques Rousseau, and the more recent John Rawls.

Finally, feminist ethics. Rather than being "a simple, uniform approach" to what one should do and how one should live, feminist ethics insists that we should give heed to how it is that women, in contrast with men, generally approach being, living, and doing. The point is not necessarily that there *is* a monolithic *woman's way of doing things*, or that it is always better than a man's (assuming there is such a man's way), but that it is or can be significantly different—a difference, feminist ethicists contend, that can and should equally contribute to the human quest to be, live, and do well, based on the feminist assumption that men and woman share moral equality. What is the factual or observational basis of this difference? In large part it has to do with the "experiences of women." As identified by Russ Shaefer-Landau, these are the "first-hand knowledge of physical, emotional, and financial vulnerability, a sense of interdependence with and responsibility to friends and family members, and a long history of exclusions from various offices, positions, and privileges."[7] As with the other approaches to ethics, feminist ethics has also been influenced by virtue ethics. Well-known practitioners of feminist ethics are Mary Wollstonecraft and Simone de Beauvoir. As for antiquity, we may point to the worldview of the Greek poet Sappho of Lesbos, though her focus was not ethics.

Now that we've very briefly run through each of the other approaches in "normative ethics," let's take a look at virtue ethics, an approach that was directly inspired and influenced by the ancient Greeks, chiefly by Aristotle and, to a lesser extent, perhaps, by Plato and Socrates.

Initially, when it was first developed mid-twentieth century, virtue ethics was a response to the above-mentioned normative theories, but in particular to consequentialism and deontology, which both propose precise moral principles or prescriptions or maxims that one may utilize to know how to act in any given situation (for example, John Stuart Mill's "Greatest Happiness Principle" or Immanuel Kant's "Categorical Imperative"). For a number of reasons, the philosopher Elisabeth Anscombe criticized this approach in her paper, "Modern Moral Philosophy" (1958). In its place, she proposed what came to be known as "virtue ethics," an approach that focuses on a person's intellectual and emotional states (those that occur in what has traditionally been called the soul—and so the significance of human psychology in virtue ethics, from the Greek *psyché* or soul), character and virtue (both ongoing dispositions), and end, that is, the end or goal of flourishing as a human being (rather than, say, any other animal or kind of being, such as an angel or god). Others took up the standard of virtue ethics. Well-known and influential individuals include Philippa Foot, Alasdair MacIntyre, Martha Nussbaum, Rosalind Hursthouse, Michael Slote, Christine Swanton, and Julia Annas.[8]

What, then, *is* virtue ethics? If we look at it in terms of its fundamental question, as we did above with the other approaches, we observe that rather than primarily asking, "What should I do in *this* specific situation?" virtue ethics more broadly queries, "What sort of person should I be so that I may generally flourish as a human being?" Allied questions are, "How should I live?" and, "What is the good or happy life?"

Since the ancient Greek philosopher Aristotle forms the foundation of virtue ethics, we'll begin with him in answering these questions and thereby lay the groundwork for virtue ethics' more recent developments.[9] For Aristotle, the human good or end or goal (*telos*) "is the activity of the soul that accords with excellence or virtue (*ar-etē*)."[10] Such activity is happiness (*eudaimonia*), and so the human good or end is happiness. Accordingly, the answer to the question, "What sort of person should I be?" is, "One who acts in accord with virtue." If we ask why we should act in such a manner, the response is, "So that we may flourish as a human being," which is to say, "so that we may be happy." Virtue itself is a disposition cultivated and established (it is an ongoing, steady thing, a habit or possession) by means of doing acts of one virtue or another until we finally possess a virtuous disposition or character. How do we know whether some disposition or act is virtuous? We do, according to Aristotle, because it allows for the flourishing, the blooming, the excellence of one aspect or another of human nature. For instance, relative to other animals, we humans are rational; therefore, we act virtuously when we act in accord with reason. At bottom, the key factors of Aristotle's virtue ethics are human nature (particularly relative to the soul), the good or end or goal of human life (human flourishing or happiness), and the means by which or the way in which we may live out this end in an ongoing, steady manner (virtue, character).

Recent virtue ethics has emphasized various aspects of Aristotle's approach. What follows is an all-too-brief and admittedly inadequate account of each major branch of virtue ethics.[11]

Eudaimonism or eudaimonist virtue ethics centers on the notion of the overall goal of human life, which is *eudaimonia*, happiness or human flourishing. One may protest, But isn't that consequentialism? Isn't one shooting for some end or goal, some consequence, one called *eudaimonia*? The simple answer is, Yes. But the difference is huge. Whereas consequentialism notes a fundamental distinction between the act, which is neutral in itself, and the consequence or goal, which is good, useful, advantageous or not, eudaimonist virtue ethics sees both as one and the same: the virtuous human life *is one and the same with* the happy, flourishing human life. To be virtuous *is* to flourish. The difference may be illustrated with one statement each from Epicurus and Aristotle. In typical consequentialist fashion, Epicurus states that "We choose the virtues *for the sake of* pleasure and not on their own account, even as we take medicine for the sake of health." By contrast, Aristotle observes that "happiness *is* an activity of the soul that *accords with* perfect virtue."[12]

If eudaimonist virtue ethics identifies certain activity ("activity of the soul that accords with perfect virtue") with happiness and human flourishing, then agent-based virtue ethics—while accepting the eudaimonist tie of acting and *eudaimonia*—takes a deeper look, we might say, at what is going on in the human being who is engaged in such activity. What is the virtuous individual's ongoing motivation or motivations for acting in accord with virtue? How does he feel—what are his emotions—as he does so? What are his enduring dispositional states? And furthermore, how does such a person serve as an example, an exemplar, for others who wish to live virtuously?

Finally, target-centered virtue ethics focuses on the end or target of a virtuous act or virtuous behavior. In this case, the target is not *eudaimonia* per se, though it is not excluded, but the particular aim of a specific virtue. For example, the point or aim of courage is to deal with danger and the fear that typically arises with danger.

There's more, of course, to each of these branches of virtue ethics, and there are other takes as well. For instance, we could explore how the Roman Catholic Church has largely used what may be termed a virtue ethics approach to morality and the good life from its inception down to today.[13] But for now, and given the focus of this book—what the ancient Greeks had to say about *aretē*, about excellence or virtue—, these summary overviews will have to suffice. We turn, then, to the contents of this book.

The Organization of *Aretē*: Excellence or Virtue

Whatever we may think about virtue ethics and excellence today, what is certain is that the Greeks had their own thoughts about and unique uses of the term *aretē* for a period spanning well over a millennium. Beginning with the epic poetry of Homer some 2,700 years ago, many Greeks recorded these notions in works of poetry, drama, comedy, history, rhetoric, satire, philosophy, and the like. To name just a few, there were the poets Sappho of Lesbos, Theognis of

Megara, and Simonides of Ceos; the playwrights Aeschylus, Sophocles, and Euripides; the historians Herodotus, Thucydides, and Diodorus Siculus; the philosophers Socrates, Plato, and Aristotle, not to
mention the many other philosophers up to Plotinus, who wrote a
thousand years after Homer; the satirist Lucian of Samosata; and the
orators Isocrates, Demosthenes, and Dio Chrysostom.

Given the wealth of testimony relative to our subject, the
straightforward goal of *Aretē: Excellence or Virtue* is to present *in
their own words* what the Greeks felt, thought, and said about *aretē*.
Although there are drawbacks to such a presentation, the strength
is that the Greeks can speak directly to us. What did the farmer-
poet Hesiod say about *aretē*? And what about Diotima, the prophetess and teacher of Socrates? Or the Cynic philosophers Diogenes
of Sinope or Crates of Thebes? And how did the Theban leader
Epaminondas exhibit *aretē* in battle? Or in what way did Epicrates,
the young man dear to and mentored by the orator Demosthenes,
demonstrate his laudable *aretē*? And finally, how did Lucian of Samosata lampoon all the eager philosophical discussion about *aretē*
and other abstract concepts, as well as the failure to practice *aretē*?

Prior to the advent of philosophy in the sixth and fifth centuries
BC, there was no truly systematic thinking among the Greeks about
the nature of *aretē*. Consequently, we typically find some idea of
aretē in the mouth of a hero in an epic poem, or expressed by the
chorus in a tragedy, or displayed by one man, woman or another in
a history. That there were general and even consistent notions of
aretē, we can affirm. To discover more precise, carefully mapped
out ideas, however, we must wait for philosophers such as Pythagoras and Socrates. We are told by the ancient biographer Diogenes
Laertius that the latter philosopher "was the first to talk about the
conduct of life" in terms of the best way of living. Diogenes adds
that Socrates "investigated ethical or moral matters in workshops
and in the marketplace"—including, as we know from Plato and
Xenophon, the nature and way of *aretē*.[14]

This shift over time from non-systematic to systematic presenta-
tions of *aretē* explains the basic organization of this volume. Reflecting the shift, *Aretē: Excellence or Virtue* is divided into several parts.

Part 1, "The What, Who & How of Aretē," mostly presents the various masks worn by *aretē* before the coming of Socrates and moral philosophy. (I say "mostly" because the philosophers are included at times.) Part 1 answers several questions: What things, human or otherwise, could be termed *aretē*? What was *aretē*'s basic nature? How or by what means did a thing or person possess *aretē*? Aside from answering these questions, Part 1 affirms that *aretē* was a significant goal of life for most early Greeks. It also presents many models or examples of *aretē*. Part 2, "Thinking about Aretē," offers Greek philosophy's systematic exploration of *aretē* and the virtuous life in the form of lively dialogues, quips, lecture notes, and expository writing. Each philosopher's view is summarized at the end of each chapter. Then, just as we are growing serious with the philosophers, Part 3, "Comic Interlude," comes along and lampoons their abstractions and their, at times, inept approach to actually living the virtuous life. It is our chance to laugh a bit at all our (and the Greeks') earnestness and, yes, failures. Finally, getting serious again, Part 4, "Talking about Aretē," presents selections from the speeches of four orators that offer an idea of what each thought about *aretē*, though not in systematic fashion.

We should note that although it is broadly representative, *Aretē: Excellence or Virtue* is not a comprehensive survey of Greek beliefs about *aretē*. Instead, as the Cave Bonfire Series tagline suggests, it is the best of Greek thinking and speaking on the topic. This means that some of what the Greeks had to say is left out. For instance, you will not find here the short work attributed (falsely) to Aristotle titled, *Virtues and Vices*. Nor will you find any selections from the biographer and moral writer Plutarch's several essays on or related to virtue. The reason is not that these are worthless—*au contraire!* Rather, it is because they do not present anything essentially new. The same could be said of other authors and works.[15]

We should also glance at another issue, that of terminology. We've already noted that *aretē* is a multivalent term, one with many possible meanings. Nevertheless, in this book *aretē* is translated with two words alone: excellence or virtue. The general rule is that, prior to the philosophers, *aretē* is given as "excellence," whereas after philosophy and thus with the philosophers, it is given as "virtue." (This also holds for Part 1 when the philosophers occasionally show up.) Regardless, whenever you spot the words "excellence" or "virtue," you should know that *aretē* is the Greek term lurking beneath. We leave it up to you to substitute other words in place of these. For instance, in battle situations, "valor" could have been given in place of "excellence" (and often has been in other translations). Or when we see in Hesiod that "the immortal gods have put sweat in front of Excellence," we could have exchanged "Excellence" for "Success."[16]

One last point before we launch. Read *Aretē* in whatever order you wish. If you read it from beginning to end, you will have a strong sense of how Greek feeling, thinking, and speaking about excellence and virtue changed over time, from roughly 700 BC to the end of the third century AD and beyond (the final author, Procopius, who appears a few times, hails from the sixth century AD). On the other hand, if you wish to read it more meditatively, contemplating reflections on *aretē* and the good life, now from this author and now from another, you may wish to skip around. Either plan will work. (For a few other features of the book, see "NOTE" below.)

Let's Go!

However you read, and however familiar you already are with virtue ethics or other conceptions of excellence or virtue, you will likely pick up a new or refined way of looking at *aretē*.

It is this new way, this new understanding, that is at the heart of *Aretē: Excellence or Virtue* and many other books in the Cave *Bonfire* Series. Yes, the quest is to learn about history, about what the Greeks thought and said. But more, the goal is the discovery of the earliest light the Greeks have to offer us for a brighter light today. So, in learning something new, we will be learning something old, something that has been tested over time and found valuable.

Anyway, let's go! There's much to hear and learn from the Greeks, and just as much to practice.

NOTE: from here on, aretē is mostly no longer italicized and often appears on its own without definition or further explanation. If you require a reminder as to what aretē means, please consult the Glossary toward the back. As for each chapter in *Aretē*, you'll notice a few common features. First, each one begins with a brief introduction that will serve to orient you to the contents of the chapter, or, if the chapter presents a single thinker or writer, to the central facts about that author's life, works, and ideas. Next the material coming after the subtitle IN THEIR OWN WORDS presents the thoughts and words of the Greeks from the many works that have come down to us. Interspersed in *italics* are short commentaries explaining the content or purpose of the selections and passages that follow.

As for the different authors, the following is how each will be mentioned in *Aretē*. Typically, the author of the text is given in italics before offering his or her own words. For example: *Bacchylides* I declare—and I will declare—that the greatest glory is to possess excellence. (Note: there are no quotation marks as we know these are the poet Bacchylides' own words.) That said, if the author is presenting someone else's thoughts or words, as with Socrates in Plato's dialogues, or the chorus in Sophocles' plays, or a politician in Thucydides' history, then the speaker is noted in parentheses. To give an example: *Sophocles (the Chorus is speaking)* "Soon the glorious voice of the flute will go up for you . . . divine music responsive to the lyre. For the son of Zeus and Alcmene is rushing home, carrying the spoils of every excellence." Lastly, if a whole chapter is devoted to an author, as is the case in parts 2-4, or if the author is obvious from the surrounding text, then mention of the author is absent.

NOTES

[1] According to Anthony Everitt, the latter admonition inspired the Greek conqueror Alexander the Great and the Roman statesman and orator Cicero, as well as countless other Roman boys, "to be the best and the bravest." See *Cicero: The Life and Times of Rome's Greatest Politician* (New York: Random House), 46.

[2] We should note that "subjective" here is not a matter of mere feeling or how one "identifies," to use recent parlance, without any objective reference; rather, the subjective implies or points to the objective, whether one's roles, talents, relationships, responsibilities, and the like. It refers to the specific or individual rather than the general or universal.

[3] Regarding virtue or the virtues, the Wisdom of Solomon declares, "There is nothing more valuable in the life of man" (8.7). Isaiah 43.21 reveals God's motivation for preserving his people: they were "to declare my virtues."

[4] Rosalind Hursthouse and Glen Pettigrove, "Virtue Ethics," in *The Stanford Encyclopedia of Philosophy* (Winter 2016 Edition), Edward N. Zalta, ed., https://plato.stanford.edu/archives/win2016/entries/ethics-virtue/.

[5] That the Stoics were deontologists is only true from one angle. From another and perhaps better perspective, they were simply virtue ethicists — to use modern terminology. For more, see chapters 11 and 12. See also *The Best of Early Stoicism* (Sugar Land: The Classics Cave, 2021).

[6] Epicurus, *The Principal Teachings* 33, in Diogenes Laertius, *Lives and Opinions of Eminent Philosophers* 10.150. See the Cave's *The Best of Epicurus* (Sugar Land: The Classics Cave, 2021).

[7] Russ Shafer-Landau, "Introduction to Part XII," in *Ethical Theory: An Anthology*, 2nd ed. (Oxford: Blackwell Publishers, 2013), 689.

[8] Virtue ethics has also influenced the field of psychology, particularly that of "positive psychology." See "Character Strengths" (Chapter 6), in Christopher Peterson, *A Primer in Positive Psychology* (Oxford: Oxford University Press, 2006), 137-164. See also, C. Peterson and M.E.P. Seligman, *Character Strengths and Virtues: A Handbook and Classification* (New York: Oxford University Press; Washington DC: American Psychological Association, 2004). For a study of virtue within various cultures and through time, see K. Dahlsgaard, C. Peterson, and M.E.P. Seligman, "Shared Virtue: The Convergence of Valued Human strengths across Culture and History," *Review of General Psychology* 9 (2005): 203-213.

[9] For Aristotle's view in his own words, see 9, "Aristotle."

[10] Aristotle, *Nicomachean Ethics* 1.7.15-16 (1098a).

[11] For a general introduction to each, see Part XI, "Virtue Ethics," in the above-cited *Ethical Theory: An Anthology* for essays on various aspects and kinds of contemporary virtue ethics. See also, the *Stanford Encyclopedia of Philosophy*'s article on virtue ethics referenced above.

[12] Diogenes Laertius, *Lives* 10.138. Aristotle, *Nicomachean Ethics* 1.7.15-16 (1098a). See also Diogenes Laertius, *Lives* 7.96-97 for how the Stoics taught that the virtues were both means and ends.

[13] For a brief introduction, see Article 7: The Virtues, in the *Catechism of the Catholic Church* (Washington, DC: United States Catholic Conference, 1994), 443-450. For a more extensive treatment, see People Benedict XVI, *The Virtues* (Huntington: Our Sundar Visitor, 2010), and Peter Kreeft, *Back to Virtue* (San Francisco: Ignatius Press, 1992).

[14] Diogenes Laertius, *Lives* 2.20-21.

[15] This asserted, if we at the Cave have overlooked and left out anything essential, please contact us at www.theclassicscave.com to let us know. Emendations are always in order.

[16] As is found in the Cave's *The Best of Hesiod's Theogony & Works and Days* (Sugar Land: The Classics Cave, 2021).

PART 1

The What, Who & How of *Aretē*

DETERMINING THE GOAL
ARETĒ AS THE *TELOS* OF LIFE

W HAT IS THE goal of life? Or goals? What is the overall objective? Is there such? What target or targets should we shoot for? As they are for us, these were vital questions for the ancient Greeks, posed in their quest to figure out how best to live.

The central Greek term of their quest was *telos*, a word that meant not only "goal," "objective," and "target" but also "end," "chief matter," and "good." The *telos* of life, then, was what people pursued; it was the most important thing to do or get in life, that which would make life worthwhile or good, and, according to some, happy or blessed.

Nearly all ancient Greek philosophers held that aretē, excellence or moral virtue, was the goal of life, the highest good. An exception was Epicurus, who taught only that virtue was the means to pleasure, the actual goal of life. Athenaeus of Naucratis, for instance, reports that Epicurus, in his work *On the Goal of Life*, taught that one "should . . . honor that which is morally noble and the virtues and everything like that if they produce pleasure. But if they do not produce pleasure, then we should have nothing to do with them."[1] Still, even Epicurus' intended meaning is not entirely clear.[2]

The question remains: what about other ancient Greek writers and thinkers? The truth is that, aside from the philosophers, no one from Homer on clearly stated that "the goal of life is aretē." Nevertheless, it is easy to detect the general conclusion.

In the following selections, we see that the Greeks by and large judged aretē to be the goal of life. It was the one good for which no amount of toil was too great, that for which they gave everything to achieve. It was what people hoped for, strove and prayed for; it was what they admired, honored, and rewarded. Finally, it was, they believed, that which outlasted the death of the body in the form of everlasting glory.

IN THEIR OWN WORDS

The following selections are mostly presented chronologically. They are passages from the late eighth century BC (Homer and Hesiod) to the sixth century AD (the Byzantine historian Procopius).

In the first few selections from Homer, aretē (excellence) is a gift to pray for (for others). It is battle excellence, the excellence of the hero or warrior, the "might and manhood" that reveal "the best of men." As such, it is the absence of shame. It is that for which a father earnestly prays for his son, that which a son must be—outstanding, the best—when around others.

Homer (Odysseus is speaking to the Phaeacians) "As for those of you staying here, may you happily delight your wedded wives and children, and may the gods give you every kind of excellence, and may misfortune be absent from among the people."[3]

Homer (Odysseus, Telemachus, and Laertes are speaking) And at once Odysseus said to Telemachus, his dear son, "Having come to battle where the best of men are separated in distinction from the rest, now you will learn never to shame your family line, for we have always excelled in might and manhood throughout all the land."

In turn mindful Telemachus answered him, "If you wish, dear father, you will see me—given my present spirit—bring no shame on the family line, as you say."

That's what Telemachus said, and glad, Laertes spoke, saying, "What kind of day is this for me, dear gods? I absolutely rejoice! My son and my son's son are battling over excellence!"[4]

Homer (Glaucus is speaking) "My father sent me to Troy and insistently ordered me to always be the best and to stand out among other men and not dishonor or shame the family of my fathers who were the best in Ephyre and in wide Lydia."[5]

Homer (Nestor is speaking) "Old Peleus enjoined his child Achilles to always be the best and to stand out among other men."[6]

Homer (Hector is praying for his son, indicating the nature of an excellent man) After playing with his son Astyanax like this, Hector spoke in prayer to Zeus and all the gods. "Zeus and the other gods, grant that this child, my boy, may be as I am. Make him outstanding among all the Trojan men, preeminent in forceful strength and noble bravery, and may he powerfully rule Ilium. And when someday he returns home from battle carrying the gory spoils of the enemy man he has slaughtered—the dead man's shield and armor—may some man say, 'He's even better than his father was!' And let his mother rejoice and delight in her heart!"[7]

For Hesiod, aretē is the excellence of the farmer. It is the destination toward which the path of an ordered life consisting of hard and constant work leads. It is success in terms of prosperity, honor, and happiness (eudaimonia).

Hesiod Listen, Perses, you big fool. I will proclaim all this noble knowledge for you. It is easy to grab at Deficiency (Kakotēs). It is there in abundance for you. The way is smooth to her, and she dwells very near to you. But the immortal gods have put sweat in front of Excellence (Aretē). The path to her is long and steep. And so it is rough-going at first. Nevertheless, when one comes to the highest point, then the path becomes easy.[8]

One thousand years later, St. Basil the Great recognizes Hesiod's call to the goal of aretē in his work on How to Benefit from Reading Greek Literature. *Interestingly, he observes that "everyone is singing" these lines of Hesiod about aretē—though note his shift to moral virtue.*

Basil the Great What else, if not an exhortation for the young to virtue, are we to assume Hesiod had in mind when he composed the following verses that everyone is singing? That—"the steep road that leads to virtue is at first rugged and hard to travel, full of much sweat and lengthy toil."[9]

In the following Homeric Hymns, *we hear the singer praying for aretē along with "happy prosperity" (olbos—another Greek term for happiness).*

Hymn to Heracles Rejoice, lord, son of Zeus, and give me both excellence and happy prosperity.[10]

Hymn to Hephaestus Be gracious, Hephaestus, and give me both excellence and happy prosperity.[11]

For the Spartan Tyrtaeus, aretē is the "best prize among human beings," which is to say it is the most important goal of life, "the most beautiful for a young man to carry off." As with Homer, aretē is battle excellence. Most importantly, it is persistence in the fight, "never relaxing from war."

Tyrtaeus of Sparta This is excellence, the best prize among human beings, the most beautiful for a young man to carry off. . . . This is the excellence that each man should now aspire to in his spirit, never relaxing from war.[12]

A millennium on, the general Belisarius echoes the view of Homer, Tyrtaeus, and others—that one should live up to and fight for the standard of excellence.

Procopius (the general Belisarius is speaking to his army before battle) "And let the strongest motive that rouses men come to your minds, namely, pride in past achievements. For it is a shame, for those at least who have reason, to fall short of one's own self and to be found inferior to one's own standard of excellence."[13]

Solon and Cleobulus, two of the seven wise men of ancient Greece, both highly valued and pursued aretē—every excellence.

Diodorus Siculus In wisdom and learning, Solon surpassed all the men of his time. Being by nature far superior in excellence relative to the rest of men, he diligently cultivated excellence that wins applause—for he devoted much time to every branch of knowledge and became practiced in every kind of excellence.[14]

Diogenes Laertius Cleobulus advised men to practice bodily exercise . . . and to be friendly to excellence and hostile to deficiency.[15]

For the Greeks, to be wise was, in some sense, to be excellent, which was praiseworthy.

Diogenes Laertius The story told by Andron . . . that the Argives offered a tripod as a prize for excellence to the wisest of the Greeks.[16]

The following poets, all in their own way, promote aretē as a significant goal of life—the thing to keep in mind, strive for, and leave behind as a memorial. It is a secure foundation and one's glory.

Xenophanes of Colophon It is fitting to praise that one of men who, when drinking, shows and proclaims noble things, so that there is the memory of excellence—a rope pulling us thereto.[17]

Theognis of Megara Wear yourself out for the sake of excellence. *And,* The great glory of excellence will never be destroyed. *And,* Excellence and beauty accompany few men. Happy the one who is allotted both of these.[18]

Simonides of Ceos These men once lost their shining youth at Eurymedon River . . . when they perished, they left behind the noblest memorial of their excellence.[19]

Phocylides Seek after the means of life, and whenever you already have life, then seek after excellence.[20]

Bacchylides of Ceos I declare—and I will declare—that the greatest glory is to possess excellence. *And,* The light of a man's excellence is not dimmed with the demise of his body.[21]

Sophocles The only secure acquisitions are those tied to excellence.[22]

For the historian Thucydides (or the speakers whose speech he records), bravery and excellence go hand in hand, both deserving to be honored with prizes.

Thucydides (the Peloponnesian commanders are speaking) "The brave will be honored with the appropriate prizes for excellence."[23]

From the historian Herodotus, we learn that the Greeks competed in the Olympic games for the sake of excellence rather than for any other prize.

Herodotus Bringing these men into the king's presence, the Persians inquired of them what the Greeks were doing. . . . When the Arcadians told them that the Greeks were holding the Olympic games and viewing athletic contests and horse races, the king asked about the prize on offer for which they competed. They told him about the crown of olive leaves that was given to the victor. Then Tigranes, the son of Artabanus, said something that was most noble—even though the king judged him a coward for it. When he heard that the prize was not money but a crown, he could not keep quiet, but said, "Mardonius! What kind of men are these that you have pitted us against? It is not for money that they compete but for excellence!" This is what he said.[24]

For the Athenian orator Isocrates, aretē is the goal of education and training. As such, it is good to listen to stories about "the excellences of men." Aretē is that which abides, even unto old age.

Isocrates The fact, then, that our city was governed in those times better than the rest of the world I would justly credit to her kings, of whom I spoke a moment ago. For it was they who trained the multitude in the ways of excellence.[25]

Isocrates Most of all I am concerned with those who, in preference to any other, will gladly listen to a discourse which celebrates the excellences of men and the ways of a well-governed state.[26]

Isocrates Excellence, when it grows up with us in our hearts without alloy, is the one possession that abides with us in old age.[27]

With the historian Diodorus Siculus (of Sicily), we observe in his introduction to the Library *what was a common concern for ancient historians—to provide examples of* aretē *and its opposite so that men and women would behave excellently. The point is the same as we find in Isocrates' above remark about "discourses which celebrate the excellences of men." But we could also mention other ancient writers (Herodotus, Polybius, Plutarch, and the Roman historian Livy) who were all, to one degree or another, interested in highlighting the excellent relative to the not-so-excellent.*[28]

Diodorus Siculus Throughout our entire treatise . . . we have justly praised good men for their noble deeds and criticized base men whenever they have missed the mark. We believe that, by this means, we will lead men, whose nature fortunately inclines them to excellence, to undertake, because of the immortality that fame and reputation accords them, the noblest deeds, whereas by appropriate criticism we will turn men of the opposite character from their impulse to vice.[29]

The final selections present the views of philosophers and the ancient schools of philosophy. Up to this point we've mostly given aretē *as "excellence." Now, with the philosophers, we begin to give "virtue" since their concern was more for a moral or ethical excellence.*

Though chronologically later than the founding of the major schools of philosophy, Potamo of Alexandria indicates that all the schools held that aretē *is the* telos *(end or goal) of "all actions" in life. We see this with the Academy (Plato's school), the Cynics, the Lyceum (Aristotle's school), and the Porch (the Stoics). Aretē was the goal for all but the school of Epicurus, known as the Garden, and the Skeptics (the Pyrrhonists).*

In the following selections we hear from or about Socrates, Diotima (one of Socrates' teachers), Plato, Antisthenes the Cynic, Aristotle, Zeno of Citium (the founder of Stoicism), Apollonius of Tyana (more a religious figure), Galen (the renowned medical theorist, also a philosopher), Clement of Alexandria (a Christian theologian and Greek-influenced philosopher), and Plotinus (the founder of Neoplatonism).

Diogenes Laertius Not long ago an Eclectic school was introduced by Potamo of Alexandria, who made a selection from the tenets of all the existing schools. As he himself states in his *Elements of Philosophy*, . . . the end to which he refers all actions is a life made perfect in all virtue."[30]

Xenophon Socrates openly tried to reform young men and exhorted them to desire the most noble and magnificent virtue by which men prosper in public life and in their homes.[31]

Xenophon Socrates put a stop to these vices [impiety, lawlessness, gluttony, sexual lust, a lack of self-control] in many by making them long for virtue, and by giving them the hope that with care they might be good and noble men.[32]

Julian the emperor Socrates the Athenian . . . praised whatever ruler he knew to delight in virtue, and to cherish courage with moderation, and to love practical wisdom with justice.[33]

Plato (Diotima is speaking to Socrates) "Consider well," she said, "that it is only there with beauty itself that it will happen to him. . . . He gives birth to true virtue inasmuch as he grasps the truth—what is real and actual. So, when this man has produced true virtue, nourishing it and letting it grow, he becomes dear to the gods. And if ever immortality is granted to humans, that man, above all others, will be immortal."[34]

Diogenes Laertius Plato held that the goal of life is to become godlike, and that virtue is sufficient in itself for happiness.[35]

Diogenes Laertius The Cynics hold that the goal of life is to live according to virtue. Antisthenes says as much in his *Heracles*—just like the Stoics. . . . Therefore, some have said that Cynicism is a shortcut upon the path of virtue. Zeno of Citium [the founder of Stoicism] passed his own life in this way.[36]

Aristotle The human good, then, is the activity of the soul that accords with virtue. And if there happens to be more than one human virtue, then it is that activity which accords with the best and most complete or perfect virtue.[37]

Athenaeus of Naucratis (from a hymn to virtue attributed to Aristotle) O virtue, never but by much labor won, noblest object of all human life.[38]

Diogenes Laertius In his work *On the Nature of Man*, Zeno [of Citium] was the first to say that the end or goal of life is to live in accord with nature, which is the same as living in accord with virtue, since nature leads us toward virtue.[39]

Diogenes Laertius The epigrammatist Athenaeus speaks of all the Stoics in common as follows: "You who are acquainted with the words of the Stoic Porch. You who have committed to your divine books the best of human teachings, that virtue of the soul is the only good. Her decrees alone protect the lives of men and cities. But those other men who declare the goal of life is the enjoyment of the flesh are ruined by one of the Muses, the daughters of Memory."[40]

Philostratus the Athenian (Apollonius of Tyana is speaking) "The gods care most for those who pursue philosophy together with virtue."[41]

Galen I especially favor that exercise which promotes sufficient health for the body, harmonious development of its parts, and virtue in the spirit.[42]

Clement of Alexandria God is always urging us on to virtue.[43]

Plotinus Since evils are here in this realm, and since these evils "prowl about this realm by necessity," and since the soul wishes to flee these evils, then "we must flee from this realm." But what is the nature of this flight we must take? Plato says that it is in becoming like god—like the divinity. And this, he says, is found if one "is becoming just and holy, and in one who is beginning to live by means of practical wisdom"—which is to say the whole of virtue.[44]

NOTES

[1] Athenaeus of Naucratis, *Deipnosophists* 12.67. For the same lines, see also 7.11.

[2] It is unclear because Epicurus otherwise equates virtue with living pleasantly. Therefore, it seems that one *cannot* live pleasantly—with pleasure—without living virtuously. For Epicurus' position, see Diogenes Laertius, *Lives and Opinions of Eminent Philosophers* 10.32. From now on, *Lives*.

[3] Homer, *Odyssey* 13.44-46.

[4] Ibid., 24.505-515.

[5] Homer, *Iliad* 6.207-210. Recall that "best" is the Greek *aristos*, a word etymologically related to *aretē*.

[6] Ibid., 11.783-784. Again, "best" is the Greek *aristos*, a word etymologically related to *aretē*.

[7] Ibid., 6.475-481. Recall from the Introduction that the root word of "excellence" is related to a "hill" that rises above the flatlands; therefore, to be "outstanding" or "preeminent" (as Hector prays for his son) is to be excellent.

[8] Hesiod, *Works and Days* 286-292. "Excellence" (Aretē) could have been given as "Success." If Homer sings about the path of the heroic warrior, Hesiod describes the way of the heroic farmer.

[9] Basil the Great, *How to Benefit from Reading Greek Literature* 5.3, in *The Best of Basil the Great on Reading Literature and Education* (Sugar Land: The Classics Cave, 2020), 53. Lilah Grace Canevaro reports that this one Hesiodic passage alone "is quoted some twenty-six times in extant literature dating from 70 BC to AD 300." See Lilah Grace Canevaro, *Hesiod's Works & Days: How to Teach Self-Sufficiency* (Oxford: Oxford University Press, 2015), 8. If we reference earlier Greek literature, the number of citations expands, including writers such as Plato and Xenophon.

[10] Homeric *Hymn 15 to Heracles* 9.

[11] Homeric *Hymn 20 to Hephaestus* 8.

[12] Tyrtaeus of Sparta, in Stobaeus, *Anthology* 4.10.1.

[13] Procopius, *History* 4.1.17.

[14] Diodorus Siculus, *Library* 9.1.1.

[15] Diogenes Laertius, *Lives* 1.92.

[16] Ibid., 1.30.

[17] Xenophanes of Colophon, in Athenaeus, *Deipnosophists* 11.462c.

[18] Theognis of Megara 465; 867; 933-934.

[19] Simonides of Ceos, in *Palatine Anthology* 7.258.

[20] Phocylides, in Alexander of Aphrodisias on Aristotle, *Topica* 3.118a6.

[21] Bacchylides, *Victory Ode* 1.159-160; 3.90-91. See also 1.181-184 in which Bacchylides declares how a man must obtain excellence with much toil, yet in the end, even after the man dies, he has much glory.

[22] Sophocles, *Eriphyle* fragment 201d.

[23] Thucydides, *The Peloponnesian War* 2.87.

[24] Herodotus, *Histories* 8.26.

[25] Isocrates, *Panathenaicus* 12.138.

[26] Ibid., 12.136.

[27] Isocrates, *To Demonicus* 1.7.

[28] For "Models of Aretē," see Chapter 6.

[29] Diodorus Siculus, *Library* 15.1.1.

[30] Diogenes Laertius, *Lives* 1.Prologue.21.

[31] Xenophon, *Memorabilia* 1.2.64.

[32] Ibid., 1.2.2.

[33] Julian the emperor, *The Heroic Deeds of Emperor Constantius, or On Kingship, Oration II* 79.

[34] Plato, *Symposium* 212a.

[35] Diogenes Laertius, *Lives* 3.78.

[36] Ibid., 6.104.

[37] Aristotle, *Nicomachean Ethics* 1.7.15-16 (1098a).

[38] Athenaeus, *Deipnosophists* 15.1.

[39] Diogenes Laertius, *Lives* 7.87.

[40] Ibid., 7.30.

[41] Philostratus, *Life of Apollonius* 2.39.

[42] Galen, *On Exercise with the Small Ball*. Translation from Stephen G. Miller, *Aretē: Greek Sports from Ancient Sources* (Berkeley: University of California Press, 2012), 123.

[43] Clement of Alexandria, *Exhortation to the Greeks*, Chapter 1.

[44] Plotinus, *Enneads* 1.2.1.

THE *ARETĒ* SPECTRUM
FROM INANIMATE TO DIVINE *ARETĒ*

T HE EARLY STOICS taught that "excellence is in one sense the perfection of anything in general, say of a statue."[1] This seems to
have been the common view of the ancient Greeks. They recognized
aretē in many things extending from the non-living to the living.

Though the Greeks did not explicitly do so, we may call this
range of excellence *the aretē spectrum*, a field of high quality, merit,
and perfection that spanned from inanimate things like soil, cotton,
bread, and compositions on the one hand, to living things such as
horses, dogs, human beings, and gods on the other.

In this chapter, we'll begin with the inanimate side of the aretē
spectrum before passing through the range of animals, humans,
and gods, all of which possess excellence.

IN THEIR OWN WORDS

Inanimate things. *On one side of the aretē spectrum are inanimate or
non-living things. Some are excellent things existing in nature or given
by the gods, things such as the land or soil, cotton, or a particular fish for
food (and so a non-living thing). Others are drawn from nature or in some
other manner perfected by human beings—things such as certain breads,
literary qualities and compositions, or statues (all related, in some sense,
to human excellence, but not the perfection of human being itself).*

*We begin with dirt, with excellent, which is to say fertile, soil or land—
something the Greeks lived very close to and knew very well. It was from the
soil that they raised everything that helped them survive and thrive.*

Herodotus It seems to me that there is in no part of Libya any great
excellence for which it should be compared to Asia or Europe—

except in the region that is called by the same name as its river, Cinyps. And this region is a match for the best farmland bearing the fruit of Demeter. Nor is it at all similar to the rest of Libya. For the soil is black and well-watered by springs—there's no fear of drought. . . . Its yield of grain is similar in measure to the land of Babylon. The land inhabited by the Euhesperitae is also good—it yields at the most a hundredfold. But the land of the Cinyps region yields three hundredfold.[2]

Thucydides The best land [in Greece] was always most subject to this change of inhabitants. Examples are the land now called Thessaly, Boeotia, most of the Peloponnese—though, not including Arcadia—and the best parts of the rest of Hellas. It was thanks to the excellence of the land that some men became more and more powerful. This led to faction and civil war, which was the source of ruin. It also invited invasion.[3]

Isocrates The Egyptians have come to a perfect state of happiness—regarding the excellence of their land and the extent of their plains, they reap the fruits of the Greek mainland.[4]

Diodorus Siculus Ducetius, after founding Palice and enclosing it with strong walls, portioned out the neighboring countryside in allotments. And it came to pass that this city, because of the excellence of the land and the multitude of colonists, enjoyed a rapid growth.[5]

Diodorus Siculus In Italy the city of Thurii came to be founded for the following reasons. When in former times the Greeks had founded Sybaris in Italy, the city had enjoyed rapid growth because of the excellence of the land. For situated as the city was between two rivers, the Crathis and the Sybaris, from which it derived its name, its inhabitants, who tilled an extensive and fruitful countryside, came to possess great riches.[6]

Dio Chrysostom The Trojans were distinguished not only for their wealth and excellence of soil and number of inhabitants but also because human beings born at Troy were very beautiful, both men and women, and horses were very swift.[7]

Athenaeus of Naucratis Polybius, in his seventh book, says that the inhabitants of Capua in Campania, having become exceedingly rich through the excellence of their soil, fell into habits of luxury and extravagance, exceeding all that is reported of the inhabitants of Crotona or Sybaris.[8]

Next, Herodotus reports the excellence of a "wool" that "grows on wild trees" in India. Though he doesn't have a word for it, what he means is cotton.

Herodotus The most outlying nations of the world have somehow drawn the finest things as their lot, exactly as Greece has drawn the possession of the best seasons by far. As I said a moment ago, India lies at the world's most distant eastern limit. And in India all living creatures, both four-footed and flying, are much bigger than those of other lands—except the horses, which are smaller than the Median horses called Nesaean. Moreover, the gold there, whether dug from the earth or brought down by rivers or obtained as I have described [with the help of ants], is very abundant. There, too, wool more beautiful and excellent than the wool of sheep grows on wild trees. These trees supply the Indians with clothing.[9]

Athenaeus of Naucratis identifies various excellent foods —excellent eels (a delicacy in the ancient world) and the nature of excellent fish. As explained, they are included here among the non-living because their excellence is discussed relative to their being food rather than living, swimming beings.

Athenaeus of Naucratis I praise all kinds of eels. But by far the best is that eel which fishermen take in the sea opposite to the strait of Rhegium, where you, Messenius, who daily put this food in your mouth, have more of a share of this food than most mortals. Still, no one can deny the greatness of the glory and excellence that belong to Strymonian and Copaic eels, for they are large and wonderfully fat.[10]

Athenaeus of Naucratis For fish whose flesh is by nature soft and fat, it is enough to sprinkle them with salt and lightly anoint them with olive oil. I say this because these fish possess their own excellence and delight.[11]

Finally, we have a few selections that present excellent inanimate human products. In discussing the excellence (or not) of various loaves of bread, Athenaeus of Naucratis claims that oven-baked bread is the best. Otherwise, Dionysius of Halicarnassus hints at the excellent qualities of literature and identifies as excellent the "well-mixed" composition.

Athenaeus of Naucratis And Galen, when we were just about to lay hands on the loaves, said, "We will not begin supper until you have heard what the sons of the Asklēpiadai [i.e., physicians] have said about loaves of bread . . .

"Diphilus the Siphnian, in his treatise on *What is Wholesome to Be Eaten by People in Health and by Invalids*, says, 'Loaves made of wheat are by far more nutritious and by far more digestible than those made of barley, and are in every respect superior to them . . .'

"Philistion the Locrian says, 'The loaves made of similago are superior to those made of groats, as far as their strengthening properties go. And next to them he ranks loaves made of groats, then those made of sifted flour. But the rolls made of bran give a much less wholesome juice, and are by far less nutritious. And all bread is more digestible when eaten hot than cold. . . . Bread baked in the ashes is heavy and difficult for digestion because it is not baked in an equal manner. . . . But bread baked in the oven has every possible excellence, for it gives a pleasant and wholesome juice, and it is good for the stomach, digestible, and it agrees exceedingly well with everyone—for it never clogs the bowels and never relaxes them too much.'"[12]

Dionysius of Halicarnassus Let no one think me ignorant of the fact that the so-called "pedestrian character" is commonly regarded as a vice in poetry, or attribute to me, of all persons, the folly of ranking any bad quality among the excellences of poetry or prose.[13]

Dionysius of Halicarnassus The third kind of composition is a mean between the two I have already mentioned. I call it "well-mixed" for lack of a proper and better name. It has no form peculiar to itself but is a sort of judicious blend of the two others and a selection from the most effective features of each. This kind, it seems to me, deserves to win the first prize. I say this because it is a sort of mean—and, according to Aristotle and the other philosophers of his school, excellence in life and conduct and skill is a mean.[14]

Animals. *Next along the aretē spectrum are living things or animals. Since the Greeks dwelled close both to domesticated and wild animals, they had clear views about what was best or excellent among them (recall that aristos, the Greek word for "best," is related to aretē). In the* Iliad, *for instance, Homer reports that the eagle has the "best eyesight," and in the* Works and Days, *Hesiod declares that nine-year-old oxen are "the best for working." In the selections that follow, we encounter excellent horses and dogs.*

Homer (Achilles is speaking) "You know how much my steeds are better in excellence than all others—for they are immortal. Poseidon gave them to my father Peleus, who in turn gave them to me."[15]

Homer When now the swift horses were completing the last stretch of the course back toward the grey sea, then their excellence was manifest.[16]

Homer Of the horses, those of the son of Pheres were by far the best. They were as fast as birds are, the same age and color, and perfectly matched in height. Apollo of the silver bow had bred them in Pereira—both of them mares and dreadful as Ares in battle.[17]

Bacchylides of Ceos As yet the golden-haired god Apollo holds dear the city-state of Syracuse and honors Hieron, the city's lawful ruler. For thanks to the excellence of his swift-footed horses, his praises are sung as a Pythian victor for a third time nearby the navel of the land with high cliffs.[18]

Herodotus And everything everywhere was filled with his power. Accordingly, Darius now first produced and set up a carved stone, upon which was cut the figure of a horseman, with this inscription: "Darius, the son of Hystaspes—with the help of the excellence of his horse, and of Oebares, his righthand horseman—won the kingdom of Persia."[19]

Isocrates The man entered a larger number of teams of horses in competition than even the mightiest cities had done. And these teams were so excellent that he won first, second, and third.[20]

Diodorus Siculus While Alexander was wasting the countryside with fire, . . . some of the local men made a sudden rush and carried off the best one of the royal horses. This horse had come to Alexander as a gift from Demaratus of Corinth and had carried the king in all his battles in Asia. . . . Because of the excellence of this animal, the king was infuriated at his loss and ordered that every tree in the land be felled, while he proclaimed to the local inhabitants through interpreters that if the horse were not returned, they would see the country laid waste to its farthest limit and its people slaughtered to a man. Since he began immediately to carry out these threats, the local inhabitants were terrified and returned the horse and sent with it their costliest gifts. They also sent fifty men to beg forgiveness.[21]

Diodorus Siculus Sopeithes presented to Alexander many impressive gifts, among them one hundred fifty dogs remarkable for their size, strength, and other advantages. People said that they had a strain of tiger blood. He wanted Alexander to test the excellence of the dogs in action. And so he brought into a ring a full-grown lion and two of the poorest of the dogs. He set these on the lion, and when they were having a hard time of it, he released two others to assist them.[22]

Sextus Empiricus Now the dog—that animal upon which, by way of example, we have decided to base our argument—makes a choice for that which is fitting and flees from that which is harmful, in that it hunts after food and avoids a raised whip. . . . Nor is the dog without virtue. I say this because if justice consists in rendering to each his due, then the dog, which welcomes and guards its friends and benefactors but drives off those who are not its friends and who lack justice, cannot be lacking in justice. But if he possesses this virtue, then, since the virtues are interdependent, he also possesses all the other virtues. . . .

That the dog is also brave, we see by the way he repels attacks. He is also intelligent, as Homer testified as well, when he sang how Odysseus went unrecognized by all the people of his own household and was recognized only by the dog Argos. The latter dog was neither deceived by the bodily alterations of the hero nor had he lost his original direct apprehension or apprehending presentation, which he evidently retained better than other men.[23]

Homer (describing the homecoming of Odysseus and his encounter with his old dog, Argos) A dog that lay there raised his head and pricked up his ears—Argos, Odysseus' dog. . . . In days gone by, the young men used to take the dog out to hunt wild goats and deer and hares. But now he lay neglected in the deep dung of mules and cattle . . .

Odysseus looked aside and wiped away a tear. . . . And he questioned the swineherd, saying, "Eumaeus, it is strange that this dog lies here in the dung. His form is beautiful, but I do not clearly know whether he has the speed to match this beauty or whether he is merely one of those dogs that their masters keep for show."

In reply, the swineherd Eumaeus said, ". . . If this dog were but in form and in action such as he was when his master left him and went to Troy, you would soon be amazed at seeing his speed and his strength. No wild creature that he pursued in the depths of the thick wood could escape him. And he knew well how to track them. But now he's in misery."[24]

Human beings. *After non-human animals (living things) on the* aretē *spectrum, come human beings. True, for the Greeks, humans are animals or living beings. Even so, they are different from the animals we've already encountered (dogs, horses, and the like). If we follow Aristotle and other philosophers, they are so in that they are "rational animals" rather than ones that live according to "impulse" alone.*

In the first selection, Xenophon tells us that the poetry of Theognis of Megara was about human excellence.

Xenophon The subject matter of this poet Theognis is about nothing other than human excellence and non-excellence. The poem is a written speech about human beings, just as if a horseman were to write about horsemanship.[25]

With the next statement of Meno, who was a well-to-do man from Thessaly and a budding philosopher, we learn that human virtue varies—that men and women and the various stations of life have different virtues.

Plato (Socrates and Meno are conversing about virtue; Meno offers his view) Socrates: "Tell me, what is your own account of virtue?" . . .

Meno: "No problem, Socrates. First, if you want to look at the virtue of a man, it is easily stated that a man's virtue is this: that he be competent to manage the affairs of his city, and to manage them so as to benefit his friends and harm his enemies, and to take care to avoid suffering harm himself. Or take a woman's virtue: there is no difficulty in describing it as the duty of ordering the house well, looking after the property indoors, and obeying her husband. And the child has another virtue—one for the female and one for the male. And there is another for elderly men. And one, if you like, for freemen, and yet another for slaves. And there are very many other virtues besides, so that one cannot be at a loss to explain what virtue is—for it is according to each activity and age that every one of us, in whatever we do, has his virtue. And as I understand it, Socrates, the same also holds for vice."[26]

Others also contemplated how excellence shifts, or how there are different excellences, through human life. The statesman Solon of Athens, for example, wrote a poem dividing the life of a man into ten stages, each lasting seven years, some possessing specific excellences. With others, we gain an idea of what excellence is through the course of human life.

Solon of Athens In the fourth hebdomad, everyone reaches the peak of strength that is the mark of excellence. . . .

In the seventh and eighth hebdomads, he is by far the best in mind and the use of language — this for a total of fourteen years.

In the ninth portion, he is still able and strong enough, but his use of language and wisdom have declined from their peak excellence.[27]

Euripides (the Chorus is speaking) "If the gods had demonstrated intelligence and wisdom as we men understand them, men would have twice experienced youth, a visible mark of excellence."[28]

Diodorus Siculus Alexander called the boy to him and treated him with affection. And when he saw that he was fearless and not at all terrified, he remarked to Hephaestion that at six years of age the boy showed an excellence beyond his years and was much better than his father.[29]

Euripides "There are three virtues that you must practice, my child. Honor the gods, your parents, and the common laws of Greece. In doing so, you will always have a noble garland of glory and reputation."[30]

Next, we learn how the excellence or virtue of women is the same — or not — as that of men. A few selections list details regarding these excellences. For specific examples of excellent women, see 6, "Models of Arete."

Diogenes Laertius (the Cynic philosopher Antisthenes is speaking) "Virtue is the same for a woman as it is for a man."[31]

Julian the emperor Now I would judge it strange indeed if we were eager to applaud men who are noble and good and not judge it worthwhile to give our tribute of praise to a good woman, supposing, as we do, that virtue is the attribute of women no less than of men.[32]

Diodorus Siculus It is proper that excellence be honored — also when it is exhibited by women.[33]

Thucydides (the Athenian statesman Pericles is speaking) "If I must say anything about the excellence of women to those of you who will now be widows, it will be included in this brief exhortation. Great will be your glory in not falling short of your natural character. And greatest will be your glory who is least talked about among the men, whether for excellence or for something blameworthy."[34]

Julian the emperor Homer was not ashamed to praise Penelope and the wife of Alcinous and other women of exceptional goodness, or even those whose claim to excellence was slight. No—nor did Penelope fail to obtain her share of praise for this very thing.[35]

Euripides (Andromache is speaking to Hermione) "It is not because my drugs that your husband despises you. No, it is because you are unfriendly and useless to live with. But this is also a love-charm. Women do not delight their husbands with beauty but with excellences."[36]

Athenaeus of Naucratis Bards in those days were sensible and self-controlled, cultivating a disposition like that of philosophers. Accordingly, Agamemnon leaves his bard as the guardian and counselor to his wife Clytemnestra. The bard, going through all the excellences of women, endeavored to inspire her with a love for honor in nobility and goodness.[37]

Lucian of Samosata Where perfection of the body goes hand in hand with soul virtue, I maintain that there alone is true beauty. I could show you many a woman whose outward loveliness is marred by what is within—who has but to open her lips and beauty stands revealed a faded, withered thing, the unlovely handmaid of that odious mistress, her soul. Such women are like Egyptian temples. The shrine is beautiful and big, built with costly stone, decked out with gilding and painting, but seek the god within and you find an ape, a bird, a goat, a cat. This same thing is true for so many women! Beauty unadorned is not enough. And her true adornments are not clothing of purple and necklaces, but those I mentioned before—excellence, moderation, equity, humanity, and anything like these.[38]

From Homer we learn that the loss of liberty—when one is enslaved—entails a loss of excellence.

Homer (Eumaeus is speaking) "Slaves, when their masters lose power, are no longer interested thereafter in doing honest service. I know this because Zeus, whose voice is carried afar, takes away half the excellence of a man when he is enslaved."[39]

In the final selections having to do with human excellence on the aretē spectrum, we encounter various groupings of excellent human beings—cooks, artists, rowing men, barbarians and Greeks, and, among the Greeks, Athenians, Lacedaemonians (Spartans), and Syracusans.

Athenaeus of Naucratis But Euphron, whom I mentioned a little while ago . . . in his play called the *Brothers*, represented a certain cook as a well-educated man of extensive learning, and enumerated all the artists before his time, and mentioned what particular excellence each of them had, and what he surpassed the rest in.[40]

Diodorus Siculus And Cimon, taking the fleet that had been equipped with excellent rowing men and abundant supplies, sailed to Cyprus.[41]

Philostratus the Athenian Homer took the story of the Trojan War as his subject, in which fortune brought together the excellences of the Greeks and the barbarians.[42]

Herodotus Among the Greeks, the Tegeans and Athenians conducted themselves nobly, but the Lacedaemonians surpassed all in excellence.[43]

Diodorus Siculus The Athenians fell back to the Lacedaemonians and joined them in assaulting the Theban walls. They did so against those Persians who had taken refuge within. Both sides struggled greatly—the barbarians fighting bravely from their fortified positions and the Greeks storming the wooden walls. And many were wounded as they fought on desperately. And not a few were also slain by the many missiles. And these courageously submitted to death. Still, the powerful Greek attack could not be resisted—neither by the barbarian's wall nor by their great number. But the Greeks forced all resistance to give way. This was so because the leading Greeks were competing with each other—the Lacedaemonians and the Athenians. And both were buoyed up thanks to their former victories and to the confidence they had in their own excellence.[44]

Diodorus Siculus Elated by his good fortune, the Spartan man Pausanias came to despise the Lacedaemonian training and way of life. So, he began to copy the Persians in their license and luxury—the very man who least of all had any reason to esteem the customs of the barbarians. I say this because he had not learned about their ways from others, but in person he had been exposed to them and had tried them, and he was aware of how greatly superior his ancestor's way of life was relative to excellence compared with the luxury of the Persians.[45]

Thucydides (Athenian envoys are speaking) "The Lacedaemonians, when their own interests or their own land's laws are in question, are the most excellent men alive. Regarding their behavior toward others, a good deal may be said. But no clearer idea of their conduct could be given than by briefly stating that of all the men we know, they are the most conspicuous in acknowledging that, on the one hand, the noble is whatever is pleasant or agreeable, and that, on the other hand, the just is whatever is expedient or useful."[46]

Thucydides (the Athenian statesman Nicias is speaking) "Remember that the Lacedaemonians are sensitive to their own disgrace. Their sole thought now is how they might find a way, if possible, to make us fall, thereby repairing the harm that has come to their own reputation, given how much and for how long they have trained to win their reputation for excellence."[47]

Diodorus Siculus Now among the Athenians, each citizen was required to write on a broken piece of ceramics the name of the man who, in his view, was most able through his influence to tyrannize over his fellow citizens. Among the Syracusans, by contrast, the name of the most influential citizen was written on an olive leaf, and when the leaves were counted, the man who received the largest number of leaves had to go into exile for five years. They thought that they would lessen the pride of the strongest men in these two cities. . . .

This legal custom remained in place among the Athenians for a long time. But among the Syracusans it was soon repealed for the following reasons. They did so because the greatest, most influential men were being sent into exile—those who were most highly educated and refined, and, thus, those who were able, because of their own excellence, to fix many things for the community. Instead, these men were missing in action relative to the business of the people. They were taking care of their own wealth and leaning toward soft living. Meanwhile, the basest, most worthless citizens were giving their attention to public affairs and urging on the many to disorder and revolution.[48]

The gods or divine excellence. *Lastly, and perhaps most excellent on the* aretē *spectrum, are the gods. The notion of excellence or virtue is not usually paired with the gods in non-philosophical Greek literature.[49] Still, the idea that the gods are by nature excellent or virtuous was common — or, at very least, common was the idea that they should be so, even when not.[50] The following selections show both.*

Homer (Phoenix is speaking) "You must conquer your great anger, Achilles. There's no need to have such a pitiless heart. No—even the gods are willing to bend, those whose excellence and honor and might are greater than ours."[51]

Isocrates Now I, for my part, think that not only the gods but also their offspring have no share in any vice. Rather, they themselves are by nature endowed with all the virtues and have become for all mankind guides and teachers of the most honorable conduct.[52]

Epicurus The gods always receive those men who are like them since they make every virtue their own, while rejecting everything that does not belong to them.[53]

Euripides (Amphitryon is speaking, chastising Zeus for his apparent lack of aretē) "Zeus, in vain did I get you to share my wife. In vain did I call you my son's partner. Rather, it seems you are less a friend than you pretended to be. So it is that even though you are a great god, I have prevailed over you in excellence since I have not deserted the children of Heracles. But you who know how to sleep in another bed secretly, you who know how to take the wife of another man without his permission, you do not know how to help and save your friends! Either you are some ignorant god, or you are unjust by nature."[54]

Euripides (Ion is speaking, encouraging Apollo to "chase after excellence") "But I must admonish Phoebus Apollo. What is the state of his mind? Does he rape virgins by strength? Does he engender children only to leave them to die? Let me tell you—don't do it anymore! Rather, since you have power, chase after excellence. I say this because if any mortal man is bad, the gods punish him. How then is it just for you to write laws for mortals, even though you yourselves are guilty of injustice? And if you make us humans pay for rape, then you gods—Apollo, Poseidon, and Zeus—you will empty your temple treasuries in paying for your crimes, for you unjustly pursue your pleasures so eagerly and without foresight. Therefore, it is not right to speak badly about men—if, that is, we are merely imitating what the gods present as noble. Rather, we should speak this way about the ones who taught us these things."[55]

We finish with two New Testament passages (both Greek, albeit Christian, literature) that pair aretē with God, as well as one that calls on humans to cultivate aretē.

St. Peter You are a chosen people, a royal priesthood, a holy nation, God's own people—this so that you may proclaim the virtues of the one (God) who called you out of darkness into his marvelous light.[56]

St. Peter God's power has given us everything necessary for life and piety through the full knowledge of the one who has called us by his own glory and virtue. Through these he has given us his precious and most magnificent promises so that you may become a partner in the divine nature after escaping the corruption engendered by worldly desire. For this reason, earnestly make every effort to add virtue to your faith. And to virtue, add knowledge. And to knowledge, self-control. And to self-control, patient endurance. And to patient endurance, piety. And to piety, brotherly love. And to brotherly love, unconditional love.[57]

Notes

[1] Diogenes Laertius, *Lives* 7.90.

[2] Herodotus, *Histories* 4.198. The Cinyps today is the Wadi Ka'am in Libya. For another example of excellent soil or land in Herodotus, see ibid., 7.5, which reads: "After Darius' death, the royal power descended to his son Xerxes. Now Xerxes was at first by no means eager to march against Hellas—rather, it was against Egypt that he mustered his army. But Mardonius, the son of Gobryas, . . . was with the king and had more influence with him than any other Persian. He argued as follows: 'Master, it is not fitting that the Athenians should go unpunished for their deeds—not after all the evil they have done to the Persians. For now you should do what you have in hand. Then, when you have tamed the insolence of Egypt, lead your armies against Athens so that you may have fair fame among men, and so that others may be wary about invading your realm in the future.' This argument was for vengeance. But he kept adding that Europe was an extremely beautiful land, one that bore all kinds of orchard trees, a land of highest excellence, worthy of no mortal master but the king."

[3] Thucydides, *The Peloponnesian War* 1.2. The explanation is given to explain why Attica, where Athens is located, had been relatively stable—thanks to its "thin or poor soil."

[4] Isocrates, *Busiris* 11.14.

[5] Diodorus Siculus, *Library* 11.90.1.

[6] Ibid., 12.9.1-2.

[7] Dio Chrysostom, *First Tarsic* 33.21.

[8] Athenaeus, *Deipnosophists* 12.36.

[9] Herodotus, *Histories* 3.106. For the gold and the help of the ants, see ibid., 3.102.

[10] Ibid., 7.53. "Best" here is the superlative form of *kratos*, a word that generally means "strength" and thus "strong," but applied to things it carries the connotation of "best, most excellent."

[11] Ibid., 7.117.

[12] Athenaeus, *Deipnosophists* 3.83.

[13] Dionysius of Halicarnassus, *The Arrangement of Words* 26.

[14] Ibid., 24. For Aristotle, "the mean" is that which comes between two extremes, a deficiency and an excess. For more, see 9, "Aristotle."

[15] Homer, *Iliad* 23.276-278.

[16] Ibid., 23.373-375.

[17] Ibid., 2.763-767. Recall that "best" is the Greek *aristos*, a word etymologically related to *aretē*.

[18] Bacchylides of Ceos, *Victory Ode* 4.2-6.

[19] Herodotus, *Histories* 3.88.

[20] Isocrates, *On the Team of Horses* 16.34. The "man" was Alcibiades.

[21] Diodorus Siculus, *Library* 17.76.7-8.

[22] Diodorus Siculus, *Library* 17.92.1-2. What happens? In short, the four "excellent" dogs defeat the lion.

[23] Sextus Empiricus, *Outlines of Pyrrhonism* 1.66-68. Sextus Empiricus, of the Pyrrhonist or Skeptical school of philosophy, makes these points only to argue against the "dogmatist" (in this case, "Stoic") position that there is a significant difference between human beings and "the so-called irrational animals," such as dogs. We give aretē as virtue rather than excellence because the general point is about human virtue.

[24] Homer, *Odyssey* 17.291-318. Though the specific term aretē does not appear in the text, its every mark is manifest. Speed and strength and skill in the hunt make for an excellent dog. Argos was beautiful, the best of dogs.

[25] Testimony regarding the poet Theognis of Megara, in Stobaeus, *Anthology* 4.29.53. We do not know if this Xenophon is Xenophon of Athens, the statesman and author, or another commentator.

[26] Plato, *Meno* 71d-72a.

[27] Solon in Philo, *On the Creation of the World* 104. A hebdomad is a group of seven, in this case a period of seven years. Again, "best" is the Greek *aristos*, a word etymologically related to aretē.

[28] Euripides, *Heracles* 655-658.

[29] Diodorus Siculus, *Library* 17.38.2.

[30] Euripides, fragment from *Heraclidae*. Modified from Arthur W.H. Adkins, *Merit and Responsibility: A Study in Greek Values* (Oxford: Oxford University Press, 1960; reprint 1975), 176.

[31] Diogenes Laertius, *Lives* 6.12.

[32] Julian, *Panegyric on the Empress Eusebia, Oration III* 104b.

[33] Diodorus Siculus, *Library* 10.24.2.

[34] Thucydides, *The Peloponnesian War* 2.45.

[35] Julian, *Panegyric on the Empress Eusebia, Oration III* 104c.

[36] Euripides, *Andromache* 205-208.

[37] Athenaeus, *Deipnosophists* 1.24.

[38] Lucian of Samosata, *Imagines* 11.

[39] Homer, *Odyssey* 17.320-323.

[40] Athenaeus, *Deipnosophists* 9.24.

[41] Diodorus Siculus, *Library* 12.3.2.

[42] Philostratus the Athenian, *Heroicus* 692.

[43] Herodotus, *Histories* 9.71.

[44] Diodorus Siculus, *Library* 11.32.4.

[45] Ibid., 11.46.3.

[46] Thucydides, *The Peloponnesian War* 5.105.

[47] Ibid., 6.11.

[48] Diodorus Siculus, *Library* 11.87.1-4. The Athenians called this means of exiling strong and influential men "ostracism" from the Greek *ostrakon* (potsherd) whereas the Syracusans called it "petalism" from the Greek *petalon* (leaf).

[49] In philosophical literature, it is often recognized that the gods — or God — are beyond virtue. For example, Aristotle states, "For there is no such thing as virtue in the case of a god" (*Nicomachean Ethics* 7.1.1).

[50] Greeks such as the Presocratic Xenophanes and later Plato (in the guise of Socrates) criticized the way the gods were depicted in much of early Greek literature, namely in Homer's and Hesiod's poems (much as Euripides does in this section through Amphitryon and Ion). For them, the gods are naturally good or excellent. Later philosophers and commentators attempted to explain the vicious behavior of the gods in Homer's and Hesiod's poems by means of allegorical interpretations.

[51] Homer, *Iliad* 9.496-498.

[52] Isocrates, *Busiris* 11.41-42.

[53] Diogenes Laertius, *Lives* 10.124 (*Letter to Menoeceus*).

[54] Euripides, *Heracles* 339-347.

[55] Euripides, *Ion* 436-451.

[56] 1 Peter 2.9. Although this is Christian literature (though written in Greek) about the God of Christians (judged to be the one and only God), it nevertheless tells us something about what the broader Greek world was thinking about divine excellence or virtue—at the very least, the idea that God possesses excellences or virtues (the Greek is plural—*aretai*).

[57] 2 Peter 1.3-7. For why this selection is included, see the note above regarding 1 Peter 2.9. Otherwise, the passage is valuable in that it repeats many qualities or virtues (particularly knowledge, self-control, patient endurance, piety, and brotherly love) that had long been considered virtues by the ancient Greeks.

THE NATURE OF *ARETĒ*
GENERAL & SPECIFIC NOTIONS OF *ARETĒ*

T HE PREVIOUS CHAPTERS have revealed two basic points regarding what the ancient Greeks generally believed about aretē. One, aretē is the goal of life; it is the objective we humans pursue, the end or good for which we live—or, rather, at our best it should be so. Two, as "the perfection of anything in general," excellence or virtue in the aretē spectrum can exist anywhere and in anything, ranging from non-living things, such as land or soil, to living things, including various animals, humans, and the gods (or God).

In this chapter we explore what the Greeks thought and said about the nature of excellence or virtue. We do so in terms of both a general definition (generally speaking, aretē is *such-and-such*) and specific instances of aretē, such as the four cardinal virtues of wisdom, courage, moderation, and justice.

IN THEIR OWN WORDS

Before getting to general definitions of aretē, let's take in Pindar's more poetic approach.

Pindar Excellence increases, rising like a tree to bursting rain, when lifted up among wise and just men to the heavens above.[1]

General definitions. *The Greeks did not produce a general definition of aretē until the appearance of philosophy when they began to look for the common source and general nature of things. It was only then, so far as we know, that someone thought to ask about the nature of aretē itself— that one reality, according to Plato, in which every other individual aretē participates.*[2]

What follows here, then, in the first set of selections, are the later definitions of aretē from philosophy. After observing these, we will peruse various specific excellences or virtues from Homer onward.[3]
Among the definitions hailing from the philosophers, we see that aretē is the general perfection or fulfilment of a thing. Another philosopher states that virtue is "the means by which a thing performs its function well." Another that it is a habit or disposition, the ongoing observance of a mean that falls between two extremes. Or it is strength, capacity, health, harmony, beauty. Finally, it is "a good condition of the soul"—a point that highlights the much more internal focus of the philosophers (on the soul) versus that of earlier and other Greeks (whose focus was much more external, on the body and more physical or tangible things—though certainly excellence of mind and feeling were highly valued). Note that with the shift to the philosophers, we give aretē as "virtue" instead of "excellence," even though we could have just as well stuck with excellence.

Diogenes Laertius (presenting the view of the philosopher Pythagoras)
Virtue is harmony and health and all that is good and the god.[4]

Plato (Socrates is speaking) In the first place, virtue signifies ease of motion, and secondly, that the flow of the good soul is always unimpeded.[5]

Plato (Socrates is speaking) It appears, then, that virtue is a kind of health and beauty and good condition of the soul.[6]

Plato (Socrates is speaking) Virtue is the means by which a thing performs its function well.[7]

Antisthenes the Cynic Virtue is a weapon that cannot be taken away.[8]

Diogenes Laertius (giving the Cynic philosopher Antisthenes' position)
Virtue is something you do—it is a matter of deeds. It doesn't require a stockpile of arguments or much learning.[9]

(Pseudo) Diogenes the Cynic To Anniceris: Virtue alone is that by which

the soul can be strengthened and delivered from its afflictions.[10]

Aristotle [Moral] virtue is a habit or disposition involving deliberate choice, consisting in the observance of a mean relative to us, as determined by reason, that is, as a wise and sensible man would determine it. Virtue is a mean that falls between two vices, that which is excessive and that which is deficient.[11]

Diogenes Laertius (reporting the early Stoic position) Virtue is in one sense the perfection of anything in general, say of a statue. Virtue may be non-intellectual, such as health, or intellectual, such as practical wisdom.[12]

Diogenes Laertius (reporting the early Stoic position) Virtue . . . is the state of the soul that tends to make the whole of life harmonious.[13]

Epictetus (in conversation with a young man) "What about a human being, then? What makes a human being beautiful?"

"Is it not the presence of a human being's virtue, his excellence?"

"Very well, then, young man. If you want to be beautiful, then strive hard to be excellent with the virtue that characterizes a human being."[14]

As the next selections reveal, most Greek philosophers and some orators held that areté was the key to happiness, to human flourishing.[15] Keep in mind that we could have just as well given "excellence" in place of "virtue."

Diogenes Laertius Plato held that the goal of life is to become godlike, and that virtue is sufficient in itself for happiness.[16]

Plato (Socrates is speaking) He who lives well is blessed and happy.[17]

Diogenes Laertius (giving the Cynic position) Virtue is sufficient for happiness.[18]

Isocrates Nothing in the world can contribute so powerfully to material gain, to good repute, to right action, in a word, to happiness, as virtue and the qualities of virtue.[19]

Aristotle Happiness is an activity of the soul that accords with perfect virtue.[20]

Diogenes Laertius (reporting the early Stoic position) The Stoics hold that virtue is sufficient in itself for happiness.[21]

Diogenes Laertius (expounding the early Stoic view) The virtues are goods that have both the nature of ends and means. Inasmuch as they produce happiness, they are means to good things. On the other hand, inasmuch as the virtues are the fulfillment of happiness, being a portion of happiness itself, they are ends.[22]

Epictetus Virtue promises happiness and tranquility and a life that flows well.[23]

Epicurus (explaining in his Letter to Menoeceus*)* The virtues have become one with living pleasantly. Living pleasantly is inseparable from the virtues. . . . We say that pleasure is the beginning point and goal of living happily.[24]

Rather than a single reality, ancient Greeks commonly held that aretē was many—that there were many excellences or virtues. In general, to be excellent or virtuous was to be the best in anything (recall that aretē is related to aristos, *the Greek for "best")—whether in fighting or rowing or planning or some other activity. More specifically, among the many excellences, we see preeminence, bodily form, stature, speed, strength, beauty, athletic skill, battle excellence (skill in battle), bravery, courage, daring, loyalty, magnificence, grace, dialectic, patient endurance, simplicity, self-control, discipline, piety, skillful knowledge, scientific knowledge, intelligence, and what came to be called the four cardinal (meaning "hinge") virtues of wisdom (whether practical or theoretical), courage (or fortitude), moderation (or temperance), and justice.[25] The next selections present some of these many excellences or virtues (aretai).*

Theognis of Megara There is every vice among men and every excellence and every plan of life.[26]

Homer (Idomeneus is speaking) Idomeneus, the leader of the Cretans, answered Meriones, "I know that you are an excellent man. You don't have to tell me. For if by the ships we were now choosing the best of all men for an ambush, you'd want to go first. Let me tell you, Meriones, that it is under circumstances like an ambush that the excellence of a man is discerned, and there that the cowardly man or the brave man reveals himself. For while the coward's skin changes from this color to another—and he can't sit without trembling or restrain the spirit in his chest, but he keeps shifting his weight from one knee to the other as his great heart rapidly beats, and he frightfully pictures the fates of death taking him, and his teeth begin to chatter—the good man's skin doesn't change, nor is he excessively alarmed when he's chosen first to participate in an ambush of men. Rather he prays to mix quickly in the deadly battle. No, Meriones—in such a situation no man would find fault with your prowess and the strength of your hands. If you were struck by an arrow or spear, you would not be hit from behind upon your neck or your back. But the weapon would hit you upon the chest or your belly as you were pressing forward to take your place in the front ranks."[27]

Homer Hector struck one man alone, Periphetes of Mycenae, the dear son of Copreus, the man who used to deliver messages from lord Eurystheus to mighty Heracles. And from him, from a father far more inferior than he was, was begotten a much better son, superior in every excellence, both in the excellence of his feet and in battle excellence, and in mind, he was among the first of the men of Mycenae.[28]

Homer Achilles raced against Polydorus, the son of Priam. Polydorus' father had always refused him permission to fight because he was the youngest of his sons and the one he loved best. He was also the fastest of his sons and could beat any other man with his feet.

So it was that right then, when Polydorus was foolishly showing off the excellence of his feet by darting through the foremost fighters, godlike Achilles struck him in the middle of the back as he was racing past him. He struck him upon the golden fastenings of his belt, where the breastplate overlapped. The point of the spear punched through his stomach, exiting his body through his belly button. Immediately, Polydorus fell to his knees, groaning, and a cloud of darkness passed over him as he collapsed, holding his own guts in his hands.[29]

Homer (Achilles is speaking) Achilles said, "Hector . . . remember every excellence—for now you need to be a spearman and a daring warrior."[30]

Homer Then thoughtful Penelope answered him, saying, "Eurymachus, the immortals destroyed my excellences—those of beautiful form and stature—when the Argives, including my husband, Odysseus, embarked for Ilium."[31]

Homer (Agamemnon is speaking) Then the soul of the son of Atreus, Agamemnon, addressed the suitor Amphimedon, saying, "Happy son of Laertes, much-able Odysseus! You acquired for yourself an excellent wife, one of great worth. How good was the heart in blameless Penelope, the daughter of Icarius! How faithful in mind to Odysseus, her wedded husband! The glory of her excellence will never fade, but the immortals will make among men on earth a graceful song for thoughtful Penelope. She didn't plot evil works like the daughter of Tyndareus [Clytemnestra]."[32]

Hesiod (relating different "best" things) Zeus gave human beings Justice, which is by far the best thing that has come to be. *And,* To be well-ordered is best for mortal human beings; mismanagement and disorder are the worst. *And,* Keep watch over the measure. Due measure is the best in all things.[33]

Simonides of Ceos (said in praise of those men who died at the battle of

Thermopylae and of Leonidas' battle excellence) Of those men who died at Thermopylae—glorious is the good fortune, and beautiful the destiny! Their tomb is an altar. For weeping they have remembrance, for their lot, praise. Mold nor all-conquering time will waste away such a funeral offering. This shrine of brave men chose the honor of Greece as their household. Leonidas himself, the king of Sparta, bears witness to this, he who left behind a great adornment of battle excellence and everlasting glory.[34]

Simonides of Ceos (on the excellence won by those who fought for liberty and died nobly) If the greatest part of excellence is to die nobly, then Fortune apportioned it to us more than others, for we struggled eagerly to bestow liberty upon Greece, and so we lie here announcing a never-fading eulogy.[35]

Pindar Our mortal existence drives us toward four excellences.[36]

Bacchylides of Ceos To have a good portion from the gods is the best thing for human beings. . . . Different men have different honors. And among men there are countless excellences. Still, one stands out from the rest—it is when a man is governed by just thoughts in everything he must do.[37]

Panyassis "Friend—come on and drink! This is now an excellence, when someone drinks the most wine during a feast . . . It is equally one for a man to be quick during a dinner banquet as during a battle."[38]

Isocrates I speak, not of excellence as that word is used in the arts or in many other activities, but of the virtue that, in the souls of noble and good men, is engendered along with piety and justice.[39]

Plato (Meno is speaking with Socrates) There are other virtues aside from justice. . . . It seems to me that courage is a virtue, as well as moderation, and wisdom, and magnificence of character, and a great many others.[40]

Diogenes Laertius (reporting Plato's view) Of perfect virtue there are four kinds or forms: practical wisdom, justice, courage, and moderation. Of these, practical wisdom is the cause of right conduct, and justice is responsible for straight dealing in partnerships and commercial transactions. Courage is the cause that makes a man not give way but stand his ground in alarms and perils. Moderation causes mastery over desires, so that we are never enslaved by pleasure but live in an orderly manner.[41]

Demosthenes For of all virtue, I say, and I repeat it, the beginning is intelligence or understanding, and the fulfillment is courage.[42]

Demosthenes All men would agree with me, I believe, that it is of the utmost importance for young men of your age to possess beauty relative to appearance, moderation relative to the soul, and manliness relative to both, and consistently to possess grace relative to speech.[43]

Munich Anthology To the lad who had turned red, Philoxenus said, "Be courageous—for this is the color of excellence."[44]

Aristotle So then, there are two kinds of virtue—intellectual or thinking virtue and moral or ethical virtue.[45]

Aristotle The virtues by which the soul achieves truth in terms of assent and denial are five in number. These are art or skillful knowledge, science or scientific knowledge, prudence or practical wisdom, wisdom or theoretical wisdom, and intelligence.[46]

Diogenes Laertius (reporting the Stoic position) Of the virtues, some are primary, and some are arranged under these primary virtues. There are four primary virtues: practical wisdom, moderation, courage, and justice.[47]

Diogenes Laertius The Stoics hold that dialectic itself is necessary and a virtue, and that it encompasses the other virtues.[48]

Diodorus Siculus Pythagoras delivered many other discourses designed to inculcate the zealous imitation of a moderate life and courage and patient endurance and the other virtues.[49]

Diodorus Siculus Lysis, the Pythagorean, came to Thebes in Boeotia and became the teacher of Epaminondas. And with respect to excellence, he developed him into a perfect man. . . . And Epaminondas, because of the incitements toward patient endurance and simplicity and every other excellence that he received from the Pythagorean philosophy, became the foremost man not only of Thebes but of all who lived in his time.[50]

Diodorus Siculus All excellences are combined in Epaminondas. For in strength of body and eloquence of speech, in splendor of soul, contempt for money, and fairness, and, most of all, in courage and understanding in the art of war, he surpassed them all by far.[51]

St. Paul Finally, brothers, whatever is true, whatever is holy, whatever is just, whatever is pure, whatever is agreeable, whatever is spoken of well—if there is any virtue and any praise, think about these things.[52]

St. Peter Earnestly make every effort to add virtue to your faith. And to virtue, add knowledge. And to knowledge, self-control. And to self-control, patient endurance. And to patient endurance, piety. And to piety, brotherly love. And to brotherly love, unconditional love.[53]

Dio Chrysostom Nearly everyone praises and calls "divine" and "holy" such things as courage and justice and practical wisdom and, in short, every virtue.[54]

Philostratus the Athenian (regarding the religious figure Apollonius of Tyana, a Neopythagorean philosopher) The conversations that Apollonius held in Olympia were about the most useful and profitable topics, such as wisdom and courage and moderation. In a word, they were conversations upon all the virtues. He discussed these from the platform of the temple, and he astonished everyone not only by the insight he showed but also by his forms of expression.[55]

Philostratus the Athenian As they made their way into Mesopotamia, the tax-gatherer who presided over the bridge . . . asked them what they were taking out of the country with them. Apollonius replied, "I am taking with me moderation, justice, virtue, self-control, courage, and discipline."[56]

Philostratus the Athenian (Thespesion is speaking to Apollonius of Tyana) "Practical wisdom is something more than a lack of foolishness, just as courage is something more than not running away from the ranks. Likewise, moderation is something more than the avoidance of adultery. And no one reserves his praise for a man who has simply shown himself to be not bad. Just because a thing is equally far from honor and punishment doesn't make that thing virtue."[57]

Athenaeus of Naucratis Now, formerly music was an exhortation to courage. Accordingly, the poet Alcaeus, one of the greatest musicians that ever lived, sets down courage before skill in music and poetry, being himself a man skilled in war even beyond duty. . . . The ancients considered courage the greatest of all civil excellences, and they attributed the greatest importance to that quality—even to the exclusion of others.[58]

Athenaeus of Naucratis The physician Dioscorides, with respect to the laws praised in Homer, says, "The poet—seeing that moderation was the most desirable excellence for young men, the first of all excellences, and the one that was becoming to everyone, and the excellence that was, as it were, the guide to all other excellences—wishing to implant moderation from the very beginning in everyone . . . appointed a simple and independent mode of life to everyone."[59]

Julian the emperor Socrates never praised Xerxes or any other king of Persia or Lydia or Macedonia, and not even a Greek general,

except for only a very few—those whom he knew to delight in virtue, and to cherish courage with moderation, and to love wisdom
with justice.[60]

Procopius For in courage and every sort of virtue, [the accountant]
John was well endowed, and to those who associated with him, he
showed himself to be gentle and fair to a degree that was quite unsurpassed. So it was, then, that he fulfilled his destiny.[61]

*In the last few selections, we observe that there were some who were skep-
tical regarding the virtues. At least they were skeptical of the "system of
virtues" as it was developed by the philosophers—the system that was
meant to bridle human passions and desires.*

Athenaeus of Naucratis Aristoxenus the musician, in his *Life of Archytas*, says that ambassadors were sent by Dionysius the younger to
the city of the Tarentines. Among them was Polyarchus, who was
surnamed "the Luxurious," a man wholly devoted to pleasures of
the body, not only in deed but in word also.

Polyarchus was a friend of the Pythagorean Archytas and not
wholly unversed in philosophy. And so, he used to come with him
into the sacred precincts and walk with him and with his friends,
listening to his lectures and arguments.

And once, when there was difficulty about the desires together
with a consideration of the bodily pleasures, Polyarchus said, "I
have often considered the matter, men, and it has seemed to me that
this system of the virtues is altogether a long way removed from
nature. For nature, when it utters its own voice, orders one to follow
pleasure, and it says that this is the conduct of a sensible and wise
man. But that to oppose nature and to bring one's desires into a
state of slavery is neither what a sensible nor a fortunate man would
do—nor one who has any accurate understanding of what the constitution of human nature really is."[62]

Athenaeus of Naucratis Sotion says that in that play, a slave named
Xanthias was represented as exhorting all his fellow slaves to a life

of luxury, saying, "Why do you talk such stuff? Why do you run around to the Lyceum and the Academy . . . hunting in vain for all the nonsense of the sophists? There's no good in it! Let us drink—drink, O Sicon! Let us amuse ourselves while time lets us gratify our souls! Enjoy yourself, Manes! Nothing has more pleasure than the stomach. That's your father!—your mother! As for the excellences and embassies and military commands, they are but noisy boasts and empty dreams. Fate will come to chill you at its destined time. Take all that you can get to eat and drink. Pericles, Codrus, Cimon—they are but dust!"[63]

Notes

[1] Pindar, *Nemean* 8.40-41.

[2] For a typical conversation illustrating how this idea may have developed, one between Socrates and Meno, see the first part of 7 "Plato & Socrates."

[3] For now, we give only the briefest idea of what each philosopher held. For a fuller treatment, see Part 2, where a whole chapter is devoted to each major philosopher or school of philosophy.

[4] Diogenes Laertius, *Lives* 8.33.

[5] Plato, *Cratylus* 415c-d.

[6] Plato, *Republic* 4.444d-e.

[7] Ibid., 1.353c. Faithful to Plato's intention (evident in Socrates' position), we have modified the line by transforming Socrates' question into a positive statement. The question: "I am asking about whether a thing that has a function performs it well by means of its own virtue . . ."

[8] Diogenes Laertius, *Lives* 6.12. Diogenes Laertius tells us that the teaching was recorded by Diocles of Magnesia (second or first century BC), who was an ancient historian and writer of biography and summaries. He concentrated on the views, sayings, and lives of the earliest philosophers.

[9] Ibid., 6.11.

[10] (Pseudo) Diogenes of Sinope, *Letter* 27 To Anniceris.

[11] Aristotle, *Nicomachean Ethics* 2.6.15-16 (1107a).

[12] Diogenes Laertius, *Lives* 7.90. Note that for the early Stoics, the aretē spectrum (as we have termed it) extended from the non-intellectual or non-contemplative (*atheōrētos*) to the intellectual or contemplative (*theōrēmatikos*) as compared to our more general expanse from the non-living to the living.

[13] Ibid., 7.89.

[14] Epictetus, *Discourses* 3.1.

[15] For the ideas of the Greek philosophers, as well as earlier conceptions of happiness, see *Happiness: What the Ancient Greeks Thought and Said about Happiness* (Sugar Land: The Classics Cave, 2021).

[16] Diogenes Laertius, *Lives* 3.78.

[17] Plato, *Republic* 1.354a. By living "well" (the Greek is *eu*) we should understand excellently or virtuously, as Plato makes clear in the remainder of the dialogue.

[18] Diogenes Laertius, *Lives* 6.11.

[19] Isocrates, *On the Peace* 8.32.

[20] Aristotle, *Nicomachean Ethics* 1.13.1 (1102a).

[21] Diogenes Laertius, *Lives* 7.127.

[22] Ibid., 7.96-97.

[23] Epictetus, *Discourses* 1.4. In the original text, the remark, presented here as a positive statement, appears as part of a conditional. Nevertheless, it is clear that Epictetus believes the "if" is positively true.

[24] Diogenes Laertius, *Lives* 10.132; 128. For Epicurus, virtue is connected to happiness through pleasure.

[25] Cardinal because every other virtue hinges upon them or is related to them.

[26] Theognis of Megara 623-624.

[27] Homer, *Iliad* 13.275-291.

[28] Ibid., 15.638-643.

[29] Ibid., 20.408-418.

[30] Ibid., 22.260-261; 268-269. The phrase "every excellence" also appears in Homer, *Odyssey* 4.725, 4.815, and 18.205, but with no accompanying hint of *which* excellences (as in the *Iliad* 22.268-269, where we see a spearman's and warrior's excellence, including daringness [from *tharsaleos*]). In the lines from the *Odyssey*, Penelope longs for Odysseus' "every excellence."

[31] Homer, *Odyssey* 18.250-253. See also 19.124-126 for the same.

[32] Ibid., 24.191-199.

[33] Hesiod, *Works and Days* 279-280; 471-472; 694. Recall that "best" is *aristos*, a word related to aretē. In a sense, "best" means "the most excellent."

[34] Diodorus Siculus, *Library* 11.11.6.

[35] Simonides, in *Palatine Anthology* 7.251. Said either about those who died at Thermopylae or of the Athenians who perished at Plataea. For this explanation, see *Greek Lyric: Stesichorus, Simonides, and Others*, ed. and trans. David A. Campbell (Cambridge: Harvard University Press, 1991), 527.

[36] Pindar, *Nemean* 3.74-75. Unfortunately, Pindar doesn't name the four excellences; however, commentators speculate that they may relate to various stages of life or to what will be known as the four cardinal virtues.

[37] Bacchylides of Ceos, *Ode* 14.1-2; 6-11. Again, "best" is *aristos*, a word related to *aretē*.

[38] Stobaeus, *Anthology* 3.18. The speech comes from a fragment of Panyassis' epic, the *Heraclea*, which is about Heracles.

[39] Isocrates, *Panathenaicus* 12.183.

[40] Plato, *Meno* 73e-74a.

[41] Diogenes Laertius, *Lives* 3.90-91.

[42] Demosthenes, *Funeral Speech* 60.17.

[43] Demosthenes, *Erotic Essay* 61.8-9.

[44] Stobaeus, *Anthology* 2.31. Presumably, the lad had turned red with shame—the color those with aretē turn when something shameful occurs.

[45] Aristotle, *Nicomachean Ethics* 2.1.1 (1103a). The Greek for "intellectual or thinking" is *dianoētikos* and for "moral or ethical" is *ēthikos*. The "or" should not be read as *either* one *or* the other, for instance, moral *or* ethical; rather, the two terms are, in this case, equivalent—that is, one can translate *ēthikos* with both words. So it goes with "intellectual or thinking" and *dianoētikos*.

[46] Ibid., 6.3.1 (1139b).

[47] Diogenes Laertius, *Lives* 7.92; 93.

[48] Ibid., 7.46. For the Stoic understanding of dialectic, see ibid., 7.42-44.

[49] Diodorus Siculus, *Library* 10.9.9.

[50] Ibid., 10.11.2.

[51] Ibid., 15.88.3.

[52] Philippians 4.8. Though a selection from early Christian (Greek) literature, the passage is valuable in that it repeats many qualities or virtues that had long been considered virtues by the Greeks.

[53] 2 Peter 1.5-7. Again, though Christian, the selection is valuable in that it repeats many qualities or virtues that had long been considered virtues by the Greeks.

[54] Dio Chrysostom, *On Virtue* 52 (or 69) 1.

[55] Philostratus the Athenian, *Life of Apollonius* 4.31.

[56] Ibid., 1.20. For other examples of specific virtues relative to Apollonius of Tyana, see ibid., 1.13, 2.5, and 5.35.

[57] Ibid., 6.21.

[58] Athenaeus of Naucratis, *Deipnosophists* 14.23.

[59] Ibid., 1.15.

[60] *The Heroic Deeds of the Emperor Constantius, or on Kingship, Oration II* 79.

[61] Procopius, *History of the Wars* 4.4.20. Earlier, Procopius notes that John "was in charge of the expenditures of the general Belisarius' household. . . . He was an Armenian by birth, a man gifted with intelligence and courage to the highest degree" (3.17.1-2).

[62] Athenaeus, *Deipnosophists* 12.64. Compare his remarks to those of the businessman Callicles (in Plato's *Gorgias*), who declares that excellence (and thus happiness) is the power and ability to satisfy any and every desire.

[63] Ibid., 8.15.

4

ARETĒ AS THE MEANS BY WHICH
COMPETITIVE, COOPERATIVE & DEIFYING EXCELLENCE

H AVING NOW SEEN what *aretē* was in terms of general definitions and specific examples, and that it was the goal of life,
and that it ranged across a spectrum from non-living to living
things, let's now turn to ask another question: what did aretē *do* for
ancient Greeks? We've already encountered the general understanding that aretē was the means by which one attained happiness
(no small thing!). But what else did aretē do for human beings?
What did aretē help one do or be?

Looking at Greek literature, we may distinguish three major
fields of function for aretē: competition, cooperation, and deification. Within these fields, aretē was the means by which one competed and cooperated excellently, and, if things went particularly
well, it was how one became divine. Accordingly, we may identify
competitive, cooperative, and deifying excellences.

The competitive excellences were how Greeks competed with
one another to satisfy their desire for, among other things, safety,
conquest, riches, power, preeminence, honor, and glory. The cooperative excellences joined Greeks together into various levels of association, from that of a guest and host, to those relationships
present in the household and city-state, to the connections established between city-states. Cooperative excellences often aided in
competition and were cultivated to achieve similar ends. Finally,
the deifying excellences (if they may be called such) helped a mortal
human being to become an immortal divine being.

IN THEIR OWN WORDS

Competitive aretē. *As we will see in the first set of selections, for the earliest Greeks onward, excellence (aretē) was how an individual or group competed to maintain safety, make a stand, gain victory, gather valued possessions and wealth, gain a spouse, take control, stand out, and win honor and glory. Since such competitive excellence was essential to survival and success, it was shameful to be found without it and a big disgrace to have your excellence marred. Many of the following could also be counted as examples of cooperative excellence.*

Homer Then the Danaans broke the enemy battle lines by means of their excellence.[1]

Homer (the hero Menelaus is speaking) "Antilochus," he said, "what have you done—you who have been so sensible and wise before now? You dishonored my racing excellence when you hindered my horses by darting yours ahead, even though yours are not as good as mine are."[2]

Homer Meanwhile, the suitors were enjoying themselves in front of Odysseus' great home. They were throwing javelins and discuses in an area cleared out and levelled—doing as they had before, weighed down with insolence. There sat Antinous and godlike Eurymachus, the leaders of all the suitors. Standing out in the excellence of manly skill, they were the best.[3]

Homer (Alcinous, the king of the Phaeacians, is speaking to Odysseus) "Stranger—you do not say these things without grace among us, but you wish to manifest the excellence you possess, indignant that this man stood by you in the gathering and schooled you in a way that no mortal man who knew in his heart how to speak suitably would do, scorning your excellence.

"No, come now and listen to my words so that you may tell another hero when you are feasting in your halls with your wife and children, remembering our Phaeacian excellence, what feats Zeus has given us from the days of our fathers until now. For while we are not faultless boxers or wrestlers, we run swiftly in the foot race, and we are the best sailors, and feasting is always dear to us, and the lyre and dance, and changing clothes, and warm baths and bed."[4]

Homer (Odysseus is speaking) "I went through the ship and cheered my men with gentle words, coming up to each man in turn, saying, 'Friends, up to this point we have experienced much sorrow. Surely this evil that assails us now is no greater than when the Cyclops penned us in his hollow cave by brutal strength. Yet even then we escaped thanks to my excellence and counsel and sense. So, too, I suppose we will one day remember these dangers."[5]

Homer (Odysseus, disguised as a Cretan man, is speaking) "I took a wife from a house that had many possessions, winning her by my excellence—for I was neither a useless man, nor was I one to flee from battle."[6]

Homer (Odysseus, Telemachus, and Laertes are speaking) And at once Odysseus said to Telemachus, his dear son, "Having come to battle where the best of men are separated in distinction from the rest, now you will learn never to shame your family line, for we have always excelled in might and manhood throughout all the land."

In turn mindful Telemachus answered him, "If you wish, dear father, you will see me—given my present spirit—bring no shame on the family line, as you say."

That's what Telemachus said, and glad, Laertes spoke, saying, "What kind of day is this for me, dear gods? I absolutely rejoice! My son and my son's son are battling over excellence!"[7]

Tyrtaeus of Sparta I would not remember a man nor give an account of his excellence in a footrace nor in a wrestling match—not even if he had the stature and strength of a Cyclops, nor if he surpassed in swiftness the Thracian Northwind, nor if he were a more graceful man than Tithonus and a richer man than Midas or Cinyras, nor if he were a greater king than Pelops, the son of Tantalus, and had Adrastus' persuasive tongue, nor yet if he possessed the greatest reputation for everything but warlike strength. For a man is not good in war if he has not endured the sight of bloody slaughter, reaching out to cut down the enemy standing nearby.

This is excellence, the best prize among human beings, the most beautiful prize for a young man to carry off.

This is a common good both for the city-state and all her people, when a man stands firm among the foremost fighters without ceasing. And making his soul and spirit abide, he forgets shameful flight altogether, and with words he emboldens the man who stands nearby. Such a man is good in war. He quickly turns the hated enemy battle lines and earnestly checks the battle-wave.

Moreover, the man who falls among the foremost fighters and loses his own dear life—that man wins praise for his city and people and father. His chest and bossed shield and breastplate struck through many times, he is bewailed by young and old alike, and painfully longed for by all the city. This man's burial mound and his children are conspicuous among men, and the children of his children and their offspring thereafter.

Never do his noble glory or his good name perish. No, even though he is beneath the earth, he has become immortal—this because he was doing nobly and abiding in the fight for his land's and his children's sake when furious Ares made an end of him.

On the other hand, if such a man escapes the doom of outstretched death, and by victory he seizes the splendid glory-boast of battle, he is honored by all, the young and old alike, and he goes down to Hades after experiencing many delights. And as he grows old, he stands out among his people, and there's no one who harms him, whether to dishonor him or act contrary to justice. All yield him a place on the benches—the young and his peers and his elders.

This is the excellence that each man should now aspire to in his spirit, never relaxing from war.[8]

Theognis of Megara The great glory of excellence will never be destroyed. No, a warlike man keeps his land and city safe.[9]

Sophocles (the Chorus is speaking) "Soon the glorious voice of the flute will go up for you . . . divine music responsive to the lyre. For the son of Zeus and Alcmene is rushing home, carrying the spoils of every excellence."[10]

Herodotus (Demaratus, a former king of Sparta, is speaking to Xerxes, the king of Persia) "King," Demaratus said, "since you call on me by all means to speak the whole truth and to say what you will not later prove false, in Greece poverty is always widespread, but excellence is acquired as the achievement of wisdom and strong law. By constant practice of this excellence, Greece drives off poverty and defends herself against tyranny.

"Now I praise all the Greeks who dwell in Dorian lands, yet I am not going to speak these words about all of them, but only about the Lacedaemonians. First, they will never accept conditions from you that bring slavery upon Greece. And second, they will meet you in battle even if all the other Greeks are on your side. Do not ask me how many these men are who can do this. They will fight with you whether they have an army of a thousand men—or more or less than that."[11]

Herodotus While Hippocrates was tyrant, Gelon . . . was one of his guard, as were Aenesidemus, the son of Pataecus, and many others. In no long time, Gelon was appointed for his excellence to be captain of the entire cavalry—for his performance had been preeminent while he served under Hippocrates in the assaults against Callipolis, Naxos, Zancle, Leontini, Syracuse, and many other of the foreigners' towns. None of these cities, except for Syracuse, escaped enslavement by Hippocrates.[12]

Herodotus There was a great struggle between the Persians and Lacedaemonians over Leonidas' body, until the Greeks dragged it away by means of their excellence and routed their enemies four times.[13]

Herodotus For as long as the Athenians were not there, the barbarians defended themselves and had a great advantage over the Lacedaemonians who did not know how to besiege walls. When the Athenians came up, however, the fight for the wall became intense and lasted for a long time. In the end, the Athenians, by excellence and constant effort, scaled the wall and breached it. And the Greeks poured in through the opening they had made.[14]

Thucydides (the Athenian leader Pericles is speaking) "I will begin with our ancestors. It is both just and proper that they should have the honor of the first mention on an occasion like the present. They dwelled in the land without break in the succession from generation to generation, and they handed the land down free to the present time by means of their excellence. And if our more remote ancestors deserve praise, much more do our own fathers, who added to their inheritance the empire we now possess and spared no pains to be able to leave their acquisitions to us of the present generation."[15]

Thucydides (the Athenian leader Pericles is speaking) "You must consider that it was by endurance, the knowledge of what had to be done, and a keen feeling of honor in action that men were enabled to acquire all this, and that no personal failure in an enterprise could make them consent to deprive the city-state of their excellence, but they laid it at her feet as the most glorious contribution they could offer."[16]

Thucydides (the Spartan commander Brasidas is speaking to his own Lacedaemonian men) "The bravery that you habitually display in war does not depend on your having allies at your side in this or that encounter, but on your own excellence."[17]

Aristophanes (the Chorus of women is speaking) "For my part, I could dance and never complain! No wearisome fatigue will ever seize my knees! I'm willing to go through anything with women as excellent as these—given their nature, their grace, their courage, their skill, their love for our city-state, and their sensible excellence!"[18]

Diodorus Siculus Solon believed that the boxers and short-distance runners and all the other athletes contributed nothing worth mentioning to the safety of states. Rather, only men who excel in practical wisdom and excellence can protect their native lands in times of danger.[19]

Diodorus Siculus (a warrior is speaking) "I deny that I am panic-stricken at the magnitude of the Persian army since excellence decides a battle, not numbers."[20]

Diodorus Siculus (the Spartan king Leonidas is speaking) "Greeks have learned from their fathers to gain land not by vicious behavior but by excellence."[21]

Diodorus Siculus (describing the heroic battle at Thermopylae) The Medes . . . attacked the defenders at Thermopylae. . . . The fight that followed was a fierce one, and since the barbarian king stood as a witness of their excellence and the Greeks kept in mind their liberty and were exhorted to the fray by Leonidas, it followed that the struggle was amazing. For a considerable time, the battle was equally balanced—the men stood shoulder to shoulder in the fighting, the blows were struck in close combat, and the lines were densely packed. But since the Greeks were superior in excellence and in the great size of their shields, the Medes gradually gave way since many of them were slain and not a few wounded.[22]

Diodorus Siculus (speaking about the Spartans who fought at Thermopylae) Who would not regard the excellence of these men with wonder? Together they did not desert the post to which Greece had assigned them, but gladly they offered up their own lives for the common salvation of all Greeks and preferred to meet their end nobly rather than to live shamefully. . . .

Consequently, what man of later times might not zealously imitate the excellence of those warriors who, finding themselves in the grip of an overwhelming situation, and though their bodies were subdued, were not conquered in spirit? These men, therefore, alone of all whom history records, have in defeat been granted a greater reputation than all others who have won the most beautiful of victories. For judgement must be passed upon brave men not by the outcome of their actions but by their deliberate purpose. In the one case Fortune rules; in the other, it is the choice that wins approval.

What man would judge any other man to be better than were those Spartans who, though not equal in number to even one thousandth part of the enemy, dared to match their excellence against their unbelievable multitudes? Nor did they have any hope of overcoming so many myriads, but they believed that in bravery they would surpass all men of former times, and they decided that, even though the battle they had to fight was against the barbarians, yet the real contest and the award of valor they were seeking was in competition with all who had ever won admiration for their excellence. Indeed, they alone of those of whom we have knowledge from time immemorial chose rather to preserve the laws of their state than their own lives, not feeling aggrieved that the greatest perils threatened them but concluding that the greatest boon for which those who practice excellence should pray is the opportunity to engage in contests of this kind.

One would be justified in believing that it was these men who were more responsible for the common freedom of the Greeks than those who were victorious later in the battles against Xerxes. For when the deeds of these men were called to mind, the Persians were dismayed, whereas the Greeks were spurred on to perform similar brave deeds. And, speaking in general terms, these men alone of the Greeks down to their time passed into immortality because of their exceptional excellence. Consequently, not only the writers of history but also many of our poets have celebrated their brave exploits.[23]

Diodorus Siculus (describing an event that took place between the Persian Wars and the Peloponnesian War) When the ships thus suddenly came to rest on dry land, the Egyptians in alarm left the Athenians in the lurch and came to terms with the Persians.

The Athenians, being now without allies and seeing that their ships had become useless, set them on fire to prevent their falling into the hands of the enemy. Then they themselves, undismayed at the alarming plight they were in, began to exhort one another so that no one would do anything unworthy of the contests they had won in the past. Consequently, with a display of excellence surpassing the men who perished at Thermopylae in defense of Greece, they stood ready to fight it out with the enemy.

But the Persian generals, Artabazus and Megabyzus, taking note of the exceptional boldness of their adversaries, and reasoning that they would be unable to annihilate such men without sacrificing many thousands of their own, made a truce with the Athenians. . . .

So, the Athenians, having saved their lives by means of their excellence, departed from Egypt.[24]

Diodorus Siculus At this time [during the Peloponnesian War], as Nicias, the general of the Athenians, surveyed the ships and measured the magnitude of the struggle, he found that he could not remain at his station on shore. Rather, leaving the land troops, he boarded a boat and made his way along the line of the Athenian triremes. And calling each captain by name and stretching out his hands to each, he implored them all—now if ever before, he said—to grasp the only hope left to them. For on the excellence of those who were about to join battle at sea depended the preservation both of themselves and of their homeland.[25]

Diodorus Siculus Now that I have reached the actions of Philip, the son of Amyntas, I will try to include the deeds performed by this king within the range of the present book. For Philip was king over the Macedonians for twenty-four years. And having started from the most insignificant beginnings, he built up his kingdom to be the greatest of the dominions in Europe. . . . It was by his own excellence that he took over the supremacy of all Greece with the consent of the city-states, which voluntarily subordinated themselves to his authority. . . . He accomplished these deeds not by Fortune but by means of his own excellence.[26]

Diodorus Siculus At that time, Alexander [the Great] had more than thirty thousand footmen and no less than three thousand horsemen, all battle-seasoned veterans of Philip's campaigns who had hardly experienced a single reverse. This was the army—with its excellence and willingness—on which he relied to overthrow the Persian empire.[27]

Pausanias The Phigalians have in their marketplace a statue of the pancratiast Arrhachion. . . . He won two victories at Olympic festivals. . . . He won because of the fairness of the chief judges and his own excellence.[28]

Inscription (dedicated to Ariston for the boys' pankration) I am Ariston, who was crowned with wild olive in the *pankration*. Whom Greece said was perfect when she saw me, though still a boy, with the excellence of a man, victorious with my blows.[29]

Procopius (the general Belisarius is speaking to his army) "Now as for the host of the Vandals, let no one of you stop to consider them. For it is neither by a great number of men nor by the size of bodies that a battle is decided but by means of soul excellence."[30]

Cooperative aretē. *Next up are examples of cooperative excellence. While the major emphasis in the ancient world was on the competitive excellences, the Greeks also esteemed various cooperative excellences. That said, these are much harder to find in explicit form in Greek literature. Still, where they are evident, the cooperative excellences brought people together for greater strength—often to compete against others.*

Aside from the competitive excellence that arose from joint action, cooperation in the form of hosting strangers and friends was an excellent act. So too was loyalty or faithfulness to family, as was the willingness to take care of the mortally ill or contagious. Finally, we see that the excellence of one or a group bolsters that of an individual.

Homer (the god Poseidon disguised as Thoas is speaking) "Excellence comes into existence even when very weak men are joined together."[31]

Homer (the swineherd Eumaeus is speaking to Odysseus) "Stranger, I will not win the good reputation and excellence I wish to have in time to come if I slay you and take away your dear life after leading you into my shelter and offering you gifts of hospitality."[32]

Homer Then the soul of the son of Atreus, Agamemnon, addressed the suitor Amphimedon, saying, "Happy son of Laertes, much-able Odysseus! You acquired for yourself an excellent wife, one of great worth. How good was the heart in blameless Penelope, the daughter of Icarius! How faithful in mind to Odysseus, her wedded husband! The glory of her excellence will never fade, but the immortals will make among men on earth a graceful song for thoughtful Penelope. She didn't plot evil works like the daughter of Tyndareus, Clytemnestra, who killed her wedded husband. Her song will be hated among men—and harsh will be the judgment that follows womankind, bringing a bad reputation even to those women who are upright."[33]

Thucydides (speaking about the plague in Athens) By far the most terrible feature of the malady was the dejection that appeared when anyone felt himself getting sick—for the despair into which they instantly fell took away their power to resist and left them a much easier prey to the disorder. Aside from this, there was the awful spectacle of men dying like sheep when they caught the infection while nursing one another. This caused the greatest numbers of death. On the one hand, if they were afraid to visit one another, they perished from neglect. Indeed, many houses were emptied of those within since there was no one to nurse them. On the other hand, if they ventured to do so, death was the consequence. This was particularly the case for those who claimed excellence—a fear of shame made them unsparing of themselves in their attendance in their friends' households, where even the members of the family were at last worn out by the moans of the dying and succumbed to the force of the disaster.[34]

Thucydides (the Mytilenian envoys are speaking) "Justice and excellence will be the first topics of our speech—particularly since we are asking for an alliance. We know that there can never be any solid friendship between individuals, or union between communities that is worth the name, unless the parties be persuaded of each other's excellence."[35]

Apollonius of Rhodes (Jason, the hero and leader of the Argonauts, is speaking) "Friends, my courage has increased thanks to your excellence. Up to now, even though I would have made my way through the pit of Hades, I will no longer let fear take hold of me since you remain steadfast amid cruel terrors."[36]

Deifying aretē. *Finally, for some ancient Greeks, aretē was the means of deification, the means by which a mortal human being became a god—a divine being, immortal and ageless.*

Sophocles (Heracles is speaking) "First, I will tell you about my own fortunes—how by means of hard work and passing through great toils, I have won the excellence of immortality."[37]

Isocrates Thanks to his excellence, Heracles was led up to the gods.[38]

Isocrates Lacedaemon offered Menelaus, who, because of his moderation and his justice, was the one man to be judged worthy to become the son-in-law of Zeus.[39]

Isocrates And so much greater honor is paid to beauty among the gods than among us that they pardon their own wives when they are vanquished by it. One could cite many instances of goddesses who succumbed to mortal beauty, and no one of these sought to keep the fact concealed as if it involved disgrace. On the contrary, they desired their adventures to be celebrated in song as glorious deeds rather than to be hushed in silence. The greatest proof of my statement is this: we will find that more mortals have been made immortal because of their beauty than for all other excellences.[40]

Isocrates I suppose that if any men of the past have become immortal by means of their excellence, then Evagoras also has been judged worthy of this gift. The sign that causes me to declare this is that the life he lived on earth has been more fortunate and more favored by the gods than those other men.[41]

Plato (the priestess Diotima is speaking to Socrates) "Consider well," she said, "that it is only there with beauty itself that it will happen to him. . . . He gives birth to true virtue inasmuch as he grasps the truth—what is real and actual. So, when this man has produced true virtue, nourishing it and letting it grow, he becomes dear to the gods. And if ever immortality is granted to humans, that man, above all others, will be immortal."[42]

Plotinus Since evils are here in this realm, and since these evils "prowl about this realm by necessity," and since the soul wishes to flee these evils, then "we must flee from this realm." But what is the nature of this flight we must take? Plato says that it is in becoming like god—like the divinity. And this, he says, is found if one "is becoming just and holy, and in one who is beginning to live by means of practical wisdom"—which is to say the whole of virtue.[43]

Julian the emperor I have heard many people say that Dionysus was a human being because he was born of Semele, and that he became a god through his knowledge of theurgy and the mysteries, and like our lord Heracles for his kingly virtue, he was taken up to Olympus by his father Zeus.[44]

NOTES

[1] Homer, *Iliad* 11.90.
[2] Ibid., 23.570-572.
[3] Homer, *Odyssey* 4.625-629.
[4] Ibid., 8.236-249.
[5] Ibid., 12.206-212.
[6] Ibid., 14.211-213.
[7] Ibid., 24.505-515.
[8] Tyrtaeus of Sparta, in Stobaeus, *Anthology* 4.10.1.

[9] Theognis of Megara 867-868.
[10] Sophocles, *The Women of Trachis* 640-645. The son is Heracles.
[11] Herodotus, *Histories* 7.102.
[12] Ibid., 7.154. Hippocrates was the tyrant of Gela in Sicily.
[13] Ibid., 7.225.
[14] Ibid., 9.70.
[15] Thucydides, *The Peloponnesian War* 2.36.
[16] Ibid., 2.43.
[17] Ibid., 4.126.
[18] Aristophanes, *Lysistrata* 541-547.
[19] Diodorus Siculus, *Library* 9.2.5.
[20] Ibid., 10.34.10.
[21] Ibid., 11.5.5.
[22] Ibid., 11.6.4; 7.1-2. The Medes are the Persians.
[23] Ibid., 11.11.1-6.
[24] Ibid., 11.77.3-4.
[25] Ibid., 13.5.1-2.
[26] Ibid., 16.1.3-4, 6.
[27] Ibid., 17.9.3.
[28] Pausanias, *Description of Greece* 8.40.1.
[29] Inscription translation from Stephen G. Miller, *Arete: Greek Sports from Ancient Sources*, 3rd ed. (Berkeley: University of California Press, 2012), 72. Rather than *excellence*, the original text in Miller reads *arete*.
[30] Procopius, *History of the Wars* 4.1.15-16.
[31] Homer, *Iliad* 13.237.
[32] Homer, *Odyssey* 14.401-405. From Eumaeus' words, we see that a good reputation and excellence is found in the cooperative acts of entertaining a guest and preserving his life.
[33] Ibid., 24.191-202.
[34] Thucydides, *The Peloponnesian War* 2.51.
[35] Ibid., 3.10.
[36] Apollonius of Rhodes, *Argonautica* 2.641-644.
[37] Sophocles, *Philoctetes* 1418-1420.
[38] Isocrates, *To Philip* 5.132.
[39] Isocrates, *Panathenaicus* 12.72.
[40] Isocrates, *Helen* 10.60. Though beauty is the chief means of deification here, the implication is that other excellences have also led to mortals becoming immortals.
[41] Isocrates, *Evagoras* 9.70.
[42] Plato, *Symposium*, 212a.
[43] Plotinus, *Enneads* 1.2.1.
[44] Julian the emperor, *To the Cynic Heracleios* 219a-b.

THE HOW OF *ARETĒ*
INHERITANCE, THE GODS, TEACHING & HARD WORK

HAVING ESTABLISHED THAT aretē is the goal of life, a general and specific understanding regarding its nature, and what it was good for, the ancient Greeks naturally turned to ask how it was that someone became excellent or possessed virtue. In the selections that follow, we see that in some cases aretē was judged something within human control, while in other cases it was not.

One idea was that aretē was passed down from one's parents and earlier ancestors. But observing that it was not always inherited by younger generations, the Greeks offered other answers. Some supposed the gods simply granted aretē to certain individuals and not to others. Others suggested that it was through praise and the desire to avoid shame that one would come to possess aretē. Though some were skeptical, others held that humans teach aretē to one another, whether by word or example. In this way, a human was trained in aretē. The key word in this situation was practice—one had to *do* excellence or virtue in order to *be* excellent or virtuous.

Regardless of the manner, it was generally acknowledged that aretē was something difficult to obtain, that it took a great deal of hard work and even suffering.

IN THEIR OWN WORDS

Inheritance. *Some held that aretē was passed down from one generation of a family to the next. For this reason, royal offspring seemed royal or kinglike (an excellence) in comparison with those who were not royal—a judgment often expressed in ancient Greek literature.*

Diodorus Siculus On his father's side, Alexander [the Great] was a descendant of Heracles, and on his mother's, he could claim the blood of the Aeacids. So it was that he inherited the nature and highly reputable excellences of his ancestors.[1]

The gods. *Many judged that aretē was something given by the gods or, to use Plato's language, "by divine providence."*

Homer (Aeneas is speaking) "As for excellence, it is Zeus who increases it for men or diminishes it as he wishes since he is the strongest."[2]

Homer (Odysseus is speaking) "Of all things that breathe and move along the earth, there's nothing weaker than a human being—I tell you, the earth nurtures no frailer thing. For as long as the gods give him excellence, and as long as his knees stand strong, he thinks he'll never suffer misfortune in the days to come."[3]

Simonides of Ceos No one ever won excellence without the gods—no city-state, no mortal man.[4]

Theognis of Megara The gods grant property to even the most vicious man, Cyrnus. But a share of excellence attends few men.[5]

Pindar Zeus, from you come great excellences to mortals.[6]

Plato (Socrates is speaking) "If through this entire discussion our searches and statements have been given well, then virtue is neither something natural nor is it something taught. Rather, it is something that comes to us by divine providence, without any understanding on our part."[7]

Praise and shame-avoidance. *Others held that praise was the water or sunshine that assisted aretē in its growth. The collaborator of praise was shame, something one wished to avoid at any cost. So it was that shame-avoidance drove one to aretē.*

Bacchylides of Ceos Excellence, when praised, flourishes like a tree.[8]

Homer (Odysseus, Telemachus, and Laertes are speaking) And at once Odysseus said to Telemachus, his dear son, "Having come to battle where the best of men are separated in distinction from the rest, now you will learn never to shame your family line, for we have always excelled in might and manhood throughout all the land."

In turn mindful Telemachus answered him, "If you wish, dear father, you will see me—given my present spirit—bring no shame on the family line, as you say."

That's what Telemachus said, and glad, Laertes spoke, saying, "What kind of day is this for me, dear gods? I absolutely rejoice! My son and my son's son are battling over excellence!"[9]

Timotheos Have respect for shame before others, the fellow workman of spear-fighting excellence.[10]

Teaching, along with training and practice. *Many believed that one could become excellent by means of teaching. In some manner, whether by word or by example, one person helped another become excellent. Such a movement toward aretē usually involved training or practice.*

Herodotus (Demaratus, a former king of Sparta, is speaking to Xerxes, the king of Persia) "King," Demaratus said, "since you call on me by all means to speak the whole truth and to say what you will not later prove false, in Greece poverty is always widespread, but excellence is acquired as the achievement of wisdom and strong law. By constant practice of this excellence, Greece drives off poverty and defends herself against tyranny."[11]

Euripides (the Chorus is speaking) "The natures of mortal men vary one from another, as do their ways and habits. But straightaway a noble man is always clear to see. Both training and education carry one a far distance to excellence. . . . It is a great thing to hunt after excellence."[12]

Critias A greater number of men are good from practice rather than from nature.[13]

Aristophanes (Aeschylus is speaking) "Look at how useful the noble tribe of poets have been from the very beginning. . . . Hesiod taught us the business of farming—when to plow and when to harvest. And divine Homer, where did he obtain his honor and glory if not from teaching profitable things—how to line up during battle, excellences, and the arming of men."[14]

Xenophon (Socrates is speaking to Critobulus, that is, his good friend Crito) "You will find on reflection that every kind of virtue named among men is increased by education and practice."[15]

Isocrates Busiris appointed the older men to have charge of the most important matters. But he persuaded the younger men to forego all pleasures and devote themselves to the study of the stars, to arithmetic, and to geometry. Some praise the value of these sciences for their utility, while others attempt to demonstrate that they are conducive in the highest measure to the attainment of excellence.[16]

Diodorus Siculus Solon was the son of Execestides, and his family was of Salamis in Attica. In wisdom and learning he surpassed all the men of his time. Being by nature far superior in excellence relative to the rest of men, he diligently cultivated excellence that wins applause—for he devoted much time to every branch of knowledge and became practiced in every kind of excellence. While still a youth, for instance, he availed himself of the best teachers, and when he attained to manhood, he spent his time in the company of the men who enjoyed the greatest influence for their pursuit of wisdom. Consequently, by reason of his companionship and association with men of this kind, he came to be called one of the seven wise men and won for himself the highest rank in sagacity, not only among the men just mentioned, but also among all who were regarded with admiration. The same Solon, who had acquired great fame by his legislation, also in his conversations and answers to questions as a private individual became an object of wonder because of his attainments in learning. The same Solon—even though the city followed the whole Ionian manner of life and luxury, and a carefree existence had made the inhabitants effeminate—worked a change in them by accustoming them to practice excellence and to vie with the deeds of truly manly men.[17]

Diodorus Siculus Croesus, the king of the Lydians, who had a large and great military force and had purposely amassed a large amount of silver and gold, used to call to his court the wisest men from among the Greeks. He would spend some time in their company and ultimately send them away with many presents. In this way he was greatly benefited toward a life of excellence.[18]

Diodorus Siculus Lysis, the Pythagorean, came to Thebes in Boeotia and became the teacher of Epaminondas. And with respect to excellence, he developed him into a perfect man. . . . Such were the remarkable deeds that Epaminondas performed . . . because of his astuteness and the excellence resulting from his education.[19]

Plato (Socrates is speaking) "Then the other so-called virtues of the soul do seem similar to those of the body since it is true that where they do not pre-exist, they are later produced by habit and practice."[20]

Diogenes Laertius (offering the Cynic Antisthenes' and the general Cynic position) The Cynics further hold that virtue can be taught, just as Antisthenes declares in his *Heracles*.[21]

Aristotle Moral or ethical virtue is born thanks to habit, which is to say customary behavior. . . . The [moral] virtues are engendered in us neither by nature nor yet in a way contrary to nature. Rather, nature disposes us to receive them, perfecting them by means of habit. We acquire the [moral] virtues . . . by doing them, by putting them into action, just as we do with the various arts or skills. For we learn an art or skill by doing that which we wish to do when we have learned it. We become builders by building and harpers by harping. And so, by doing just acts we become just, and by doing acts of moderation and courage we become moderate and courageous.[22]

Aristotle It is no small thing whether, from when we are young, we are trained up in one habit or another; rather, it is a great difference—in fact, all the difference.[23]

(Pseudo) Crates of Thebes To Orion: Virtue enters the soul by means of training—not automatically as happens with vice.[24]

Xenophon I notice that as those who do not train the body cannot perform the functions proper to the body, so those who do not train the soul cannot perform the functions of the soul—for they cannot do what they should do or avoid what they should not do. For this reason, fathers try to keep their sons, even if they are sensible and wise, out of bad company—for an association with good men is a training in virtue, but an association with bad men is virtue's undoing.[25]

Philostratus the Athenian "And for myself, O man of Tyana," Titus answered, "can you give me any principles for ruling and exercising the authority of a sovereign?"

"Only such rules," replied Apollonius, the man of Tyana, "as you have laid upon yourself. For in so submitting yourself to your father's will, it is, I think, certain that you will grow like him. And I would like to repeat to you on this occasion a saying of Archytas, which is a noble one and worth committing to memory. Archytas was a man of Tarentum, who was learned in the lore of Pythagoras, and he wrote a treatise on the education of children, in which he says, 'Let the father be an example of virtue for his children. Fathers will walk along the path of virtue with greater resolution when they see that their children are coming to resemble them.' But for myself, I propose to offer for your association my own companion Demetrius, who will attend you as much as you like and instruct you in the whole duty of a good ruler."[26]

Hard work and suffering. *For some Greeks, there was the notion that aretē was cultivated by means of hard work and sweat and the shedding of blood—again, the result of action and careful practice.*

Hesiod (to his brother, Perses) Listen, Perses, you big fool. I will pro-claim all this noble knowledge for you. It is easy to grab at Deficiency (Kakotēs). It is there in abundance for you. The way is smooth to her, and she dwells very near to you. But the immortal gods have put sweat in front of Excellence (Aretē). The path to her is long and steep. And so, it is rough going at first. Nevertheless, when one comes to the highest point, then the path becomes easy. . . .

Work is no disgrace; rather, it is not working that is the disgrace. And if you work, the man who does not work will quickly become jealous when you are wealthy because the excellence and glory of being a prominent man follow upon wealth. Whatever you are by some god, by fortune, working is better if you turn your thoughtless desires and muddled mind away from another man's possessions. Turn them instead toward work and, as I have encouraged you, think about what it takes to live.[27]

Simonides of Ceos It is said that excellence dwells upon rocky peaks that are hard to climb. . . . She guards a holy place. She may not be seen by the eyes of all mortals. Only the one who experiences heart-vexing sweat from within may see her, the one who reaches the peak of manliness.[28]

Pindar When a man wholly devotes himself to excellence, spending what is necessary and working hard, we must praise him if he achieves it.[29]

Aeschylus Excellence is bought with blood.[30]

Thucydides (the Corinthians are speaking) "We must provide for the future by maintaining what the present gives us and redoubling our efforts—for it is hereditary to us to win excellence as the fruit of hard work, and you must not change the habit."[31]

Sophocles (Heracles is speaking) "First, I will tell you about my own fortunes—how by means of hard work and passing through great toils, I have won the excellence of immortality."[32]

Euripides (Hecuba is speaking) "Your eye was fixed on Fortune, Paris, and by such a practice you were careful to follow in her steps. You were not willing to do the same for excellence."[33]

Euripides (the Chorus is speaking) "The excellences advance by means of hardship."[34]

Diogenes Laertius (giving a saying of the Cynic philosopher Antisthenes) Virtue is something you do—it is a matter of deeds. It doesn't require a stockpile of arguments or much learning.[35]

Skepticism relative to teaching and training. *Some expressed skepticism regarding aretē, suggesting that we cannot alter a person for the better through teaching or training.*

Theognis of Megara It is easier to beget and bring up a man than to instill noble thoughts in him. No one has ever devised the means by which he has made a fool wise and a base man noble. If god had given the sons of Asclepius the art of healing the base character and ruinous thoughts of men, they would have earned a great deal in wages. And if understanding could be made and put into a man, then the son of a good father would never become bad, persuaded as he would be by wise and sensible words. But by teaching you will never make the bad man good.[36]

Quietness and stillness. *Finally, at least one ancient author judged that quietness and stillness were conducive to virtue.*

Phocylides Deliberate at night since with men the mind is sharper at night. Quiet and stillness is good for one who is seeking after excellence.[37]

NOTES

[1] Diodorus Siculus, *Library* 17.1.5.
[2] Homer, *Iliad* 20.242-243.

3 Homer, *Odyssey* 18.130-133.

4 Simonides, in Theophilus of Antioch, *To Autolycus* 2.8.

5 Theognis of Megara 149-150. That excellence is given by the gods is implied.

6 Pindar, *Isthmian* 3.4.

7 Plato, *Meno* 99e-100a.

8 Bacchylides, fragment in Clement of Alexandria, *The Schoolmaster* 1.94.1.

9 Homer, *Odyssey* 24.505-515.

10 Timotheos, in Plutarch, *How the Young Should Study Poetry* 11.

11 Herodotus, *Histories* 7.102.

12 Euripides, *Iphigenia in Aulis* 558-562; 568.

13 Critias, in Stobaeus, *Anthology* 3.29.11. Good (*agathos*) here is equivalent to excellence or virtue (*aretē*).

14 Aristophanes, *Frogs* 1030-1031; 1033-1036.

15 Xenophon, *Memorabilia* 2.6.39.

16 Isocrates, *Busiris* 11.23.

17 Diodorus Siculus, *Library* 9.1.1-4.

18 Ibid., 9.2.1.

19 Ibid., 10.11.2; 15.39.2-3. For Epaminondas' remarkable deeds and more about his education, see 6, "Models of Aretē," in which he appears as a model of aretē.

20 Plato, *Republic* 7.518e.

21 Diogenes Laertius, *Lives* 6.5.

22 Aristotle, *Nicomachean Ethics* 2.1.1, 3, 4 (1103a-1103b).

23 Ibid., 2.1.8 (1103b). In speaking of habits, Aristotle is speaking of virtues, since a virtue is a habit or disposition (see ibid., 2.6.15 [1107a]).

24 (Pseudo) Crates of Thebes, *Letter* 12 To Orion.

25 Xenophon, *Memorabilia* 1.2.19-20.

26 Philostratus the Athenian, *Life of Apollonius* 6.31.

27 Hesiod, *Works and Days* 286-292; 311-316. Although the second part does not say anything directly about aretē, it is implied.

28 Simonides, in Clement of Alexandria, *Miscellanies* 4.7.48.

29 Pindar, *Isthmian* 1.42-44.

30 Aeschylus, *Fabula Incerta* 112.

31 Thucydides, *The Peloponnesian War* 1.123.

32 Sophocles, *Philoctetes* 1418-1420.

33 Euripides, *The Trojan Women* 1008-1009. The implication, of course, is that one must carefully follow in the steps of aretē with practice in order to achieve aretē.

34 Euripides, *Heracleidae* 624.

35 Diogenes Laertius, *Lives* 6.11.

36 Theognis 429-438. Though *aretē* does not appear in the text, words related in meaning do (*agathos*, good, and *esthlos*, noble).

37 Phocylides, in Orion, *Anthology* 1.22.

MODELS OF ARETĒ
EXCELLENT MEN & WOMEN

I N HIS *NICOMACHEAN Ethics*, Aristotle suggests that we can learn about the nature of aretē by observing the rationally chosen behavior of a wise and sensible person, the example of a human being who acts in an excellent or virtuous manner. To that end—though different, perhaps, than the examples Aristotle himself would offer—this chapter presents an assortment of models of aretē. These examples range from those who are excellent simply because of their family line, to those who stand out from others in a particular activity, to those who demonstrate general excellence in their own lives. They are examples of public and private aretē—excellence having to do with war and peace, or with a particular skill or quality.

Note that, aside from the usual author given at the beginning of the selection, the name of the model person or group of persons is given first, followed by a period. For instance, in the following case, Odysseus is the model: *Odysseus. Homer (Penelope is speaking)*. Aside from this identification, no other introductions are offered in this chapter. So happy reading.

Before going to the models themselves, let's hear what the ancient historian Diodorus Siculus had to say about why it is important to remember noble deeds and their opposite:

> To recount the lives of men of the past is a task that presents difficulties to writers, and yet it is of no little profit to society as a whole. For such an account that clearly portrays in all frankness their base as well as their noble deeds renders honor to the good and abases the wicked by means of the censures as well as the praises that appropriately come to each group. The praise constitutes, one might say, a reward for excellence. . . . It is a

noble thing for later generations to bear in mind, that whatever manner of life a man chooses to live while on this earth, such will be the remembrance that he will be thought worthy to have after his death. This principle should be followed so that later generations may not set their hearts upon the erection of memorials in stone that are limited to a single spot and subject to quick decay, but upon reason and the excellences in general. . . . Time, which withers all else, preserves for these excellences an immortality. . . .

Throughout our entire treatise . . . we have justly praised good men for their noble deeds and criticized base men whenever they have missed the mark. We believe that, by this means, we will lead men whose nature fortunately inclines them to excellence to undertake, because of the immortality fame and reputation accords them, the noblest deeds, whereas by appropriate criticism we will turn men of the opposite character from their impulse to vice.[1]

IN THEIR OWN WORDS

Life-sacrificing ancestors. Dinarchus the orator After facing many noble struggles for it, your ancestors have handed on to you a land that is free, in which many noble examples have been left to us of the excellence of those who gave up their own lives.[2]

Heracles. Pseudo-Hesiod (Alcmene is speaking) "My son, truly your father Zeus begot you to be the one most engaged in toils as well as the best man."[3]

Heracles. Sophocles (Heracles speaking) "First, I will tell you about my own fortunes—how by means of hard work and passing through great toils, I have won the excellence of immortality."[4]

Heracles. Euripides (the Chorus is speaking) "Here is a good theme for a hymn—Heracles, the son of Zeus. Even so, his excellence surpasses his noble birth. It was his hard work, so full of sweat and exhaustion, that established a tranquil life for mortal men, when he destroyed many terrifying beasts."[5]

Heracles. Philostratus the Athenian Prodicus of Ceos had composed a certain pleasant story in which Virtue and Vice came to Heracles in the shape of women, one of them dressed in guileful and many-colored attire, the other with common clothing. And to Heracles, who was still young, Vice offered idleness and luxury, while Virtue offered thirst and toil upon toil.[6]

Heracles. Philostratus the Athenian You have seen in paintings the representation of Heracles by Prodicus. In it Heracles is represented as a youth who has not yet chosen the life he will lead. And Vice and Virtue stand on each side of him tugging at his garments and trying to draw him to themselves.

Vice is adorned with gold and necklaces and with purple clothing, and her cheeks are painted, and her hair is delicately braided, and her eyes are lined with eyeliner. She also wears golden slippers—for she is pictured strutting around in these.

But Virtue in the picture resembles a woman worn out with toil, with a pinched look. And she has chosen for her adornment rough squalor, and she goes without shoes and in the plainest of clothing, and she would have appeared naked if she had not too much regard for her feminine decency. . . .

If then you really make the choice of Heracles, and steel your will resolutely, neither to dishonor truth nor to decline the simplicity of nature, then you may say that you have overcome many lions and have cut off the heads of many hydras and of monsters like Geryon and Nessus, and have accomplished all his other labors.[7]

Heracles, Castor, Polydeuces, Achilles, and Ajax. Athenaeus of Naucratis (a hymn to virtue by Aristotle) O excellence, never but by much labor won, noblest object of all human life. For such a prize as you there is no toil, there is no strife, nor even death which any Greek would shun. . . . For you Zeus' mighty son, great Heracles, gave up a life of ease. For you the sons of Leda, Castor and Polydeuces, sought toil and danger, following your directives with fearless and unwearied breasts. Love of you inspired and drove Achilles and Ajax to an early grave.[8]

Oeneus. Homer (Diomedes is speaking) "The third was the horseman Oeneus, who was father to my father. He was outstanding in excellence among them."[9]

Ajax, Peteos, Agamemnon, Odysseus. Homer (from the Catalogue of Ships and various bests) Ajax, son of Oileus, surpasses all the Panhellenes and Achaeans with the spear . . . Peteos, leader of the Athenians, is best at marshalling chariots and warriors . . . Agamemnon is preeminent among the heroes because he is the best and has the most men . . . Odysseus is like Zeus in being first in counsel."[10]

Calchas. Homer From among them stood up Calchas, the son of Thestor, the best of those who read bird signs, who knew all things that were, things to come, and things past.[11]

Thoas. Homer Thoas is by far the best of the Aetolians—not only is he skilled in throwing a javelin but also a good man in a close fight. And in the place of assembly, few of the Achaeans could surpass him when young men were contending in debate.[12]

Sarpedon, Glaucus, and Asteropaeus. Homer Sarpedon led the glorious allies and took with him Glaucus and warlike Asteropaeus, whom he judged the best men of the others after himself—for he himself was conspicuous by far among all the rest.[13]

Laodice. Homer Laodice is the best looking of the daughters of Priam.[14]

Helen. Sappho of Lesbos Helen far surpassed every human being in beauty.[15]

Nestor, Menelaus, Agamemnon. Isocrates The greatest cities of the Peloponnese . . . deserved the greatest possible rewards from the Hellenes because of the expedition against Troy in which they took the foremost place and furnished as its leaders men who displayed not only those excellences of the many and the non-noble but also those in which no base man is able to participate. For Messene furnished

Nestor, the wisest and most sensible of all who lived in those times. And Lacedaemon offered Menelaus, who, because of his moderation and his justice, was the one man to be judged worthy to become the son-in-law of Zeus. And Argos sent Agamemnon, who possessed not merely one or two of the excellences, but all those which anyone can name—and these not in measure but exceedingly.[16]

Penelope. Homer (the suitor Eurymachus is speaking) "We suitors will go on here, competing day after day for Penelope's excellence. We won't go after other women."[17]

Penelope. Homer (the suitor Antinous is speaking) "More so than other women, Athena granted Penelope skill in beautiful works, a noble mind, and cunning. She had these as we have never known, even in the days of old among those who were long ago fair-haired Achaean women—Tyro, Alcmene, and Mycene of the beautiful crown. Not one of these possessed understanding as did Penelope."[18]

Penelope. Homer Then thoughtful Penelope answered him, saying, "Eurymachus, the immortals destroyed my excellences—those of beautiful form and stature—when the Argives, including my husband Odysseus, embarked for Ilium."[19]

Penelope. Homer (Agamemnon is speaking) Then the soul of the son of Atreus, Agamemnon, addressed the suitor Amphimedon, saying, "Happy son of Laertes, much-able Odysseus! You acquired for yourself an excellent wife, one of great worth. How good was the heart in blameless Penelope, the daughter of Icarius! How faithful in mind to Odysseus, her wedded husband! The glory of her excellence will never fade, but the immortals will make among men on earth a graceful song for thoughtful Penelope. She didn't plot evil works like the daughter of Tyndareus, Clytemnestra, who killed her wedded husband. Her song will be hated among men—and harsh will be the judgment that follows womankind, bringing a bad reputation even to those women who are upright."[20]

Penelope and Alcestis. Crates of Thebes Do not abstain from the most beautiful adornment, but adorn yourself each day so that you may be different from others. The most beautiful adornment is the one that adorns you most beautifully. But the one that adorns you most beautifully is the one that produces a well-ordered, regular, moderate life. It is this adornment that produces this well-ordered life.

It seems to me that both Penelope and Alcestis adorned themselves in this manner. Even now they are hymned and honored for their virtue. So that you might be a match for their kind, then, try to cling to this advice.[21]

Odysseus. Homer (Penelope is speaking) "Hear me, dear ones, for the Olympian has given me grief and distress beyond all those women I grew up with. Before this I lost a good husband, lion-spirited, who surpassed the Danaans in manly excellences of all sorts whose glory is far spread through Hellas and mid-Argos."

And, "I wish that pure Artemis would even now give me so soft a death so that I might no more waste my life away with sorrow at heart, longing for the manifold excellence of my dear husband, for he was outstanding among the Achaeans."[22]

Odysseus. Homer (Zeus is speaking) "How can I forget godlike Odysseus? He surpasses all mortals in his mind, and no man offers more sacrifices to the immortal gods who hold the wide sky above."[23]

Antinous and Eurymachus (two suitors contending for Penelope's hand). Homer Meanwhile, the suitors were enjoying themselves in front of Odysseus' great home. They were throwing javelins and discuses in an area cleared out and levelled—doing as they had before, weighed down with insolence. There sat Antinous and godlike Eurymachus, the leaders of all the suitors. Standing out in the excellence of manly skill, they were the best.[24]

Queen Arete of the Phaeacians. Homer (Athena, disguised as a young maiden, is speaking) "You will first approach the queen in the palace. Arete is the name by which she is called. . . . Alcinous made her his

wife and honored her as no other woman on earth is honored. . . .
In this manner she is wholeheartedly honored by her dear children,
and by Alcinous himself, and by the people who look upon her as
though she is a goddess and greet her with many words when she
strolls through the city. For she herself possesses a noble mind and
settles quarrels if she is well disposed to do so—even among men.
If she considers you with affection in her spirit, then there is hope
that you will see those who are dear to you and come to your high-
roofed house in your own fatherland."[25]

The man with foresight. Hesiod Best of all is the man who thinks about
everything himself, pondering how things will turn out in the end
and what will be better. And noble too is the kind of man who is
won over by good advice. But good for nothing is the man who
doesn't think for himself or take to heart what he hears from another man. He is useless.[26]

Sappho of Lesbos. (Sappho is speaking) My name is Sappho. I surpassed all women in poetry as much as Maionidas [Homer] did
among men.[27]

Solon of Athens. Diodorus Siculus Solon was the son of Execestides,
and his family was of Salamis in Attica. In wisdom and learning he
surpassed all the men of his time. Being by nature far superior in
excellence relative to the rest of men, he diligently cultivated excellence that wins applause—for he devoted much time to every
branch of knowledge and became practiced in every kind of excellence. While still a youth, for instance, he availed himself of the best
teachers, and when he attained to manhood, he spent his time in
the company of the men who enjoyed the greatest influence for
their pursuit of wisdom. Consequently, by reason of his companionship and association with men of this kind, he came to be called
one of the seven wise men and won for himself the highest rank in
sagacity, not only among the men just mentioned but also among
all who were regarded with admiration. The same Solon, who had
acquired great fame by his legislation, also in his conversations and

answers to questions as a private individual, became an object of wonder because of his attainments in learning. The same Solon— even though the city followed the whole Ionian manner of life and luxury, and a carefree existence had made the inhabitants effemi- nate—worked a change in them by accustoming them to practice excellence and to vie with the deeds of truly manly men.[28]

Chilon of Sparta. Diodorus Siculus In the case of Chilon, his life agreed with his teaching, a thing one rarely finds. As for the philosophers of our time, for instance, most of them are seen uttering the noblest sentiments but following the basest practices. . . . As for Chilon, not to mention the excellence that he displayed in every deed through- out his life, he thought out and expressed many precepts which are worthy of record.[29]

Pittacus of Mytilene. Diodorus Siculus Pittacus of Mytilene was not only admired among men for his wisdom, but he was also such a citizen as the island never produced again, nor, in my opinion, could produce in time to come—not until it bears wine both more abundant and more delicious. For he was a good lawgiver. In his dealings with individual citizens, he was friendly and kind. And he freed his homeland from the three greatest evils—from tyranny, civil strife, and war. He was a man of consequence, gentle and in- clined to self-disparagement. Consequently, he was regarded by all as a man who, beyond dispute, was perfect in every excellence. As for legislation, he showed himself statesmanlike and sensible. As for maintaining trust, he was strictly just. As for distinction in armed combat, he was courageous. And as for highmindedness re- garding gain, he was one who didn't love money.[30]

Pythagoras. Diogenes Laertius Now Pythagoras was in Egypt when Po- lycrates sent him a letter of introduction to Amasis. Pythagoras learned the Egyptian language—or so we learn from Antiphon in his book *On Men of Outstanding Virtue*. And he also journeyed among the Chaldeans and Magi. Then, while in Crete, he went down into the cave of Ida with Epimenides. He also entered the Egyptian sanctuaries and was told their secret lore concerning the gods.[31]

Archytas. Diogenes Laertius Archytas of Tarentum . . . was another of the Pythagoreans. It was his letter that saved Plato when he was about to be put to death by Dionysius. He was generally admired for his excellence in all fields. So it was that he was general of his city seven times, while the law excluded all others even from a second year of command.[32]

Aristeides and Xanthippus. Diodorus Siculus The Athenian assembly chose two men, Aristeides and Xanthippus. They selected them not only because of their excellence but also because they saw that these men were active rivals to Themistocles for glory and leadership and were therefore opposed to him.[33]

Themistocles. Diodorus Siculus Themistocles was greatly esteemed by the Athenians for his excellence.[34]

A Persian woman. Diodorus Siculus The king was overjoyed that Themistocles had been saved and honored him with great gifts. So it was, for example, that he gave him in marriage a Persian woman, who was of outstanding birth and beauty and, besides, praised for her excellence.[35]

Brasidas. Diodorus Siculus In the siege that followed, Brasidas fought so brilliantly that the Athenians found themselves unable to take the stronghold and withdrew to their ships, and Brasidas, who had saved Methone by his own excellence and courage, received the admiration of the Spartans. And because of this manly goodness of his, Brasidas . . . on many subsequent occasions fought recklessly and won for himself a great reputation for courage.[36]

Diomedon. Diodorus Siculus Diomedon, one of the generals, took the floor before the people, a man who was both vigorous in the conduct of war and thought by all to excel both in justice and in the other excellences.[37]

Nicias. Diodorus Siculus When the proposal was introduced to dispatch an expedition to Sicily, Nicias, the son of Niceratus, a man who enjoyed the respect of his fellow citizens for his excellence, counselled against the expedition to Sicily.[38]

Nicias. Thucydides Of all the Greeks in my time, Nicias least deserved such a death, considering the whole course of his life had been regulated with strict attention to excellence.[39]

Achilles, Miltiades, and Leonidas. Pausanias At this time Xerxes led his great army against Greece, and Leonidas met him at Thermopylae with three hundred Lacedaemonians. Now, even though the Greeks have waged many wars . . . there are very few that have been made more glorious by the exceptional excellence of one man—in the way, for example, that Achilles did for the Trojan War and Miltiades for the engagement at Marathon. But the truth is that the success of Leonidas surpassed, in my view, all later as well as all previous achievements.[40]

Chilon of Patrae. Pausanias Chilon, an Achaean of Patrae, won two prizes for male wrestlers at Olympia, one at Delphi, four at the Isthmus, and three at the Nemean games. He was buried at the public expense by the Achaeans. It was his fate to lose his life on the field of battle. . . . Either he marched to Chaeronea with the whole army of the Achaeans or his personal excellence and daring led him alone of the Achaeans to fight.[41]

Hermogenes and Polites. Pausanias Similar in renown to Chionis was Hermogenes of Xanthus, a Lydian, who won the wild olive eight times at three Olympic festivals and was surnamed "Horse" by the Greeks. You will also consider Polites a great marvel. He was from Ceramus in Caria and showed at Olympia every excellence in running.[42]

Arrhachion. Pausanias The Phigalians have in their marketplace a statue of the pancratiast Arrhachion. . . . He won two victories at

Olympic festivals. . . . He won because of the fairness of the chief judges and his own excellence.[43]

The Attic contingent and Cydias. Pausanias On this day the Attic contingent surpassed the other Greeks in excellence. Of the Athenians themselves, the bravest was Cydias, a young man who had never been in battle. He was killed by the Gauls, but his relatives dedicated his shield to Zeus the Deliverer.[44]

Socrates (the philosopher). Xenophon All who knew what kind of man Socrates was, and all who care for virtue, all these men continue even now to miss Socrates most of all as the most helpful man in the pursuit of virtue. As for me, I have described him as he was. He was so pious that he did nothing without a sign from the gods. He was so just that he did no harm, however small, to any man. Instead, he conferred the greatest benefits on all who dealt with him. He was so self-controlled that he never chose the more pleasant thing or way over the better thing or way. He was so wise that he never erred in judging between what was better and what was worse. He did not even have to ask others about these, but he relied on himself for his knowledge of them. He was skillful in explaining and defining such things—and in testing others, and in convincing them of error, and in urging them on toward virtue and goodness. For all these points, then, he seemed to me the best of men, a truly happy man.[45]

Plato (the philosopher, whose original name was Aristocles). Diogenes Laertius Here reposes the godlike man Aristocles [Plato], eminent among mortal men for moderation and the justice of his character. He had a great deal of praise for wisdom—if anyone ever did.[46]

Crates of Thebes (the Cynic philosopher). Apuleius. Crates, the well-known disciple of Diogenes, was honored at Athens by the men of his own day as though he had been a household god. . . .

The poets tell that Hercules[47] of old by his valor subdued all the wild monsters of legend, beast or man, and purged all the world of them. Even so our philosopher Crates was truly a Hercules in the conquest of anger, envy, avarice, lust, and all the other monstrous and shameful things that plague the human soul. He expelled all these pests from their minds, purged households, and tamed vice. Not only that but he too went half-naked and was distinguished by the club he carried. And he sprang from that same Thebes where men say that Hercules was born. Even before he became Crates pure and simple, he was accounted one of the chief men in Thebes. His family was noble, his establishment numerous, his house had a fair and ample porch. His lands were rich and his clothing sumptuous.

But later, when he understood that the wealth that had been given to him came with no safeguard on which he might lean as on a staff in the course of his life, he realized that all was fragile and transitory—that all the wealth in all the world was no help in living well, in living virtuously.[48]

Zeno of Citium (the founder of Stoicism). Diogenes Laertius The people of Athens honored Zeno very much, as was shown when they entrusted him with the keys of the city walls and when they honored him with a golden crown and a bronze statue. This honor was also given him by the citizens of his hometown, who considered his statue a credit to their city. And the men of Citium living in Sidon also claimed him as their own. . . .

It has also seemed good to me to add on the decree that the Athenians passed concerning him. It reads as follows: . . .

"Whereas Zeno of Citium, the son of Mnaseas, has for many years been devoted to philosophy in the city and has continued to be a good man in all other respects, exhorting to virtue and moderation those of the youth who come to him to be taught, directing them to what is most excellent, offering to all in his own manner of living a pattern for imitation in perfect conformity with his teaching, it has seemed good to the people—and may it so happen—to bestow praise on Zeno of Citium, the son of Mnaseas, and to crown him with a golden crown according to the law, for his virtue and moderation, and to build for him a tomb in the Ceramicus out of public funds. . . ."

The Athenians buried Zeno in the Ceramicus and honored him in the decrees already cited above, bearing additional witness to his virtue.[49]

Epaminondas of Thebes in Boeotia (as well as a listing of other men of excellence). Diodorus Siculus The Thebans had leaders conspicuous for their excellences. Greatest among them were three men—Epaminondas, Gorgidas, and Pelopidas. The city of the Thebans was full of pride because of the glory of its ancestors in the heroic age, and its citizens aspired to mighty deeds. . . .

Epaminondas, by his own personal excellence, inspired his fellow citizens with patriotic spirit. . . .

He excelled by far not merely those of his own people but even all Greeks in courage and understanding in the art of war. His education was great and broad—he was particularly interested in the philosophy of Pythagoras. Besides this, being well-endowed with physical advantages, it is natural that he accomplished very distinguished achievements. So it was that even when he was compelled with a very few citizen soldiers to fight against all the armies of the Lacedaemonians and their allies, he was so far superior to these heretofore invincible warriors that he slew the Spartan king, Cleombrotus, and almost annihilated the great number of his opponents. Such were the remarkable deeds that he performed contrary to expectation because of his astuteness and the excellence resulting from his education. . . .

On one occasion, as the battle raged severely for a long time and the conflict took no turn in favor of either side, Epaminondas, realizing that victory called for the display of his own excellence, decided to be the instrument to decide the outcome. So he immediately took his best men, grouped them in close formation, and charged into the midst of the enemy. He led his battalion in the charge and was the first to hurl his javelin—and he hit the commander of the Lacedaemonians. . . .

While struggling heroically for the victory, Epaminondas received a mortal wound upon his chest. . . . He was carried back to camp still living, and the physicians were summoned. They declared that he would surely die as soon as the spear was pulled from his chest. Even so, with supreme courage he met his end. He first summoned the young man who carried his armor and asked him if he had saved his shield. When the lad said he had, and when he set it before him to see, Epaminondas asked him which side was victorious. The answer was that the Boeotians were. And at this, he said, "It is time to die." . . . And so, when the spear was withdrawn, without any commotion he breathed his last. . . .

It would not be right, we think, to pass by the death of a man of such stature with no word of note. For it seems to me that he surpassed his contemporaries not only in skill and experience in the art of war but in reasonableness and magnanimity as well. For among the generation of Epaminondas there were famous men: Pelopidas the Theban, Timotheus and Conon, also Chabrias and Iphicrates, Athenians all, and, besides, Agesilaus the Spartan, who belonged to a slightly older generation. Still earlier than these, in the times of the Medes and Persians, there were Solon, Themistocles, Miltiades, and Cimon, Myronides and Pericles, and certain others in Athens, and in Sicily Gelon, the son of Deinomenes, and still others. Nevertheless, if you compared the excellences of these with the generalship and reputation of Epaminondas, you would find the excellences possessed by Epaminondas far superior. For in each of the others you would discover but one particular superiority as a claim to reputation. In him, however, are all excellences combined. For in strength of body and eloquence of speech, in splendor of soul, contempt for money, and fairness, and, most of all, in courage and understanding in the art of war, Epaminondas surpassed them all by far.[50]

Philip, the king of Macedonia, and Alexander the Great. Julian the emperor Philip and his son surpassed in excellence all who of old ruled over Macedonia and Thrace—and I should say all who governed the Lydians, as well, or the Medes and Persians and Assyrians . . . For Philip was the first to try to increase the power of the Macedonians, and when he had subdued the greater part of Europe, he made the sea his frontier limit on the east and south, and on the north, I think, the Danube, and on the west the people of

Oricus. And after him, his son, who was raised at the feet of Aristotle, the wise Stagyrite, so far excelled all the rest in greatness of soul and, besides, surpassed his own father in generalship and boldness and the other excellences.[51]

Philip, the king of Macedonia. Diodorus Siculus Thereafter, when Philip had helped the Amphictyons give effect to their decrees and had dealt courteously with all, he returned to Macedonia, having not merely won for himself a reputation for piety and excellent generalship, but having also made important preparations for the aggrandizement that was destined to be his.[52]

Alexander the Great. Diodorus Siculus On his father's side, Alexander was a descendant of Heracles, and on his mother's, he could claim the blood of the Aeacids. So it was that he inherited the nature and highly reputable excellences of his ancestors. . . . Alexander's energy and quickness of action secured for him the leadership of all Greece and made famous the excellence of the young man.[53]

Thallestris, the Amazon queen. Diodorus Siculus When Alexander returned to Hyrcania, there came to him the queen of the Amazons named Thallestris, who ruled all the land between the rivers Phasis and Thermodon. She was remarkable for beauty and for bodily strength and was admired by her countrywomen for courage. She had left the bulk of her army on the frontier of Hyrcania and had arrived with an escort of three hundred Amazons in full armor.

The king marveled at this unexpected arrival and the dignity of the women. When he asked Thallestris why she had come, she revealed that she had in order to conceive a child. Alexander had shown himself the greatest of all men in his achievements, she explained, and she was superior to all women in strength and courage, so that presumably the offspring of such outstanding parents would surpass all other human beings in excellence.

At this the king was delighted and granted her request. So it was that he lived with her and had sex with her for thirteen days. After this time, he honored her with fine gifts and sent her home.[54]

Iamblichus. Julian the emperor Just as the myths give Argus, Io's guardian, an encircling ring of ever-wakeful eyes as he keeps watch over the darling of Zeus, so too does true report endow you, Iamblichus, the trusted guardian of virtue, with the light of the countless eyes of culture. . . . But who, my noble friend, would not genuinely admire you, since though you are inferior in no way to wise Proteus, if not even more fully initiated than he in consummate virtues, you do not begrudge humankind the noble things that you possess, but, like the bright sun, you cause the rays of your pure wisdom to shine on all men.[55]

NOTES

[1] Diodorus Siculus, *Library* 10.12.1-2; 15.1.1.

[2] Dinarchus, *Against Demosthenes* 109.

[3] Pseudo-Hesiod, *Great Ehoiai* 2, from Anonymous Commentator on Aristotle, *Nicomachean Ethics*, 3.7. Recall that "best" is the Greek *aristos*, a word etymologically related to *aretē*.

[4] Sophocles, *Philoctetes* 1418-1420.

[5] Euripides, *Heracles* 694-700.

[6] Philostratus the Athenian, *Lives of the Sophists* 1.preface. For the whole story as recounted by Xenophon, see 8, "Xenophon & Socrates," or Xenophon, *Memorabilia* 2.1.20-34.

[7] Philostratus the Athenian, *Life of Apollonius* 6.10.

[8] Athenaeus, *Deipnosophists* 15.1.

[9] Homer, *Iliad* 14.118.

[10] Homer, *Iliad* 2.530, 553-555, 577, 636. Again, "best" is the Greek *aristos*, a word etymologically related to *aretē*. Note the various senses that amount to excellence: to surpass, to be preeminent, to be first.

[11] Ibid., 1.68-70. Again, "best" is the Greek *aristos*, a word etymologically related to *aretē*.

[12] Ibid., 15.282-285. Again, "best" is the Greek *aristos*, a word etymologically related to *aretē*.

[13] Ibid., 12.101-104. Again, "best" is the Greek *aristos*, a word etymologically related to *aretē*.

[14] Ibid., 3.124. Again, "best" is the Greek *aristos*, a word etymologically related to *aretē*.

[15] Sappho of Lesbos, *Papyrus Oxyrhynchus* 1231.

[16] Isocrates, *Panathenaicus* 12.71-73.

[17] Homer, *Odyssey* 2.205-207.

[18] Ibid., 2.116-121.

[19] Ibid., 18.250-253. See also ibid., 19.124-126 for the same.

[20] Ibid., 24.191-202.

[21] Crates of Thebes, *Letter* 9 to Mnasos. We've already learned of Penelope's excellence from Homer. As for Alcestis, she was the wife of Admetus. She agreed to die in her husband's place when no other of his loved ones would do so. To the Chorus in Euripides' tragedy the *Alcestis*, she "appears noble beyond all women." Like Penelope, she was a most faithful and excellent wife.

[22] Homer, *Odyssey* 4.722-728; 18.199-205.

[23] Ibid., 1.65-67.

[24] Ibid., 4.625-629.

[25] Ibid., 7.53-54, 66-67, 69-77. Arete's name (*Arētē*) means "prayed for" or "prayed to" from the verb *araomai*, to pray to or for (something). This is fitting in that Odysseus is advised to approach Arete and grasp her knees in supplication. See Douglas Frame, *Hippota Nestor* (Washington, DC: Center for Hellenic Studies, 2009). That said, others have suspected (probably incorrectly) that her name is related to *aretē*, the Greek word for virtue, excellence. Either way, Arete is held up in the *Odyssey* as a truly excellent woman.

[26] Hesiod, *Works and Days* 293-297. Again, "best" is the Greek *aristos*, a word etymologically related to *aretē*.

[27] Sappho of Lesbos, *Palatine (Greek) Anthology* 7.15. David A. Campbell identifies Maionidas as Homer. Consequently, Sappho is equating herself in poetic excellence to the greatest and most esteemed Greek poet. See *Greek Lyric: Sappho, Alcaeus*, ed. and trans. David A. Campbell (Cambridge: Harvard University Press, 1990), 47.

[28] Diodorus Siculus, *Library* 9.1.1-4.

[29] Ibid., 9.9.1.

[30] Ibid., 9.11.1-2.

[31] Diogenes Laertius, *Lives* 8.3.

[32] Ibid., 8.79.

[33] Diodorus Siculus, *Library* 11.42.2.

[34] Ibid., 11.54.3. See also ibid., 11.59.4.

[35] Ibid., 11.57.6.

[36] Ibid., 12.43.3.

[37] Ibid., 13.102.1.

[38] Ibid., 12.83.5.

[39] Thucydides, *The Peloponnesian War* 7.86. Sadly, Nicias was butchered after being captured by the Syracusans during the expedition to Sicily against Syracuse, the very one he had voted against.

[40] Pausanias, *Description of Greece* 3.4.7.

[41] Ibid., 6.4.7.

[42] Ibid., 6.13.3.

[43] Ibid., 8.40.1.

[44] Ibid., 10.21.5.

[45] Xenophon, *Memorabilia* 4.8.11.

[46] Diogenes Laertius, *Lives* 3.43. For Plato's original name, Aristocles, and the possible origins of "Plato," see ibid., 3.4.

[47] Hercules rather than Heracles because Apuleius wrote in Latin, and the Latin version of Heracles is Hercules.

[48] Apuleius, *Florida* 22.

[49] Diogenes Laertius, *Lives* 7.6, 9-11, 29.

[50] Diodorus Siculus, *Library* 15.50.6; 38.3; 39.2-3; 86.4; 87.5-15; 88.3.

[51] Julian the emperor, *Panegyric on the Empress Eusebia, Oration III* 106d-107b.

[52] Diodorus Siculus, *Library* 16.60.4.

[53] Ibid., 17.1.5; 17.7.2. The Aeacids include Achilles and his father, Peleus.

[54] Ibid., 17.77.1-3.

[55] Julian the emperor, *Letter 79 to Iamblichus*.

PART 2

Thinking about *Aretē*—the Philosophers

PLATO
& SOCRATES

P LATO (c. 428/7-347[1] BC) WAS an Athenian philosopher. He is known and valued for his many dialogues and letters that explore the definition of terms (such as piety, justice, and courage) and offer his understanding of things (such as the nature of knowledge, the cosmos, becoming and being, the forms or ideas, human virtue, political well-being, and happiness).

Plato opened a school, the Academy, on the outskirts of Athens in order to research the nature of things in community with others, teach, and circulate his ideas, which—collectively known as Platonism—greatly informed and inspired later thinkers, including Greeks and Romans, Jews, Christians, and Muslims.

Plato's views on aretē have influenced Western ethical philosophy down to today. It is to these views that we now turn (for a summary, see the end of the chapter).

Before we do so, however, a few brief points. One, unless otherwise noted, all the following passages come from Plato. Two, there is the so-called "Socratic problem." When Socrates speaks in Plato's dialogues, it is hard to know whether Plato is giving Socrates' position or his own. It is a question that scholars have long debated. The consensus seems to be that we encounter the genuine Socrates in Plato's earlier dialogues. For now, however, having noted the problem, we'll let "Plato" stand for both Socrates and Plato, fully realizing that in point of fact the words and ideas may actually belong to one or the other alone.

IN THEIR OWN WORDS

We begin our exploration of Plato's view of aretē with parts of a dialogue

in which Socrates discusses the nature of aretē with Meno, a young man
from Thessaly, who was studying in Athens with the sophist Gorgias. Ra-
ther than answering every question, the dialogue is a discussion that raises
further questions—as Plato's dialogues often do. Socrates begins by asking
Meno what he thinks about aretē.

Socrates: Tell me, what is your own account of virtue? . . .

Meno: No problem, Socrates. First, if you want to look at the virtue of a man, it is easily stated that a man's virtue is this: that he be
competent to manage the affairs of his city, and to manage them so
as to benefit his friends and harm his enemies, and to take care to
avoid suffering harm himself. Or take a woman's virtue: there is no
difficulty in describing it as the duty of ordering the house well,
looking after the property indoors, and obeying her husband. And
the child has another virtue—one for the female, and one for the
male. And there is another for elderly men. And one, if you like, for
freemen, and yet another for slaves. And there are very many other
virtues besides, so that one cannot be at a loss to explain what virtue
is—for it is according to each activity and age that every one of us,
in whatever we do, has his virtue. And as I understand it, Socrates,
the same also holds for vice.

Socrates: I seem to be in luck, Meno, for in seeking one virtue I
have discovered a whole swarm of virtues there in your keeping.
Now, Meno, to follow this image of a swarm, suppose I ask you
what the real nature of the bee is, and you replied that there are
many kinds of bees. And suppose I replied, Do you say it is by
being bees—that is, as bees—that they are of many and various
kinds and differ from one another, or is their difference found not
in that, but in something else—for example, in their beauty or size
or some other quality? Tell me, what would be your answer to this
question?

Meno: My answer would be this—that they do not differ, one
from another, as bees.

Socrates: And what if I went on to say, Here's what I want you to
tell me, Meno—What do you call this thing by which they do not differ, but by which they are all alike? I imagine you could tell me, right?

Meno: Sure.

Socrates: And likewise also with the virtues, however many and various they may be, they all have one common form or nature or kind by which they are virtues, and on which one would of course be wise to keep an eye when one is giving a definitive answer to the question of what virtue really is. Do you understand what I'm saying?

Meno: It seems to me that I understand—but I still do not fully grasp the meaning of the question as I would like to.

Socrates: Does it seem to you, Meno, that it is only in the case of virtue that one can say there is one kind that belongs to a man, and another to a woman, and so on with the rest? Or is it the same in the case of health and size and strength? Do you suppose that there is one health for a man and another for a woman? Or is the form or nature of health the same for everyone, whether for a man or anyone else?

Meno: I think that health is the same for both a man and a woman. . . .

Socrates: So then, human beings are all good in the same way since they become good by means of the same things. . . . *Continuing, he asks,* Is justice virtue—virtue itself—or is it a virtue?

Meno: What do you mean by saying that?

Socrates: I mean what I would in any other case. Take roundness, for example. I would say that it is a shape and not shape pure and simple—shape in itself. I would do so because there are other shapes besides roundness.

Meno: You'd be right to do so—just as there are other virtues besides justice.

Socrates: What are they? Tell me. In the same way that I can tell you, if you call on me to do so, what other shapes there are, tell me about the other virtues.

Meno: Okay, then. It seems to me that courage is a virtue, as well as moderation, and wisdom, and magnificence of character, and a great many others.

Socrates: Once more, Meno, we are in the same plight. Again, we have discovered many virtues when we were seeking one . . . the one that is common to them all.

After Meno suggests that "virtue is the ability to procure goods," goods such as health, wealth, gold, and political honors and offices, and that justice, holiness, moderation, and other virtues are key to procuring goods, Socrates responds that it is not the ability or power to procure goods that is good, but the means by which we do so, that is, the various virtues. But, he says, these are merely the parts of virtue.

Socrates: After I asked you to speak of virtue as a whole, you said not a word as to what it is in itself, but you told me that every action is virtue as long as it is done with a part of virtue . . . The truth is you are splitting virtue up into fragments! I think, therefore, that you must face the same question all over again, my dear Meno. What is virtue? . . . Do you suppose that anyone can know a part of virtue when he does not know virtue itself?

When Socrates admits his ignorance regarding the nature of virtue, confessing, "I have no idea what virtue is," Meno introduces an all-important question.

Meno: How then—in what direction—will you search for something, Socrates, about which you know absolutely nothing at all? How will you set up something you don't even know as the object of your search? And if you happened to come upon it, how will you know it is the thing you did not know in the first place?

In response to this question—what Socrates calls "a debater's argument"—Socrates reveals what he once learned from certain priests and priestesses—that learning is actually remembering or recollection. As such, even though we may not begin a query by knowing precisely what something is, nevertheless, because we've known it before in a prior existence, we are able to take our first steps in the right direction.

Socrates: The soul is immortal and has been born many times. She has seen all things, both in this world and in the underworld, and so she has learned about everything. Thus, we should not be surprised if the soul is able to recollect all that she knew before about virtue and other things. . . . Consequently, it seems that searching for something and learning about it are wholly recollection. . . . Putting my trust in the truth of this point, I am willing to join you in searching for the nature of virtue.

Continuing in their search for the nature of virtue, Socrates and Meno hit upon the idea that virtue is "wholly or partly practical wisdom."

Socrates: Then may we assert this as a universal rule, that in human beings all other things depend on the soul, while the things of the soul herself depend on practical wisdom if they are to be good. And so, by this account the profitable will be practical wisdom—and virtue, we say, is profitable? . . . Therefore, do we conclude that virtue is either wholly or partly practical wisdom? . . . If this is so, then good men cannot be good by nature.

If good men are not good or virtuous by nature, they must be virtuous by means of teaching. The problem is that they (Meno, Socrates, and Anytus, who has joined the conversation) cannot find anyone who knows how to teach virtue or make anyone good—including parents or the sophists. And "if there are no teachers, then there can neither be students." Therefore, concludes Socrates, "virtue cannot be taught."

Meno wonders if good men actually exist—and, if so, then what process it is by which they come to exist. Socrates suggests that even though one may not be able to teach virtue by means of exact knowledge, still one may point another in the direction of virtue by means of right or true opinion—just as one may give directions to a town without having actually been there before. "Therefore, true opinion is as good a guide to acting rightly as is knowledge." Still, true opinion, Socrates argues, is an uncertain possession. He claims that he speaks as "one who does not know but only guesses." The conclusion?

Socrates: If through this entire discussion our searches and statements have been given well, then virtue is neither something natural nor is it something taught. Rather, it is something that comes to us by divine providence, without any understanding on our part.[2]

*As the following selections demonstrate, there is in other dialogues of Plato
further discussion of whether virtue is one thing or many. The conclusion,
however elusive or inconclusive it seems at times, is that virtue itself is
one in some manner—whether as a participation in wisdom and knowledge,
or as the manifestation of Virtue itself, the form or idea of virtue (just as
beautiful things participate in or manifest Beauty itself, and other things
manifest other forms or ideas).*

*Before we get to the conclusion, however, let's look at a variety of pro-
posed ideas. The first example from the* Laches *proposes that virtue is essentially a kind of knowledge whereby a person knows "all good things."
Here we listen to Socrates dialoguing with Nicias, who assents to Socrates'
propositions.*

Socrates: Then courage is knowledge not merely of what is to be
dreaded and what dared, for it comprehends goods and evils not
merely in the future, but also in the present and the past and at any
stage, like the other kinds of knowledge. . . .

So the answer that you gave us, Nicias, covers only about a third
part of courage—whereas our question was about the nature of
courage as a whole. And now it appears, according to your own
view, that courage is knowledge not merely of what is to be
dreaded and what dared but practically a knowledge concerning
all goods and evils at every stage . . .

Now do you think, my excellent friend, there could be anything
lacking in the virtue of a man who knew all good things, and all
about their production in the present, the future, and the past, and,
similarly, about all evil things? Do you suppose that such a man
could be lacking in moderation or justice or holiness? . . .

Therefore, what you now describe, Nicias, will be not a part but
the whole of virtue.[3]

The second example from the Protagoras *explores whether various virtues
are actually a single thing, or they are somehow related to a single thing, as
the parts of a face to the face as a whole, or a brick of gold divided into parts.
In it Socrates is dialoguing with the sophist Protagoras.*

Socrates: "You said that Zeus had sent justice and respect to mankind, and, furthermore, it was frequently stated in your discourse that justice, moderation, holiness, and the rest were all but one single thing—virtue. Go on, then, and deal with these in a more precise exposition, stating whether virtue is a single thing, of which justice and moderation and holiness are parts, or whether the qualities I have just mentioned are all names of the same single thing. This is what I am still yearning to know."

"Well, the answer to that question is easy, Socrates," he replied. "It is that virtue is a single thing and the qualities in question are parts of it."

"Do you mean parts," I asked, "in the sense of the parts of a face—the mouth, nose, eyes, and ears? Or do you mean it as in the parts of gold? Is there no difference among the pieces, either between the parts or between a part and the whole, except in greatness and smallness?"

"I mean it in the former sense, I think," Socrates, "as the parts of the face are to the whole face."

Though this is the initial conclusion, it is not the final one. The Protagoras *covers many other points, and we find Socrates at dialogue's end still declaring,* "For my part, Protagoras, observing the extraordinary tangle into which we have managed to get the whole matter, I am most anxious to have it thoroughly cleared up. And I would like to work our way through it until at last we reach what virtue is, and then go back and consider whether it is teachable or not."

Regrettably, Protagoras postpones the discussion to another time, suggesting, "Let's pursue the subject on some other occasion."[4]

The third, fourth, and fifth examples, all from the Laws *(in which "the Athenian" is speaking in dialogue with Clinias of Crete and Megillus of Sparta), suggest two major points. One, a city-state's legislation should aim at promoting the whole of virtue. Two, although there are many terms that identify different ends or objectives or virtues, they all actually refer to the same end or objective—to virtue itself.*

The Athenian: We assert, then, that this type of man proves himself

. . . a far better man than the other [*who is courageous alone without the other virtues*] in the measure in which justice, moderation, and practical wisdom, combined with and bolstered by courage, are better than courage alone. For a man will never prove himself loyal and sound in times of faction unless he has the whole of virtue, whereas there are plenty of hired combatants . . . Now, to what does our argument conclude? . . . The legislation of Lycurgus of Sparta and Minos of Crete was framed in the interest of virtue as a whole, not of one fragment of it.[5]

The Athenian: I must ask you not to be surprised that we have already more than once proposed certain ends as those to which the legislator must look, and that our proposals have not always appeared to be identical. You must consider that when we say he must look to moderation, or again to practical wisdom, or to friendship, these ends are not distinct but identical. And if we find ourselves using a further variety of expressions to the same effect, we must not be confused by that.[6]

The Athenian: Take our language about the four types of virtue. If there are four of them, obviously we must hold that each type by itself is one. . . . And yet we give one name to all of them. In fact, we speak of courage as virtue, of practical wisdom as virtue, and similarly the other two. And this implies that they are not really several things but just this one thing—virtue. . . .

It looks as though the guardians of our god-given constitution too must be compelled, first and foremost, to observe exactly what is the identity permeating all the four virtues—the unity to be found, as we hold, alike in courage, moderation, justice, and practical wisdom that allows them all to be called by the one name, virtue.[7]

The final example regarding the unity or plurality of virtue comes from the Republic. *In it Socrates reinforces the conclusion that virtue is one.*

Socrates: And truly, I said, now that we have come to this height of discourse, I seem to see as though from a point of outlook that there is one form of virtue, and that the forms of vice are infinite.[8]

Whatever—exactly—virtue is, and whether it is one thing or many, Plato contends that virtue, which is to say, living well, is central to happiness and human flourishing. In the next few selections, we learn that virtue is the means by which we are happy.[9]

Diogenes Laertius Plato held that the goal of life is to become god-like, and that virtue is sufficient in itself for happiness.[10]

The Athenian: One kind of life is sweeter than the other . . . In short, in comparison with a vicious life, the virtuous life in body and soul is not only more pleasant but it also rises above the other in terms of beauty, correctness, flourishing, and good reputation. Consequently, if a man lives with virtue, he will live with complete happiness.[11]

Socrates: Will the soul be able to perform its own function well if it is lacking its own virtue? Or will it be unable?

Thrasymachus: Unable.

Socrates: Necessarily, then, a bad soul rules and manages things badly, and a good soul does everything well?

Thrasymachus: Necessarily. . . .

Socrates: But he who lives well is blessed and happy.[12]

If happiness comes about by means of virtue, then what is virtue? We are thus led back to the central question.

According to Plato, virtue is the easy, unimpeded flow of the good soul. It is the soul's beauty, its healthy, good condition. Most importantly, per-haps, in terms of definition, virtue is "the means by which a thing performs its function well."

Socrates: In the first place, virtue signifies ease of motion, and sec-ondly, that the flow of the good soul is always unimpeded.[13]

Socrates: It appears, then, that virtue is a kind of health and beauty and good condition of the soul.[14]

Socrates: Virtue is the means by which a thing performs its function well.[15]

If virtue is "the means by which a thing performs its function well," then what is a thing's function or work? With the first statement, Socrates offers a simple definition of "the function of a thing." The second passage explains "function" with several examples, ending with the prior simple definition.

Socrates: The function of a thing is that which it alone can do, or what it does better, than anything else.[16]

Socrates: Would you say that a horse has a specific function or work?

Thrasymachus: Sure.

Socrates: Would you be willing to define the function or work of a horse—or of anything else for that matter—to be that which one can do only with it or best with it?

Thrasymachus: I don't understand.

Socrates: Well, let me express it this way. Aside from the eyes, is there anything else by which you can see?

Thrasymachus: Of course not.

Socrates: Again, can you hear with anything other than the ears?

Thrasymachus: There's no other way.

Socrates: Isn't it right, then, to say that seeing is the function of the eyes and hearing the function of the ears?

Thrasymachus: Yes, by all means.

Socrates: Once more, you could use a dagger, a sword, a butcher knife, and many other instruments to trim vine branches. . . . But I imagine that nothing will work or perform as well in comparison with a pruning-knife.

Thrasymachus: True.

Socrates: Must we not assume, then, that pruning is the function of a pruning-knife?

Thrasymachus: We must.

Socrates: I imagine you will now better understand that the function of a thing is that which it alone can do, or what it does better, than anything else.[17]

Since for Plato happiness corresponds to virtue, and virtue corresponds to a thing's function, and because a thing's function corresponds to its nature (a point Plato makes in the Timaeus *and the* Cratylus*), then we must investigate what a human being is, that is, what human nature is. First, there is general human nature, which is a composite of body and soul.*

Socrates: The whole [human being], composed of a soul and a body, is called an animal, that is, a living being.[18]

What is the body? The body serves the soul as its means of locomotion; it is, as it were, the soul's chariot.

Timaeus: The offspring of the creator-god made the mortal body to be the chariot of the soul. . . . It is the means of easy transportation . . . upon the earth, which has all manner of heights and hollows.[19]

What is the soul? The soul itself has three parts, here (in the Phaedrus*) compared to a charioteer and the two horses hitched to the chariot, one of which is good and noble, whereas the other is not. We'll discover more about these three parts of the soul in a moment.*

Socrates: The soul is like the composite union that arises from a yoked pair of winged horses and their winged charioteer. . . . As for human beings, the charioteer of the soul holds the reigns, driving and guiding the pair of horses. Yet another point: one of the horses is good and noble, of noble stock, whereas the other horse is quite the opposite. This is why driving the chariot of the soul is necessarily difficult and troublesome for us.[20]

Plato offers another image of the soul in the Republic, *a dialogue that explores the nature of justice. In order to understand what justice is, Socrates and his interlocutors search for it in an imaginary city. The city itself has three basic parts: the ruling, the auxiliary guarding and law-enforcing, and the producing-trading-money-making parts. The question is whether the soul is like the city, and so whether it similarly has three parts.*

Socrates: Our inquiry is to see whether the soul possesses these three parts, or forms, or not. [*"These three parts" refers to the three parts of the city.*] We are agreed that the same number and same kinds, or parts, are in both the city and the soul.[21]

Shortly after their agreement, Socrates and Glaucon (Plato's brother) attempt to discover the three parts of the soul. Corresponding respectively to the three parts of the city mentioned a moment ago, they are the rational, the spirited, and the desiring parts.

Socrates: It would be reasonable, then, to state that these two parts of the soul are different from each other. We'll call the part of the soul by which it calculates and reasons the rational part. And the part with which it desires, hungers, and thirsts, and feels the passionate excitement of other longings, we'll call the non-rational and desiring part of the soul—the companion of various fill-me-ups and pleasures.

Glaucon: Yes, it would be reasonable. . . .

Socrates: Let us assume, then, that these two parts, or forms, have been separated from each other and marked off in the soul. Still, is the *thumos*—the heart or spirit, that by which we are provoked and feel angry—a third, spirited part, or is it the same as the rational or desiring part? . . . Again, is this high-spirited *thumos* a third part in the soul just as we found three separate kinds of people that held the city together—the counselor-deliberators, the auxiliary guardians, and the money-makers?

Glaucon: It must be a third part.[22]

If there are three parts of the soul, then each part must have its own function (what it alone can do, or what it does better, than anything else) and virtue (the means by which it performs its function well). The same must be true for the body, as well as for the whole of human nature operating as a unity, body and soul (just as a city as a whole may operate well).

Let's look at each of these virtues in turn, beginning with the body and working our way through each part of the soul until we get to the excellence of the whole. As for the body, health is its excellence.

Socrates: Physical training and medicine combine into a single art to care for the body. *And,* Simplicity in physical training or exercise begets health in bodies.[23]

The general nature of the soul is self-motion—that is, by nature a soul is something that can move itself. To do so, however, the soul must decide where to go. Consequently, the general function of the soul is to deliberate and direct.

Socrates: The very nature of the soul is self-motion.[24]

Socrates: The function of the soul is . . . management, rule, deliberation, and the like.[25]

But what is the function of each part of the soul? And so, what is the virtue of each part?
      The function of the rational part is to rule and direct the whole soul. It does this by means of wisdom, its virtue.

Socrates: It is the rational part's function to rule since it is altogether wise and exercises foresight on behalf of the whole soul. . . . *The rational part* will rule the desiring part . . . and guard the whole soul and body . . . by taking counsel and by deliberating. . . . We call a man wise because of the small part in him that rules and delivers these orders and exhortations, and by its knowledge of what is beneficial for each part and for the whole soul, the community of the three parts.[26]

Socrates: The truth is that when wisdom is present, he who has it has no need for good luck.[27]

The function of the spirited part of the soul is to obey and carry out the rational part's directives. Given the fight put up by the oftentimes disobedient desiring part, as well as the agitation caused by pleasure and pain (what the desiring part moves toward or away from), this function requires courage, the spirited part's virtue.

Socrates: The spirited part's function is to listen to, obey, and be allied with the rational part of the soul. . . . *With the rational part, it will* guard the whole soul and body . . . by carrying out the rational part's resolutions by means of courage. . . . We call a man courageous, I suppose, because of the spirited part in him—when the spirited part carries out, through both pleasure and pain, the orders and exhortations of the rational part regarding what is to be feared and what is not.[28]

Next, the desiring part of the soul. As we see in the Symposium, *for Plato, desire itself is a kind of lacking. Generally speaking, what is lacking is what is necessary. Therefore, the function of the desiring part of the soul is to seek what is generally necessary for survival and sufficient for well-being.*

As Plato sees it, the problem with desire is not the yearning we may feel for wisdom (this is philosophy, the desire for or love of wisdom) or the desire we may feel to know and experience the Good or the Beautiful. Instead, for most people the problem appears relative to things like honor, money, food, wine, and sex. Rather than desiring enough food for health, for instance, or enough sex for reproduction and the continuance of the species, humans desire and seek these things in excess, in ways that are oftentimes positively unhealthy.

Corresponding to the above function, then, the virtue of the desiring part of the soul is moderation, that excellence by which it listens to and obeys the ruling part of the soul and so properly directs desire toward what is necessary for each person's survival and well-being. When this happens, the whole soul operates together well.

Socrates: Moderation is some kind of order—power over and control of certain pleasures and desires. It is what people mean when they use the term, "self-control." . . . The intended meaning of speaking this way seems to me to be that the soul of a man has a better part and a worse part, and to say "self-control" or "having power over oneself" means the control of the worse part by the naturally better part of the soul.[29]

Socrates: The most significant features of moderation for most people are the following: one, listening to and being obedient to the rulers, and two, ruling over the pleasures of eating, drinking, and having sex.[30]

Socrates: Moderation spreads throughout the whole soul, making the strongest, weakest, and intermediate parts sing in unison.[31]

Socrates: The wise man is moderate because of the friendship and concord of the three parts of the soul, when the ruling part and the ruled agree that reason should rule.[32]

The aforementioned "friendship and concord" point to the function and virtue of the soul as a whole. It is to operate in such a way that each part performs its own function well and does not interfere with or do the work of the other parts.

It may be useful to recall the imaginary city that runs well when each part does what it is supposed to do. Some in the city rule. Some enforce the directives of the ruling part. And some produce goods and trade these goods for the survival and well-being of the city. When each part functions well and does not interfere with the work of the other parts, the whole city thrives with harmony and well-being.

The same is true for the soul. When the rational part rules with wisdom, the spirited part enforces the directives of the rational part with courage, and the desiring part moderately desires, heeding the rule of the rational part, then the whole soul operates in harmony. Like a string trio, it is a harmonious unity. This harmony is justice, the virtue of the soul as a whole, the means by which the soul does well.

Socrates: Justice is doing one's own work and not doing this, that, and the other thing that are not your own.[33]

Socrates: The just man does not allow each part of the soul to perform the function or do the work of another part, or to interfere and meddle with another part's function or work. Rather, the just man does a good job arranging what is his own—ruling, ordering, and befriending himself, and harmonizing the three parts of the soul like three notes or intervals in a musical scale, high, low, and middle. And having joined and bound all three together, and all those in between, he himself becomes a harmonious unity, entirely one. . . . The just man believes that in everything the just, noble, and beautiful action is the one that preserves and brings about this harmonious condition of the soul, and that wisdom is the knowledge that presides over and supports such action."[34]

We see in the report of the biographer Diogenes Laertius how wisdom, courage, moderation, and justice were the key virtues for Plato.

Diogenes Laertius (reporting Plato's view) Of perfect virtue there are four kinds or forms: practical wisdom, justice, courage, and moderation. Of these, practical wisdom is the cause of right conduct, and justice is responsible for straight dealing in partnerships and commercial transactions. Courage is the cause that makes a man not give way but stand his ground in alarms and perils. Moderation causes mastery over desires, so that we are never enslaved by pleasure but live in an orderly manner.[35]

As for the how of virtue, Plato never precisely states how one becomes virtuous. Rather, various ideas are presented and discussed. Certain virtues, for instance, are acquired thanks to the directives of the law, which is to say the rational direction of a city-state's constitution. Others are attained by means of habituation and practice. Finally, some come about more mysteriously, by a turning of the soul in understanding, inspiration, or by direct contact with What Is, whether the Good or the Beautiful itself.

The Athenian: Responsiveness and pliability to virtue—that is clearly what the legislator hopes to achieve in all his legislation.[36]

Socrates: If through this entire discussion our searches and statements have been given well, then virtue is neither something natural nor is it something taught. Rather, it is something that comes to us by divine providence, without any understanding on our part.[37]

Socrates: Then the other so-called virtues of the soul do seem similar to those of the body since it is true that where they do not pre-exist, they are later produced by habit and practice. But the virtue related to thinking wisely, it seems, is certainly of a more divine quality, a thing that never loses its power, but, according to the way it is turned, it becomes useful and beneficial or useless and harmful.[38]

Socrates: It is easy to imagine into what creatures all the other kinds of soul will go—they will do so in accord with their own practices in life. . . . The happiest people, those who come to the best place, are those who have pursued, without philosophy or understanding, the democratic and social virtues by means of habit and practice. . . . They are happiest because they will probably pass again into some other kind of social and tamed creature such as bees, wasps, and ants—or even back into humankind again . . . But no one who has not been a philosopher, and who is not wholly pure when he departs from this life, is allowed to come into the presence of the divine kind, the gods. No, that is only for the lover of knowledge, the one yearns to understand.[39]

The prophetess Diotima of Mantinea is speaking to Socrates "In this state of life above all others, my dear Socrates," the woman from Mantinea said, "a man finds it truly worthwhile to live, as he contemplates the Beautiful itself. Once this is acknowledged, you will not imagine that the beautiful has anything to do with gold and clothing and beautiful boys and young men—those who, if you see them now, drive you out of your senses, making you and many others who look at the boys and always spend time with them ready to go without eating and drinking, if that were possible, just as long as you can look at them and be with them.

"But tell me," she said, "what would happen if a man were able to look upon the Beautiful itself—simple, pure, and unmixed, and untouched by the flesh and the decorative embellishments belonging to men and all the other nonsense having to do with mortal creatures? What if this man could behold the divine Beautiful itself in its one form?

"Do you suppose," she went on, "it is a pitiful life for a man to lead—looking that way and gazing over there as he should, and joining with it?

"Consider well," she said, "that it is only there with Beauty itself that it will happen to him. Seeing the beautiful through that which makes it visible, he does not give birth to an image of virtue inasmuch as he is not in touch with images; rather, he gives birth to true virtue inasmuch as he grasps the truth—what is real and actual.

"So, when this man has produced true virtue, nourishing it and letting it grow, he becomes dear to the gods. And if ever immortality is granted to humans, that man, above all others, will be immortal."[40]

SUMMARY OF ARETĒ FOR PLATO (AND SOCRATES)

For Plato (and Socrates), every specific virtue or excellence is a manifestation of or participation in virtue itself, which is a unity.

Generally speaking, virtue (or a specific virtue) is "the means by which a thing performs its function well," where a thing's function is "that which it alone can do, or what it does better, than anything else." For example, the virtue of a pruning knife is the sharpness of its uniquely shaped blade that works to trim grapevines (its designed function that follows from its given nature or unique shape) rather than any other function it may have or work it may otherwise accomplish (to cut meat, for instance, or to serve as a papyrus weight or toothpick).

For human beings, virtue manifests itself relative to human nature (something designed and given by the creator) and its composite parts, the body and soul—the latter being for Plato the most significant. The virtue of the body is health. As the vehicle of the soul, the body must be healthy enough for the soul to perform its proper function. The general virtue of the soul is to direct the human person by means of deliberation.

More specifically, the virtues of the soul correspond to its three parts. Each part of the soul has its own function and matching virtue. The rational part of the soul rules by means of wisdom. The spirited part enforces the rule of the rational part by means of courage. The desiring part listens to and obeys the rational part and thus moves toward what is necessary and sufficient for the body and soul by means of moderation. Together, when each part of the soul performs its own proper function well, without interfering with the work of the other parts, the soul harmoniously operates as a whole. This harmony is justice, the soul's virtue as a whole.

When soul justice (harmony) occurs, the whole person is living well and happily, deliberating, directing, and acting in accord with wisdom. So it is that Plato concludes that virtue, or living well, is central to happiness and human flourishing. Virtue is the means by which we humans are happy.

By contrast, vice is the means by which a thing fails to perform its function well, as with the opposites of the aforementioned virtues—ignorance, cowardice, immoderation, and injustice, which, Plato suggests, is "a kind of civil war between the three parts of the soul."[41] If the virtuous person is happy, then the vicious person is not. The obvious thing to do, then, is to strive toward virtue, a venture that involves intuition, education, training, practice, legislation, and a (somewhat mystical) turning toward and participation in What Is—toward the True, the Good, and the Beautiful.

NOTES

[1] Though most give 428 or 427 BC as Plato's date of birth, some scholars, including *The Oxford Classical Dictionary*, give 429 BC.

[2] Plato, *Meno* 71d; 71e-72d; 73c; 73e-74a; 79b-c; 80d; 81c; 88e-89a; 99e-100a. Although we (in 88e-89a) give *phronēsis* as "practical wisdom," one should note that, broadly speaking, *phronēsis* means thoughtfulness or wisdom.

[3] Plato, *Laches* 199c-e.

[4] Plato, *Protagoras* 329c-e; 361c.

[5] Plato, *Laws* 1.630a-e.

[6] Ibid., 3.693b-c.

[7] Ibid., 12.963c-d; 12.965c-d.

[8] Plato, *Republic* 4.445c.

[9] Many of the following examples are taken from *Happiness: What the Ancient Greeks Thought and Said about Happiness* (Sugar Land: The Classics Cave, 2021).

[10] Diogenes Laertius, *Lives* 3.78.

[11] Plato, *Laws* 5.734d-e.

[12] Plato, *Republic* 1.353e, 1.354a. To reiterate the point, for Plato, to "live well" means to live according to virtue.

[13] Plato, *Cratylus* 415c-d.

[14] Plato, *Republic* 4.444d-e.

[15] Ibid., 1.353c. Faithful to Plato's intention (evident in Socrates' position), we have modified the line by transforming Socrates' question into a positive statement. The question: "I am asking about whether a thing that has a function performs it well by means of its own virtue . . ."

[16] Ibid., 1.353a. This definition of function appears at the end of the next selection. The Greek for function or work is *ergon*.

[17] Ibid., 1.352d-353a.

[18] Plato, *Phaedrus* 246c.

[19] Plato, *Timaeus* 69c and 44d-e.

[20] Plato, *Phaedrus* 246a. Interestingly, a similar analogy appears in Indian philosophy in the *Katha* Upanishad 3.3 ff.

[21] Plato, *Republic* 4.435c.

[22] Ibid., 4.439d-e; 4.440e-441a. Socrates further compares the three to a shepherd (the rational part), his sheep (the non-rational desiring part), and the sheepdogs (the spirited part) that help the shepherd guide the sheep (see ibid., 4.440d).

[23] Plato, *Gorgias* 464b and *Republic* 3.404e.

[24] Plato, *Phaedrus* 245e.

[25] Plato, *Republic* 1.353d.

[26] Ibid., 4.441e; 4.442a-c. "Wise" is *sophos*, the adjectival form of *sophia* (wisdom).

[27] Plato, *Euthydemus* 280b. Wisdom is *sophia*.

[28] Plato, *Republic* 4.441e; 4.442a-c. Courage is *andreia*.

[29] Ibid., 4.430e; 4.431a. Moderation is *sōphrosunē*. Self-control is *enkrateia*.

[30] Ibid., 3.389d-e.

[31] Ibid., 4.432a.

[32] Ibid., 4.442c-d.

[33] Ibid., 4.433a-b. Though this definition of justice is intended for justice in general, it may equally be applied to the soul and its parts. Justice is *dikaiosunē*.

[34] Ibid., 4.443d-e.

[35] Diogenes Laertius, *Lives* 3.90-91. Rather than Plato's use of *sophia* for wisdom, Diogenes Laertius uses *phronēsis* (what Aristotle terms "practical wisdom.)"

[36] Plato, *Laws* 4.718c.

[37] Plato, *Meno* 99e-100a.

[38] Plato, *Republic* 7.518d-519a. We may expand "habit and practice" to training. If health is produced in the body by physical training or exercise, then health of the soul—virtue—may be assumed to be cultivated, in some measure, by soul training or exercise. For physical training (*gumnastikos*) see Plato, *Republic* 3.404e.

[39] Plato, *Phaedo* 82a-c.

[40] Plato, *Symposium*, 211d-212a.

[41] Plato, *Republic* 4.444b.

XENOPHON
& SOCRATES

X ENOPHON (c. 430-354 BC) WAS an Athenian statesman and historian. He is known for, among other works, the *Anabasis*, or the *Expedition Up*, an account of the harrowing escape of the Ten Thousand, a Greek Mercenary force, after the Battle of Cunaxa (401 BC). In the attempt to flee, Xenophon himself led the Ten Thousand in a march to the Black Sea. Drawing on his experience with Socrates, he also wrote the *Apology*, a work recounting Socrates' defense before the Athenian assembly, and the *Memorabilia*, *Oeconomicus*, and *Symposium*, works also centered on Socrates and his conversations with others.

It is from these latter Socrates-centered works that we will listen to Xenophon at times and Socrates at others speaking about virtue or things related to virtue (for a summary, see the end of the chapter).

Before getting to virtue, we should note that the same "Socratic problem" arises with Xenophon as did with Plato. In this case, the problem is that the Socrates we encounter in Xenophon is different—at least somewhat different—from the Socrates in Plato. While from one angle this is a problem, from another it is quite a boon. Assuming both men presented the Socrates he actually knew, we may conclude we are getting something approximating the real Socrates through two sets of spectacles, as it were—those of Plato and Xenophon.

If this conclusion is something close to the truth, then what we have with Xenophon is the presentation of a man he greatly admired. In fact, at one point he declares that "Socrates seemed to me the best of men, a truly happy man."[1]

As with Plato, all passages are from Xenophon's own work unless otherwise noted.

IN THEIR OWN WORDS

Before getting to what Xenophon himself thought and wrote about virtue, let's first turn our attention to much later testimony regarding the man himself and how he encountered Socrates and became his student in the matter of how men "become noble and good."

Diogenes Laertius The story goes that Socrates met Xenophon in a narrow passageway in the marketplace. Socrates held out his staff to prevent him from walking on and asked Xenophon to tell him where each kind of food was sold. Upon receiving a reply, he asked another question. "And where do men go to become noble and good?" he asked. Xenophon had no idea. "Then follow me," Socrates responded, "and learn." From that moment on he was Socrates' student.[2]

Eunapius of Sardis Xenophon the philosopher was unique among all philosophers in that he adorned philosophy not only with words but with deeds as well—for on the one hand, he writes of the moral virtues both in discourses and historical commentaries, while on the other, he excelled also in actual achievement.[3]

The remaining selections come from Xenophon's Memorabilia. *In the first, Xenophon makes the case that one must continue to train in virtue. Association with good men is a significant part of this training.*

Xenophon: But many self-styled lovers of wisdom may reply that a just man can never become unjust. And a sensible and wise man can never become insolent and outrageous. In fact, no one, once he has learned any kind of knowledge, can become ignorant of it. But I do not agree with this view.

I notice that as those who do not train the body cannot perform the functions proper to the body, so those who do not train the soul cannot perform the functions of the soul—for they cannot do what they should do or avoid what they should not do. For this reason, fathers try to keep their sons, even if they are sensible and wise, out of bad company—for an association with good men is a training in virtue, but an association with bad men is virtue's undoing.[4]

In the second set of selections, Xenophon speaks of Socrates' virtue and his promotion of the same—contrary to the charges brought against him in court.

Xenophon: So far was Socrates from "rejecting the gods," as charged in the indictment, that no man was more conspicuous for his devotion to the service of the gods. So far was he from "corrupting the youth," as his accuser actually charged him, that if any among his companions had worthless desires, he openly tried to reform them and exhorted them to desire the most noble and magnificent virtue by which men prosper in public life and in their homes.[5]

Xenophon: It is amazing to me that some believed the charge brought against Socrates of corrupting the youth. . . . Of all men, he was self-controlled relative to the desire for sex and the gluttony of the belly. Moreover, he was fully capable of endurance relative to cold and heat and hard work of every kind. Besides, his needs were so schooled in moderation that whenever he had very little, he was nevertheless very content. Such was his own character. How then is it possible that he led others into impiety or lawlessness or gluttony or sexual lust or a lack of self-control? On the contrary, Socrates put a stop to these vices in many by making them long for virtue, and by giving them the hope that with care they might be good and noble men. To be sure, he never professed to teach this, but by letting his own light shine, he led his students to hope that they would be like him if they imitated him.[6]

Next, Socrates himself argues that self-control is the foundation of every virtue.

Socrates: Men, if we were at war and wanted to choose a leader most capable of helping us to save ourselves and conquer the

enemy, would we choose one whom we could tell was no match for
the belly or for wine or for lust or hard work or sleep? . . . Or, if at
the end of life, we wanted to entrust someone with the education of
our boys or the protection of our girls or the safeguarding of our
property, would we consider the man lacking in self-control to be
trustworthy in these matters?

No, we would not. Rather, says Socrates, Every man should hold
self-control to be the foundation of virtue. And everyone should accordingly establish this foundation within his soul. For without this
foundation, who can learn any good or practice it in a worthy manner? No, the man enslaved to these pleasures is in a shameful condition in both body and soul.[7]

Speaking with the hedonist Aristippus,[8] *Socrates explores two paths one may
take in life—the path of virtue and the path of vice. In doing so, he mentions
Hesiod's famous description of the two paths available to one in life and
Prodicus' story of Heracles encountering Virtue and Vice personified.*

Socrates: Self-indulgence and enjoyment will never have the power
to bring the body into its highest conditioning and health, as the
trainers of athletes say. Nor does such sluggish satisfaction produce
any knowledge in the soul worth talking about. Rather, as good men
say, it is patient, enduring attention and work that leads to noble and
good results.

For instance, Hesiod somewhere says, "It is easy to have Vice.
She's there in abundance for you. The way to her is smooth, and
she dwells very near to you. But the immortal gods have put sweat
in front of Virtue. The path to her is long and steep, and so it is
rough going at first. Nevertheless, when one comes to the highest
point, then the path becomes easy—however hard it is at first."

We also have the witness of Epicharmus' with the line, "The
gods ask for toil as the high price of every good thing." . . .

Yes, and the wise man Prodicus makes the same point regarding
virtue in his tale about Heracles. When Heracles was making his
way from boyhood to young manhood, and so he was on the path
to becoming his own master, he came to the point where he had to

choose between a life of virtue or one of vice. So, he went out to a quiet spot and sat there puzzling over which path he should take. Sitting there, two very tall women appeared and walked up to him. One was fitting and noble in appearance—her body ordered with purity, her eyes adorned with modesty, and her bearing generally expressing discretion. She wore a white robe. But the other! She was plump and soft, with an unnatural pink and white face all made up, and an upright spine to exaggerate her height, and eyes wide open. As for her robe, it hung so as to reveal everything—all her charms. She eyed herself and looked away to see if anyone noticed her. She would also glance at her own shadow.

Socrates explains that it is these two women who approach Heracles, each making their case to him. The latter woman speaks first. Heracles should be her friend, she urges—if, that is, he wants to follow along the easiest and pleasantest road. He'll have the best of everything—food, drink, sex, sleep, scents, and every other pleasure. All sweets! No hardship! No war or worries! And no toil because he'll simply seize what he wants from others.

So then, Socrates said, when Heracles had heard her claims, he asked, "Lady, what is your name?" She responded, "My friends call me Happiness, but those who hate me have nicknamed me Vice."

Now the other woman speaks. She promises a good result if Heracles will only follow her path. Yet, she says, it won't be easy. "Of all that is truly good or noble, the gods give nothing to men without toil and effort."

This woman goes on to explain what a man must do to get various goods. Favor from the gods requires worship. Goodwill from friends calls for kindness. A city's honor demands service. Greek admiration—the hard work of excellence. Fruits require cultivation; an increase in flock numbers, shepherding; and defense and power, training in the art of war. Lastly, a strong body demands the mind's command and much toilsome, sweaty training.

Socrates went on, saying, As Prodicus tells it, Vice here interrupted and said, "Have you considered, Heracles, how long and hard this road to enjoyment is that this woman Virtue is mapping for you? I will lead you along a short and easy road to happiness."

Virtue strongly disagrees and declares, "But I associate with the gods and with good men, and no fine action, whether the deed of a god or of a man, is done without me. . . . So, Heracles, child of good parents, if you toil hard along the path that I, Virtue, have mapped for you, you can acquire the most blessed happiness."

Finishing Prodicus' story, Socrates said, Anyhow, Aristippus, you would do well to think about these matters and consider the life ahead of you.[9]

Next, Socrates argues that virtue is increased by learning and practice, and that the thoughts of the wise make for virtue.

(Speaking to Critobulus) Socrates: You will find on reflection that every kind of virtue named among men is augmented by education and practice.[10]

(Speaking to Euthydemus) Socrates: The thoughts of the wise enrich their possessors with virtue.[11]

In the final selections, Xenophon discusses Socrates' views on virtue and how Socrates himself was a virtuous man and led others to virtue.

Xenophon: Socrates drew no distinction between wisdom and moderation. But if a man knew and practiced what is noble and good, and knew and avoided what is base and shameful, then he judged that man to be both wise and moderate. . . . He said that justice and every other virtue is wisdom. For just actions and all forms of virtuous activity are noble and good. He who knows the noble and the good will never choose anything else. . . . So it is that the wise do what is noble and good.[12]

Xenophon: All who knew what kind of man Socrates was, and all who care for virtue, all these men continue even now to miss Socrates most of all as the most helpful man in the pursuit of virtue. As for me, I have described him as he was. He was so pious that he did nothing without a sign from the gods. He was so just that he did no harm, however small, to any man. Instead, he conferred the greatest benefits on all who dealt with him. He was so self-controlled that he never chose the more pleasant thing or way over the better thing or way. He was so wise that he never erred in judging between what was better and what was worse. He did not even have to ask others about these, but he relied on himself for his knowledge of them. He was skillful in explaining and defining such things—and in testing others, and in convincing them of error, and in urging them on toward virtue and noble goodness. For all these points, then, he seemed to me the best and happiest man.[13]

SUMMARY OF ARETĒ FOR XENOPHON (AND SOCRATES)

For Xenophon (and Socrates), virtue is something that is truly noble and good. It is an association with the gods and with good men, the expression of fine action. Virtue is the means by which we may achieve happiness.

Many in number, every virtue may nevertheless in some sense be identified with wisdom. Self-control relative to various pleasures and pains is virtue's foundation. Other virtues are endurance, moderation, piety, knowledge, order, and justice—though this list is not comprehensive. Vices are the opposite of these.

How do we attain virtue? We must first realize that the path to virtue is long and hard, a way requiring great effort and endurance. Not only that but once we have accomplished some measure of virtue, we must vigorously continue to train in it. Association with good men is a significant part of this training.

NOTES

[1] Xenophon, *Memorabilia* 4.8.11.

[2] Diogenes Laertius, *Lives* 2.48. Noble is *kalos* (a word that primarily means beautiful, but in a moral sense, noble or good). Good is *agathos* (which can also mean noble or brave). Taken together (*kalos kai agathos*, noble and good), they were contracted by the ancient Greeks to *kalokagathos* (noble and good). Thus, a noble and good person possessed *kalokagathia* (the character of a noble and good person), which was equivalent to aretē. For the latter point, see Xenophon, *Memorabilia* 3.9.5: "For just actions and all forms of virtuous activity are noble and good."

[3] Eunapius, *Lives of the Philosophers and Sophists* introduction.

[4] Xenophon, *Memorabilia* 1.2.19-20.

[5] Ibid., 1.2.64.

[6] Ibid., 1.2.1-3.

[7] Ibid., 1.5.4-5.

[8] Aristippus (c. 435-356 BC) was a philosopher from Cyrene (Libya). Originally a companion of Socrates, Aristippus is known as the founder of Cyrenaicism (called such after his home city), a philosophy that promotes pleasure as the chief goal of life. Happiness consists of the collection of particular pleasures. Bodily pleasures are superior to soul pleasures.

[9] Ibid., 2.1.20-34 (italicized portions indicate summarized parts).

[10] Ibid., 2.6.39.

[11] Ibid., 4.2.9.

[12] Ibid., 3.9.4-5.

[13] Ibid., 4.8.11. As we have before with other Greeks, we see again the connection between aretē and being the best (*aristos*), as well as being happy—here superlatively happy.

ARISTOTLE

A RISTOTLE (c. 384-322 BC) WAS a philosopher from Stagira in ancient Macedonia. He studied with Plato in the Academy for 20 years before engaging in research outside Athens and serving for a number of years as the tutor of Alexander the Great. Returning to Athens, he opened his own school, the Lyceum.

Aristotle is known for his wide-ranging interests and work in the fields of natural science, literature, rhetoric, politics, economics, and philosophy (including epistemology, logic, natural philosophy, metaphysics, and ethics).

It is primarily in Aristotle's work on ethics that we encounter his thinking about the good life and virtue (for a summary, see the end of the chapter). Much of this work influenced later thinking, including that of Medieval Christianity. For instance, St. Thomas Aquinas' treatment of the virtues is largely based on Aristotle, whom he calls "the Philosopher."

The following passages are selected from the *Nicomachean Ethics*, a work that explores the goal (*telos*) of life, the nature of happiness (*eudaimonia*), and so the nature and practice of aretē. Accordingly, the voice is always that of Aristotle.

IN THEIR OWN WORDS

In his most significant work on ethics, the Nicomachean Ethics, *Aristotle seeks to understand what the highest goal or good is for human beings—a good that is ultimately linked with happiness. He begins his study by investigating "man's proper function." In this way, he is like Plato (and Socrates) in associating the goal or good of human existence with human nature and its various functions. He concludes that proper human function is "an activity of the soul in accordance with reason." This rational soul activity is itself excellent or virtuous. Therefore, he concludes, "happiness is an activity of the soul that accords with perfect excellence or virtue."*

Given the conclusion that the virtuous life is the happy life, we begin Aristotle's treatment of virtue with his search for happiness—a search that involves human function and virtue. From there, we will move on to look at Aristotle's view of the soul and of virtue itself.

The human good, then, is the activity of the soul that accords with virtue or excellence. And if there happens to be more than one human virtue, then it is that activity which accords with the best and most complete or perfect virtue.[1]

Happiness is an activity of the soul that accords with perfect virtue. Accordingly, we must now consider the nature of virtue. . . . Now the kind of virtue we must study is human virtue . . . By human virtue, we are not referring to virtue of the body but to that of the soul. So it is that we define happiness as an activity of the soul.[2]

To call happiness the highest good is perhaps to speak in terms of clichés. Therefore, what we need is a clearer account of what, exactly, happiness is. It is possible we will be able to do this when we have ascertained man's proper function. . . .

What can this function possibly be? Can it be living itself? No, life and the act of living is clearly something that men have in common with plants—and what we are seeking is something that mankind alone does. Let us therefore eliminate the life-act of nutrition and growth. The next possibility is sense perception, that is, some form of perceptive living or life. But this form of living also seems to be something common to horses, oxen, and every other animal. There remains, then, a kind of active or practical life that follows reason or some rational principle. . . . Therefore, man's proper function or work is an activity of the soul in accordance with reason—at the very least not independent of reason.[3]

If, as Aristotle concludes, the highest human good is happiness, and happiness is an excellent or virtuous activity of the soul that accords with reason, then we must next grasp Aristotle's understanding of the soul—its parts and their corresponding virtues. The following sketch presents his views in summary form.[4] Afterward, and letting Aristotle speak for himself, we will explore in greater detail what he calls the moral or ethical virtues and the intellectual or thinking virtues.

Aristotle taught that the soul has two major parts, the rational and the non-rational part. (By the way, he left aside the question of whether these parts are real. At the very least, he judged, they are real in terms of function and activity.) The rational part itself has two parts or aspects with corresponding virtues. One is reason itself, which knows for the sake of knowing. Its general virtue is theoretical wisdom (sophia) *(philosophical or intellectual wisdom), whereby we understand truth or what is—that is, the necessary and universal truth of things and that which follows from this truth. The other part shares in reason by listening to it. It knows for the sake of guiding and acting. Its virtue is practical wisdom (or prudence)* (phronēsis), *the ability to deliberate well about and thus apprehend how best to act toward an end or goal. Other virtues corresponding to the rational part include scientific knowledge* (epistēmē), *which has to do with the understanding and demonstration of truth; art or applied science or skillful knowledge* (technē), *which is the ability to produce things; and intelligence* (nous), *which apprehends fundamental principles.*

As for the other part of the soul, the non-rational, it also has two parts or aspects. One is the appetitive or desiring part, the part that feels desire or aversion. It may or may not participate in reason—that is, it may or may not listen to and obey reason. This part has a number of moral or ethical virtues, including courage, moderation, justice, generosity, magnificence, magnanimity, gentleness, truthfulness, wittiness, friendliness, and proper shame. The other is the nutritive, or vegetative (plantlike), part. It has no virtue in itself since it operates automatically, having no part in reason.

Now that we've seen the general nature of the soul in terms of its parts and virtues, let's take a closer look at virtue itself and the soul's virtues.

Regarding virtue itself, Aristotle concludes that there are two general kinds.

So then, there are two kinds of virtue—intellectual or thinking virtue and moral or ethical virtue.[5]

Let's first turn to the moral or ethical virtues and a summary definition. Aristotle offers the following digest of the general nature of moral virtue — a summary that will make more and more sense as we proceed.

We have now discussed the common properties of the [moral] virtues. We've looked at an outline of their general nature—that they are means that fall between two extremes, and that they are habits, which is to say a trained ability or disposition. Further, we've shown that the virtues render us apt to do the same actions as those by which they are produced, and to do them in a manner commanded by right reason, and that the virtues depend on us and are voluntary.[6]

The next question has to do with how a person becomes virtuous. Aristotle explains that we acquire the moral virtues by means of training, habituation, and doing what is morally excellent. Acts of virtue lead to further acts of virtue, which ultimately result in the habit of being virtuous, the possession of a virtuous disposition. Therefore, it is important for children to grow up practicing virtue and for city-states to enact legislation promoting it.

Moral or ethical virtue is born thanks to habit, which is to say customary behavior. In fact, moral virtue gets its name, with a slight variation of form, from that word.[7]

The [moral] virtues are engendered in us neither by nature nor yet in a way contrary to nature. Rather, nature disposes us to receive them, perfecting them by means of habit.[8]

We acquire the [moral] virtues . . . by doing them, by putting them into action, just as we do with the various arts or skills. For we learn an art or skill by doing that which we wish to do when we have learned it. We become builders by building and harpers by harping. And so, by doing just acts we become just, and by doing acts of moderation and courage we become moderate and courageous. This conclusion is confirmed, as well, by what occurs in city-states. Those who craft the laws make the citizens good by means of accustomization or habituation, that is, by getting used to good habits. This is the purpose of all legislators, and if they don't do this well, then they miss the mark. Indeed, this is what distinguishes a good from a bad constitution.[9]

In a word, moral habits or dispositions are formed as a result of similar activities or actions. So it is that we should control the nature of our activities since the quality of our habits depends on the quality of these. Consequently, it is no small thing whether, from when we are young, we are trained up in one habit or another; rather, it is a great difference—in fact, all the difference.

So then, unlike other branches of study, our present inquiry does not merely have a speculative aim. We are not looking into the nature of virtue only to know what it is. On the contrary, we are doing so in order to become good. Otherwise, the whole enterprise would be without an advantage.[10]

Having said all this, Aristotle observes the complicated nature of discussing moral virtue—of excellence having to do with conduct. Any such discussion must necessarily be a sketch, an outline, offering generalities rather than specifics, what is more-than-likely rather than certain.

Let it be understood that all reasoning relative to matters of practice, of conduct, must merely be offered in the form of an outline rather than with any precision. For, as we said at the beginning, we should realize that the kind of reasoning used in any inquiry will vary according to the subject. Accordingly, there is nothing fixed or invariable about practical matters and questions of expediency—any more than with matters of health. And if our general conclusions are inexact in this way, still more will be our reasoning about particular cases. For these fall under no established skill or art or set of rules or precepts. Instead, the one acting, the agent, must always consider for himself what the specific occasion demands, just as with medicine and navigation.[11]

Generally speaking, the mean between two extremes produces, increases,

and preserves moral habits (virtues). By contrast, whatever is extreme,
that is, any deficiency or excess, degrades and ultimately destroys them.

Let us observe that moral habits are such that both deficiency and
excess destroy them. To illustrate what we cannot see by what we
can see, this is clear in the case of strength and health. Too much
and too little exercise alike destroy strength. Similarly, to take too
much or too little food and drink is ruinous to health. By contrast,
an appropriate amount, that is, one of due measure, produces and
increases and preserves them. The same holds true for moderation
and courage and the other virtues. The man who runs away from
everything in fear, and never makes a stand or endures anything,
becomes a coward, while the man who fears nothing at all but
marches on toward everything is overly bold, rash. Similarly, the
man who enjoys every pleasure and abstains from none is undisciplined. So it is that moderation and courage are destroyed by whatever is excessive and whatever falls short or is deficient, whereas
they are preserved by whatever is in the middle, the mean.[12]

How do we know where we stand relative to moral virtue? Aristotle ex-
plores how, while engaged in specific behaviors, our experience of pleasure
and pain reveals who we are in terms of the virtues. Moral virtue is some-
thing that exists—or not—relative to pleasure and pain.

The pleasure or pain that accompanies our actions may serve as a
sign indicating our moral habits or dispositions. For instance, the
man who abstains from bodily pleasures and rejoices in the abstinence is moderate, whereas the one weighed down by or annoyed
by such an abstinence is undisciplined. More: a man is courageous
who is glad to take a stand before danger or endure it—or at least it
does not distress him. But the distressed man is a coward.[13]

Moral virtue is concerned with pleasure and pain. . . . We may propose, then, that moral virtue makes us do what is best in things that
entail pleasure and pain, while moral badness, which is to say vice,
has the contrary effect.[14]

Men become worse through pleasures and pains, that is, either by pursuing and fleeing from the wrong pleasures and pains, or by pursuing and fleeing from them at the wrong time or in the wrong manner or in any other way of going wrong that may be distinguished. This is why some people go so far as to define the virtues as a kind of impassivity and quietude or rest. But they err in stating this absolutely instead of qualifying their definition by the addition of "right and wrong manner," and "time," and all the rest.[15]

Next, Aristotle explains how virtuous acts must be done with knowledge, deliberate choice, and from a permanent disposition. In this way, they are different from the various arts or crafts or skills.

The case of the arts (or crafts or skills) is not really analogous to that of the virtues. Works of art possess wellness or excellence in themselves, so that it is enough if they are produced so that they have a certain quality of their own. But virtuous acts, that is, acts done in conformity with the virtues, are not done justly or moderately, for example, if they themselves are merely of a certain kind of act; rather, they are so only if the agent, the doer, is also in a certain condition or state. First, he must act with knowledge, knowing what he is doing. Second, he must deliberately choose the act, and choose it for its own sake. Third, the act must be the expression of a firm and unchangeable habit or disposition.[16]

Considering virtue and the various states of the soul in terms of genus or general kind, Aristotle suggests that virtue must be either an emotion (feelings such as desire, anger, fear, or joy, most of which are accompanied by pleasure or pain), or a capacity (the means by which we may feel the various emotions), or a habit or disposition (by which we are well or ill-disposed to the emotions). Of the three possibilities, he concludes that virtues are habits or dispositions.

The virtues are neither emotions nor capacities. It remains that they are habits or dispositions. So then, we have stated what virtue is in terms of its genus.[17]

*Aristotle further explains what it means to feel (that is, experience emo-
tion) or to act in an excessive or defective manner, or, by contrast, to act
in accord with the mean.*

Moral virtue has to do with emotions and actions in which there is
the possibility of an excess and a deficiency, as well as a mean. For
instance, one can feel afraid or be bold, feel desire or anger or pity,
and generally experience pleasure and pain either too much or too
little—not well in either case. By contrast, to feel these feelings at the
right time, on the right occasion, toward the right people, for the right
purpose, and in the right manner, is to feel them in the best way according to the mean—the very thing that is virtue. The same holds
true for actions—there is an excess, a deficiency, and a mean.[18]

*In the next few selections, Aristotle briefly offers the various aspects and a
more complete definition of moral virtue. Virtue is both that which allows
a thing to perform its function well and a kind of perfection or excellence.
It involves reasoned choice that determines the mean. Notice the role that
"a wise and sensible" person plays in bringing reason to life. Although
Aristotle doesn't explicitly say it, and despite his oftentimes tedious aca-
demic approach, his is not a dry, rational virtue that works everything out
by cold logic or categorical imperative, but one founded on human beings
who think and act excellently. We might even say they are heroes. But that
may be going too far for Aristotle. If they are heroes, then their feet are
planted firmly on the ground. Regardless, to know what is good, we must
look to exemplars, to model men and women.*

Every virtue has a twofold effect on the thing to which it belongs: it
not only makes the thing well or good in itself, but it also allows the
thing to perform its function well.[19]

Virtue is a habit or disposition involving deliberate choice, consisting
in the observance of a mean relative to us, as determined by reason,
that is, as a wise and sensible man would determine it. Virtue is a
mean that falls between two vices, that which is excessive and that
which is deficient.[20]

There are three dispositions: two vices, one of excess and one of defect, and one virtue that is the observance of the mean.[21]

Aristotle observes that for some behaviors and feelings, such as adultery and shamelessness, for example, there is no mean, no excellent middle ground.

Some actions and emotions do not permit the observance of the mean. In fact, the very names of some directly imply that which is bad. Take, for example malice, shamelessness, and envy, and, of actions, adultery, theft, and murder. All these and similar actions and emotions are judged bad in themselves—but not for their excess or deficiency. No, it is impossible to remain upright with them. Rather, in feeling or acting in such a way, one always misses the mark. Nor in their case does doing well or not depend on the circumstances—for instance, whether one commits adultery with the right woman, at the right time, and in the right manner. No, to act in any of these ways whatsoever is to miss the mark.[22]

As for other emotions, actions, and areas of life, what we may call the field of virtue (that which the virtue is "relative to"), there is a mean that falls between the excess and the defect.

The observance of the mean relative to fear and boldness is courage. The man who is excessively fearless is not designated by any special name (such is the case with many virtues and vices). By contrast, the man who is overly bold is rash. He who is too fearful and not bold enough is a coward.

Relative to pleasures and pains, though not all of them, and less so relative to pain, the observance of the mean is moderation. The excess is immoderation or licentiousness. Though there are few who are deficient regarding the enjoyment of pleasures, and so such a condition has not been given a name, we may nevertheless call it insensibility or a lack of sensation or feeling.[23]

In addition to courage and moderation, Aristotle catalogues other virtues (other means), along with their fields and their vices, their excesses and defects, as follows (summarized). Relative to getting and spending money, liberality or generosity is the mean, prodigality or extravagance is the excess, and illiberality or meanness is the defect. There's also magnificence (the mean), tastelessness or vulgarity (the excess), and stinginess (the defect).

Relative to honor and dishonor there are magnanimity and proper ambition (means), vanity and over ambition (excesses), and pusillanimity and a lack of ambition (defects).

Regarding anger, there is gentleness or mildness (the mean), irascibility (the excess), and spiritlessness or a lack of spirit (the defect).

The mean regarding self-expression is truthfulness; the excess is boastfulness; the defect is self-depreciation.

The mean, excess, and defect regarding conversation is wittiness, buffoonery, and boorishness, respectively.

Regarding social conduct, they are friendliness, obsequiousness or flattery, and quarrelsomeness.

Regarding shame, they are modesty or proper shame, shyness or bashfulness, and shamelessness.

Finally, relative to indignation, they are righteous indignation, envy, and malice or malicious enjoyment or spitefulness.[24]

Aristotle recognizes that the mean (and so the virtue) does not always fall precisely between the excess and defect.

In some cases, the defect is more opposed to the mean. In others, it is the excess. For instance, relative to courage, the defect cowardice is more opposed to the mean than is the excess rashness or overboldness. With moderation, the excess immoderation or licentiousness is more opposed than the defect insensibility.[25]

Aristotle fully recognizes the challenge in knowing what the mean is and in achieving moral excellence. It is hard work. Accordingly, he offers several tips regarding how to hit the target of the mean.

Moral virtue is a mean. . . . between two vices—one vice that is marked by excess and the other by defect. It is a mean insofar as it is able to hit the midpoint amid emotions and actions. This is why it is hard work to be morally excellent. It is hard work to apprehend the middle of anything. For example, not everyone is able to find the center of a circle. Only one with knowledge can do so. So then, anyone can get angry. That's easy. . . . But to be angry . . . at the right person, and in the right amount, and at the right time—this is not easy for everyone. Rather, to do so well is rare, praiseworthy, and noble.[26]

The first rule in aiming at the mean is that we should point ourselves away from the extreme that is more opposed to the mean. . . . The second rule is that we should look into and examine the errors that we are most likely to commit. . . . then we must drag ourselves away in the opposite direction. . . . The third rule is that we must in everything be on guard against pleasure and what is pleasant. . . . These are the things we may do that will best enable us to hit the mean.[27]

According to Aristotle, one may move from what he terms "brutishness" to virtue, or moral excellence. What does such a movement on what we may call "the ladder to virtue" look like? In short, one moves from acting on irrational impulse (brutish, animal-like behavior) to moral viciousness, where one mistakes evil for good. Next one knows the good but is unable to pursue it consistently, given one's own moral weaknesses. With long practice, however, one is finally able to overcome various unhealthy desires, and so comes to a place of moral strength. Beyond this is virtue or excellence, where the unhealthy desires vanish altogether, and good habit is the rule. In brief, the rungs on the ladder go from brutishness (the lowest rung) to moral viciousness, moral weakness, moral strength, and, finally, up to virtue.[28]

Given that virtues have to do with actions, Aristotle investigates what it means for an action to be voluntary or involuntary. The question is: What makes for a voluntary or involuntary act?

An involuntary act is one that is done under compulsion or because of ignorance, whereas a voluntary act would seem to be an act of which its beginning is in the agent himself, who knows the particular circumstances in which he is acting.[29]

Aristotle moves on to the nature of choice, which "appears to be something voluntary," *he says.*[30] *Choice is not the same as desire, passion, wish, or opinion. As for the latter, Aristotle states that* "It is our choice of the good or the bad that determines who we are, not the opinions we hold."[31]

After determining that choice is not any of the above four (desire, passion, wish, opinion), Aristotle explores the relationship between choice and deliberation, and then the nature of deliberation itself.

What, then, is the nature of choice? . . . On the one hand, it appears to be something voluntary. . . . Perhaps it is a kind of deliberation since choice involves reasoning and some process of thought. And this is indicated by the term itself, *prohairesis*, which means something taken or chosen *before* other things.[32]

We deliberate about things that are in our control and are attainable by action.[33]

Matters of deliberation, then, are matters in which there are rules that generally hold good, but in which the result is uncertain or there is an element of indeterminacy. In important matters, we distrust our own powers of judgment and call on others to assist us in our deliberations.[34]

We deliberate not about ends but about means to ends. A physician does not deliberate about whether he is to heal his patient . . . ; rather, [he] takes the end for granted.[35]

Choice, then, is a deliberate desire for things that are within our power. For we first deliberate, and then, having decided based on the deliberation, we desire according to the deliberation.[36]

Along with the many moral or ethical virtues catalogued above (with their mean, excess, and defect), Aristotle also discusses the general nature of justice and its various kinds.

It is clear that the law-abiding man and the fair man are both just. "The just man or thing," therefore, signifies that which is lawful and that which is equal or fair.[37]

Justice that is coextensive with the whole of virtue is the practice of virtue in general toward another.[38]

The parts of justice include two kinds—distributive justice (concerning the distribution of honor, wealth, and the other divisible assets of the community of citizens that may be allotted to its members in equal or unequal shares), . . . and corrective justice, which offers a corrective principle in private transactions.[39]

Such were Aristotle's views regarding moral or ethical virtue. Next, we must look at what he thought about intellectual virtue.

In the first lines of Book 6 of the Nicomachean Ethics, *Aristotle recognizes that we choose the mean and avoid excess and deficiency with the help of "right reason." The conclusion begs several points of discussion. As Aristotle states them, they are: What is the* "exact definition of right reason"*? and,* "What is the standard that determines it?"[40]

As for the latter question, the general answer is the intellectual virtues, which have to do with the rational part of the soul and its two rational faculties, "one whereby we contemplate those things whose first principles are invariable, that is, they cannot be other than they are, and one whereby we contemplate those things that allow for variation."[41] *Aristotle calls the first the "scientific faculty," the part which is capable of knowledge. He terms the second the "calculative faculty," the part which is endowed with reason and is practiced in calculating.*

The attainment of truth is the function of both intelligent or intellectual parts of the soul. Accordingly, their respective virtues are those habits or dispositions that will allow each to best attain the truth.[42]

The virtues by which the soul achieves truth in terms of assent and denial are five in number. These are art or skillful knowledge, science or scientific knowledge, practical wisdom or prudence, wisdom or theoretical wisdom, and intelligence.[43]

Let's look at each intellectual virtue in turn—scientific knowledge, art or skillful knowledge, practical wisdom or prudence, intelligence, and wisdom or theoretical wisdom. When we get to practical wisdom, notice the reference again to people, to the example of virtuous individuals—in this case, to a prudent person, one who possesses and practices practical wisdom.

Scientific knowledge . . . may be made clear as follows. We all suppose that a thing that we can know with scientific knowledge cannot vary, that is, it cannot be other than it is. . . . A thing known by scientific knowledge, therefore, necessarily exists. Accordingly, it is eternal . . . and thus ungenerated and incorruptible, having no beginning or end. Further, we suppose that all scientific knowledge is teachable, and so what is scientifically knowable is learnable. . . . Scientific knowledge is the habit or disposition whereby we make demonstrations or construe explanations.[44]

Scientific knowledge is conviction about universal and necessary truths. And demonstrated truths and all scientific knowledge are derived from first principles (since scientific knowledge operates by means of reason). . . . First principles are apprehended by intelligence.[45]

An art or skillful knowledge is a habit or disposition that produces or makes things by means of reason or calculation that is truthful. . . . Architectural skill, for example, is an art or skillful knowledge.[46]

As for practical wisdom, we may grasp it by considering the nature of those people we say have practical wisdom. Now, we suppose that those who have practical wisdom are those who can deliberate well and nobly about those things that are good and useful for themselves. We suppose this not only relative to one area of life—for instance, to those things that are good and useful for health or strength—but relative to living well in general.[47]

Practical wisdom is not scientific knowledge since matters of conduct (*what practical wisdom is concerned with*) allow for variation.[48]

Practical wisdom is a truth-attaining rational habit or disposition concerned with action, that is, matters of conduct, relative to things that are good and bad for human beings. . . . This point accounts for the word "moderation," which means "preserving practical wisdom." Moderation does indeed preserve our conviction regarding what is good and bad. For pleasure and pain do not destroy or pervert all our convictions. For example, they do not destroy or pervert the conviction that three angles of a triangle are, or are not, together equal to two right angles. They only do so relative to those things having to do with action or matters of conduct.[49]

Of the two parts of the soul that have reason, practical wisdom is the virtue of one part, namely, the one that forms opinions or judgments, since, as practical wisdom does, opinion deals with that which can vary.[50]

First principles are apprehended by intelligence.[51]

It is clear that wisdom or theoretical wisdom must be the most perfect, that is, precise, kind of knowledge. The wise man, therefore, must not only know the conclusions that follow from the first principles, but he must also know the truth about these first principles. Thus, wisdom or theoretical wisdom must be a combination of intelligence and scientific knowledge—it is the crowning completion of knowledge, as it were, the knowledge of those things most valued and honored.[52]

Given the skepticism and even derision of others, Aristotle explains how men such as Thales and Anaxagoras (two early Presocratic philosophers or natural scientists) may be counted wise in terms of theoretical wisdom but not so in terms of practical wisdom. This is because theoretical wisdom is not concerned with those things that are good and useful for human beings, whereas practical wisdom is.

Practical wisdom is concerned with the affairs of men. *Aristotle goes on to assert,* Practical wisdom is in fact the same habit or disposition as political knowledge, though their essence, to be sure, is different."[53]

As Aristotle seems to admit, there is still some question as to why practical and theoretical wisdom are useful. Nevertheless, he goes on to affirm their benefit.

We have stated, then, what practical wisdom and theoretical wisdom (or wisdom) are—what each has to do with, that is, its proper sphere of activity, and that each is the virtue of a different part of the soul.

Even so, one may raise further questions about the usefulness of these two virtues. For one, since theoretical wisdom is only concerned with *what is* rather than *what is coming to be*, it contemplates none of the things that make a man happy. And even though practical wisdom does consider *what is coming to be*, or changing, varying realities, we may nevertheless ask why we need it. True, practical wisdom concerns itself with just, noble, and good things for a man. But these are the things that a good man *does*. Therefore, since the virtues are habits or dispositions, we are no more able to act in such a manner simply because we know about them—just as we are not actually healthy and well simply because we know about such things. . . .

First, let us say that, even *if* neither one of them produces anything, theoretical wisdom and practical wisdom are necessarily desirable and choiceworthy in themselves because they are virtues corresponding to different parts of the soul. Second, in point of fact they *do* produce something. They do so not as the art of medicine produces health, however, but as health itself produces health. In this way, theoretical wisdom produces happiness since theoretical wisdom is part of virtue as a whole, and so it makes a man happy by being possessed and by actualizing itself. Third, a man performs his proper function, or brings his work to completion, by means of both practical wisdom and moral or ethical virtue. This is so because moral virtue makes us aim at the right target, and practical wisdom makes us hit it by choosing the right means.[54]

Finally, friendship. As it was for many ancient philosophers, for Aristotle friendship is indispensable for a good life. As such it is a virtue—at least closely related to virtue.

Friendship is a virtue—or involves virtue. Moreover, it is one of the most indispensable requirements of life, for no one would choose to live without friends.[55]

There is a great deal of difference of opinion as to the nature of friendship. Some define it as a matter of similarity. They say that we love those who are like ourselves. . . . Some try to find a more profound and scientific explanation of its nature. . . . Heraclitus, for instance, says, "Opposites attract."[56]

But what sort of things arouse love or friendly affection? It seems that not everything is held dear or loved, but only what is lovable—and this is either what is good, pleasant, or useful. . . . Accordingly, there are three kinds of friendship corresponding in number to what is loveable.[57]

The three kinds of friendship are those of use or utility, pleasure, and the good.

Friends whose affection is based on use or utility do not love each other in themselves but only insofar as some benefit comes to them from each other. It is similar with those whose friendship is based on pleasure. . . .

In a friendship based on utility or on pleasure, men love their friend for their own benefit or their own pleasure . . . Consequently, friendships of this kind are easily broken off whenever friends change and no longer find each other pleasant or useful. . . .

The perfect form of friendship is that between those who are good, who resemble each other in virtue. . . . It is the ones who wish the good of their friends, for their friends' sake, who are friends in the fullest sense, since they love each other for themselves. . . . Hence the friendship of these lasts as long as they continue to be good . . . Such friendships are, of course, rare, because such men are few.[58]

SUMMARY OF ARETĒ FOR ARISTOTLE

For Aristotle, the human good "is the activity of the soul that accords with excellence or virtue." Such activity is happiness.

There are two general kinds of virtue or virtues, each corresponding to different parts of the soul. They are the moral or ethical virtues and the intellectual or thinking virtues.

The moral virtues exist relative to what we humans do. In general, they allow humans to perform human functions well relative to themselves and others, in the right manner, at the right time, and in the right place. More specifically, virtues are neither emotions nor capacities. Rather, they are habits or trained abilities or dispositions that are cultivated and established by means of acting—by doing acts of one virtue or another until we finally possess the habit or disposition.[59] Our habits (virtues) are revealed by "the pleasure or pain that accompanies our actions." Virtue helps us to do well, "what is best," relative to "things that entail pleasure and pain." Each moral virtue is a mean that falls between two extremes, the excess and defect. For example, courage is the mean that falls between rashness and cowardice. Similarly, moderation falls between immoderation or licentiousness on the one hand and insensibility or a lack of sensation or feeling on the other. Finally, moral virtue involves a voluntary act and choice. As such, and given the indeterminate nature of human life, it involves deliberation, which is the process by which we rationally consider the means by which we may achieve some goal or hit some target that is "in our control" and "attainable by action." We deliberate and therefore choose the mean and avoid excess and deficiency with the help of right reason.

This brings us to the intellectual virtues. The intellectual virtue that primarily helps us deliberate and choose well is practical wisdom, which is "a truth-attaining rational habit concerned with action relative to things that are good and bad for human beings." Other intellectual virtues are scientific knowledge, skillful knowledge, intelligence, and theoretical wisdom.

NOTES

¹ Aristotle, *Nicomachean Ethics* 1.7.15-16 (1098a).

² Ibid., 1.13.1; 5-6 (1102a).

³ Ibid., 1.7.9-14 (1097b-1098a).

⁴ The sketch itself is derived from Aristotle's *Nicomachean Ethics*. For more on Aristotle's understanding of the soul, see his *On the Soul*.

⁵ Ibid., 2.1.1 (1103a). The Greek for "intellectual or thinking" is *dianoētikos*, and for "moral or ethical" it is *ēthikos*. The "or" should not be read as *either* one *or* the other, for instance, moral *or* ethical; rather, the two terms are, in this case, equivalent—that is, one can translate *ēthikos* with both words. So it goes with "intellectual or thinking" and *dianoētikos*.

⁶ Ibid., 3.5.21 (1114b).

⁷ Ibid., 2.1.1 (1103a). The term *ēthikos* is related to *ēthos* (custom, usage, manner; one's disposition, character, habit).

⁸ Ibid., 2.1.3 (1103a).

⁹ Ibid., 2.1.4-5 (1103a-b).

¹⁰ Ibid., 2.1.7-2.2.1 (1103b).

¹¹ Ibid., 2.2.3-4 (1104a).

¹² Ibid., 2.2.6-7 (1104a).

¹³ Ibid., 2.3.1 (1104b).

¹⁴ Ibid., 2.3.6 (1104b).

¹⁵ Ibid., 2.3.5 (1104b).

¹⁶ Ibid., 2.4.3 (1104b).

¹⁷ Ibid., 2.5.6 (1106a).

¹⁸ Ibid., 2.6.10-12 (1106b).

¹⁹ Ibid., 2.6.2 (1106b).

²⁰ Ibid., 2.6.15-16 (1107a).

²¹ Ibid., 2.8.1 (1108b).

²² Ibid., 2.6.18 (1107a).

²³ Ibid., 2.7.2-3 (1107b).

²⁴ For Aristotle's rather brief discussion of these virtues, see ibid., 2.7.4-15 (1107b-1108b). For his detailed discussion, see 3.5.23-4.9.8 (1115a-1128b).

²⁵ Ibid., 2.8.6 (1109a).

²⁶ Ibid., 2.9.1-2 (1109a).

²⁷ Ibid., 2.9.3-7 (1109a-b).

²⁸ For Aristotle's discussion of these rungs or states, see ibid., 7.1-10. For an

image of the ladder and a description of each rung, see Part 5, Ways of Practice Following *Aretē*, Practice 2: My Place on the Ladder to Virtue & Climbing Up.

[29] Ibid., 3.1.20 (1111a).

[30] Ibid., 3.2.1; 2 (1111b).

[31] Ibid., 3.2.11 (1112a).

[32] Ibid., 3.2.16-17 (1112a).

[33] Ibid., 3.3.6 (1112a).

[34] Ibid., 3.3.10 (1112b).

[35] Ibid., 3.3.11 (1112b).

[36] Ibid., 3.3.19 (1113a).

[37] Ibid., 5.1.8 (1129a).

[38] Ibid., 5.2.10 (1130b).

[39] Ibid., 5.2.12 (1130b-1131a).

[40] For the general conclusion and two points of discussion, see ibid., 6.1.1, 3 (1138b).

[41] Ibid., 6.1.5 (1139a).

[42] Ibid., 6.2.6 (1139b).

[43] Ibid., 6.3.1 (1139b). The "or" simply points to another word that may be used to translate the Greek, which is, respectively, *technē, epistēmē, phronēsis, sophia,* and *nous.*

[44] Ibid., 6.3.2-4 (1139b).

[45] Ibid., 6.6.1-2 (1140b-1141a).

[46] Ibid., 6.4.3 (1140a). The post-ellipsis part is actually prior to the first part in Aristotle's text, but since it is an illustration of *technē,* we have placed it second.

[47] Ibid., 6.5.1 (1140a).

[48] Ibid., 6.5.3 (1140b). The italicized material in parentheses is explanatory (not Aristotle's).

[49] Ibid., 6.5.4-6 (1140b). Aristotle seems to combine the words *sōzein* (to save, preserve) and *phronēsis* (practical wisdom) to get *sōphrosunē* (moderation). Hence, his remark, "This point accounts for the word 'moderation,' which means 'preserving practical wisdom.'"

[50] Ibid., 6.5.8 (1140b).

[51] Ibid., 6.6.2 (1141a).

[52] Ibid., 6.6.2-3 (1141a). Aristotle again makes the last point a few lines later.

[53] Ibid., 6.7.6; 6.8.1 (1141b).

[54] Ibid., 6.11.7-6.12.1; 6.12.4-6 (1143b; 1144a).

[55] Ibid., 8.1.1 (1155a).

[56] Ibid., 8.1.6 (1155b).

[57] Ibid., 8.2.1; 8.3.1.

[58] Ibid., 8.3.1-3, 6, 8 (1156a-1156b).

[59] As such, although Aristotle does not explicitly make the point, we may distinguish between "acts of virtue" and "virtuous acts"—the one being an act independent of one's ongoing disposition and the other stemming from one's ongoing disposition. For instance, one may perform a brave act while nevertheless generally being a coward.

THE CYNICS
ANTISTHENES, DIOGENES, CRATES & OTHER CYNICS

T HE PHILOSOPHERS ANTISTHENES of Athens (c. 445-365 BC) and Diogenes of Sinope (c. 410-323 BC) are known as the founders of Cynicism, a philosophy and way of life that sought freedom from desire and wants by means of a self-sufficient life of radical simplicity and poverty based on virtue (for a summary of the Cynic view of aretē, see the end of the chapter).

Cynicism may be defined as the art of endurance that produces true happiness. In his philosophy and way of life, Antisthenes of Athens was inspired by the example of Socrates. Antisthenes in turn inspired Diogenes of Sinope, who was the first to be called "dog" (the Greek is *kuōn* or *kyōn*, the source of "Cynic"). As ones who wished to live "according to nature," Cynics prized the shamelessness and naturalness of dogs and other animals. Diogenes later influenced Crates of Thebes (c. 365-285 BC), who was known as the "Door-opener," since he would make his way into people's houses to advise and admonish them. Contrary to the practice of most Cynics, Crates married Hipparchia of Maroneia, a young woman who wished to pursue the Cynic way of life with him.

Though hard to detect with precision, the Cynics inspired many in their pursuit of a life of aretē based on simplicity, self-sufficiency, and self-control. This was evidently true of Christian monasticism and asceticism where individuals methodically embraced poverty, deliberately practicing an austere life.[1]

IN THEIR OWN WORDS

We begin with a few basic descriptions of Cynicism in which we find that, among other points, the Cynics believe that "the goal of life is to live according to virtue." Moreover, their way of life is, according to some, a "shortcut upon the path of virtue."

Diogenes Laertius (summary of Cynicism) Let us add . . . the philosophical teachings that the Cynics held in common—if, that is, we decide that the school is a kind of philosophy and not, as some declare, a way of life.

The Cynics hold that the goal of life is to live according to virtue. Antisthenes says as much in his *Heracles*—just like the Stoics. There is, after all, a certain community between the two schools. Therefore, some have said that Cynicism is a shortcut upon the path of virtue. Zeno of Citium passed his own life in this way.[2]

The Cynics also teach that men should live simply, procuring for themselves only necessary food and wearing only one piece of clothing, a worn garment. They think very little of wealth and reputation and noble birth. Some Cynics get by on herbs and vegetables and cold water. They live in any kind of shelter, or even large wine-jars, just as did Diogenes [of Sinope], who used to say that it was characteristic of the gods to need nothing, and that, consequently, when a man desires very little or nothing at all, he is like the gods.

They further hold that virtue can be taught, just as Antisthenes declares in his *Heracles*. Also, that once it is acquired it cannot be lost. . . . In agreement with Ariston of Chios, Cynics teach that whatever is between virtue and vice should be counted as indifferent, that is, neither good nor bad.[3]

Suda (definition of Cynicism) Cynicism is a school of philosophy. Its definition is "a short path to virtue." The goal of Cynicism is to live according to virtue, in the manner of Diogenes [of Sinope] and Zeno of Citium. The Cynics held that one should live frugally, eating sufficient food to support oneself and looking down on wealth and reputation and nobility of birth. Some of them were vegetarians, using plants for food, and they drank cold water and utilized whatever shelter they happened to find, even large wine-jars. They used to say that it was a unique characteristic of a god neither to need nor want anything—and those who need and want few things are like a god. They also hold that virtue is teachable and that it cannot be lost.[4]

Next, we see that, according to the Cynics, true wealth is a matter of soul goods, and virtue itself is counted "sufficient for happiness." The Cynics observe, however, that most people, when confronted with the short path of virtue leading to happiness, decline to follow, preferring instead an existence of pleasure, even though such a soft life ends in hardship. Still, to live in a virtuous manner is paramount.

Xenophon (Antisthenes is speaking) "I believe that a man's wealth or lack of wealth is not a matter of household goods but of soul goods."[5]

Diogenes Laertius (reporting the Cynic position) Virtue is sufficient for happiness. Virtue requires nothing more than the strength of Socrates.[6]

(Pseudo) Diogenes To Crates, Do well: Whenever they hear about a shortcut leading to happiness, the many throw themselves at it just as we do with philosophy. But when they reach the path and see how difficult it is, they retreat, going backward, as if weak or sick. And rather than complaining about their own softness, they find fault with our freedom from passion and suffering.

Well then, let them sleep with their pleasures as they are eager to do! For if they live this kind of life, then even greater hardship will befall them than those by which they slander us. And so they are shamefully enslaved in every circumstance.

As for you, keep training just as you began and earnestly set yourself in equal measure against both pleasure and hardship. . . . The one carries us off to shameful deeds, while the other, through fear, takes us away from that which is noble.[7]

(Pseudo) Diogenes To Hippon: *Rather than learning about what happens after death, something controlled by nature, Diogenes affirms that it is*

sufficient to live according to virtue and nature. *Such knowledge about death and what happens after doesn't help one become a better philosopher.*[8]

(Pseudo) Diogenes To Melesippus: It doesn't seem to me that everyone is capable of living virtuously as we understand it. *This is so thanks to the teachings of some that destroy moral values—such as those teachings of Homer, which declare Zeus the father of wicked offspring.* So then, the Cynic will only be able to do those things that are done according to virtue.[9]

Diogenes of Sinope Men strive in punching and kicking to outdo one another, but no one strives to become a noble and good man.[10]

Diogenes Laertius (offering the position of Antisthenes) Those who wish to be immortal must live piously and justly.[11]

The Cynics declare that virtue is teachable. But more than merely hearing about virtue or reading about it in a book, they believe one must train hard in virtue and flee vice. One does virtue; one lives virtue. Still, some people are apparently incapable of living virtuously.

Diogenes Laertius (offering Antisthenes' and the general Cynic position) The Cynics . . . hold that virtue can be taught, just as Antisthenes declares in his *Heracles*. Also, that once it is acquired it cannot be lost.[12]

Diogenes Laertius In his work *On the Socratic Philosophers*, Phanias relates how someone asked Antisthenes what he must do to be noble and good, and he said, "You must learn from those who know well that your vices must be rejected."[13]

(Pseudo) Diogenes To Charmides, greetings. Your acquaintance Euremus offered me many sophisms and dark sayings . . . But I don't think virtue is exalted by this sort of speech. Rather, *virtue is exalted by a simple life and simple words. . . .* Anyway, if he truly grew up with virtue, then he should have never introduced into himself

a desire for money, which is the cause of every evil. Or through holy philosophy he should have rid himself of every passion.[14]

(Pseudo) Crates of Thebes To Orion: *Living in the city or on a farm is not what makes a child good or bad. Rather, Crates argues that it is* time spent with good and bad men *that makes one good or bad. Thus, Orion should send his sons to spend time with a philosopher, a lover of wisdom.* Virtue enters the soul by means of training—not automatically as happens with vice.[15]

Pseudo) Diogenes To Crates: As for you, keep training just as you began and earnestly set yourself in equal measure against both pleasure and hardship . . . The one carries us off to shameful deeds, while the other, through fear, takes us away from that which is noble.[16]

(Pseudo) Diogenes To Epimenides, greetings: You stay at home delighting your belly and adorning your body instead of enduring by means of virtue. I hear that you profess virtue—and such an act did not seem incredible to me, for, according to Simonides, it is difficult to be good but easy to profess goodness.[17]

(Pseudo) Crates To his Students: Take care of your soul—but your body only so far as what is necessary, and externals not even that much. I say this because happiness is not a pleasure that requires external things, nor does perfect virtue require these.[18]

(Pseudo) Crates To His Students: Flee not only from the worst of the vices, injustice and a lack of self-control, but also what produces them, pleasure and enjoyment. . . . Pursue not only the best of goods, self-control and endurance, but also what produces them, hard work and toil. *In doing the latter you will exchange what is inferior for what is superior, as you would bronze for gold. Thus, you will exchange* hard work and toil for virtue.[19]

Julian, the emperor and philosopher But for my part . . . I still believe that even before Heracles, not only among the Greeks but among the barbarians also, there were men who practiced this [Cynic] philosophy. For it seems to be in some ways a universal philosophy, and the most natural, and to demand no special study whatsoever. But it is enough simply to choose the honorable by desiring virtue and avoiding evil. And so, there is no need to turn over countless books. For as the saying goes, "Much learning does not teach men to have understanding."[20]

Diogenes Laertius (giving Antisthenes' position) Virtue is something you do—it is a matter of deeds. It doesn't require a stockpile of arguments or much learning.[21]

(Pseudo) Diogenes To Melesippus: It doesn't seem to me that everyone is capable of living virtuously as we understand it.[22]

The Cynics teach that virtue is the means by which one gains strength; it is a weapon that may be used in the battle against every bad, ignoble, and shameful thing.

(Pseudo) Diogenes To Anniceris: The Spartans are at war with various illnesses and afflictions within themselves. *It is unfortunate, then, that they have banished virtue.* Virtue alone is that by which the soul can be strengthened and delivered from its afflictions.[23]

Antisthenes Virtue is a weapon that cannot be taken away.[24]

The Cynics judge that virtue is the same for women and men.

Antisthenes Virtue is the same for a woman as it is for a man.[25]

Relative to the ancient Greek concern for liberty and its opposite, the Cynics explain that vice is slavery and virtue is freedom. Anything in between is indifferent.

(Pseudo) Crates To Hipparchia: All slaves are enslaved either through the law or by means of vice.[26]

Diogenes Laertius Cynics teach that whatever is between virtue and vice should be counted as indifferent, that is, neither good nor bad.[27]

We end with various examples of virtue—lists of virtue or what virtue produces (self-control, non-vanity, freedom, and endurance, and non-envy, courage, non-superstition, and justice implied), as well as general categories of people (such as "good men" and "the well-born") and specific individuals (Heracles, Diogenes of Sinope, and Crates of Thebes). Each of the latter individuals exemplifies what it means to do and live virtue.

Julian, the emperor and philosopher And to the soul the Cynics naturally assigned supremacy, and to the body subjection. This seems to be the reason why they practiced virtue, self-control, non-vanity, and freedom, and why they shunned all forms of envy, cowardice and superstition. . . . We must say that happiness resides in our minds, in the best and noblest part of us.[28]

Pseudo Crates To His Students: Flee not only from the worst of the vices, injustice and a lack of self-control, but also from what produces them, pleasure and enjoyment. . . . Pursue not only the best of goods, self-control and endurance, but also what produces them, hard work and toil. *In doing the latter you will exchange what is inferior for what is superior, as you would bronze for gold. Thus, you will exchange* hard work and toil for virtue.[29]

Diogenes Laertius Diogenes [the Cynic] called good men images of the gods.[30]

Diogenes Laertius (reporting Antisthenes' view) The well-born and the virtuous are one and the same.[31]

Julian, the emperor and philosopher The better sort of Cynics assert that in addition to the other blessings bestowed on us by mighty Heracles, it was he who bequeathed to mankind the noblest example of this mode of life.[32]

Diogenes Laertius (reporting Diogenes of Sinope's view) To the man who was proud of wearing a lion's skin [Heracles' clothing], Diogenes' words were, "Stop dishonoring virtue's clothing."[33]

(Pseudo) Crates To Patrocles: [. . .] Diogenes *of Sinope* was courageous in his practice of virtue.[34]

(Pseudo) Diogenes To Hicetas, Do well: I came, Father, to Athens, and learning that Socrates' associate [Antisthenes] was teaching about happiness, I went to him. And he happened to be speaking about the paths that lead to happiness. He declared that there are two and not many paths—and that one is a shortcut and the other is long. *It is up to us to choose which path we follow, he said.*

When I heard this, I kept quiet. But when we went to him again the next day, I called on him to show to us the paths.

Quite readily, he stood from his chair and led us into the city, straight through it to the acropolis. And when we had drawn near, he showed us two paths leading upward. The one is short, steep and troublesome; the other is long, smooth and easy.

When he brought us down, he said, "Such are the paths leading up to the acropolis. And such are the paths leading to happiness. Choose the path as you wish, and I will guide you."

While the others, who were struck with fear at the troublesome and steep nature of the one path, called on him to lead them along the long and smooth one, I, superior to the hardships, chose the steep and troublesome path—for the man speeding on to happiness must go on even if it is through fire and sword.[35]

(Pseudo) Crates To Patrocles: *Do not call Odysseus the father of Cynicism simply because he put on the clothing of the Cynic.* The clothing does not produce a Cynic; rather, the Cynic the clothing. *Although Odysseus put on the typical outfit of the Cynic, his behavior was often not that of a Cynic since he honored pleasure above all else. Instead, we should call Diogenes the father of Cynicism and imitate him since he behaved like a Cynic throughout his life, conquering both toil and pleasure.* He was courageous in his practice of virtue.[36]

Julian, the emperor and philosopher Now consider whether Diogenes did not profess this belief since he freely submitted his body to hardships so that he might make it stronger than it was by nature. He allowed himself to act only as the light of reason shows us that we ought to act. And the disturbances and confusions that attack the soul and are derived from the body—to which this envelope of ours often constrains us for its sake to pay too much attention—he did not take into account at all. Consequently, by means of this discipline the man made his body stronger, I believe, than that of any who have contended for the prize of a crown in the games. And his soul was so disposed that he was happy. . . .

Let him who wishes to be a Cynic, to be an excellent man, first take himself in hand like Diogenes and Crates, and expel from his own soul and from every part of it all passions and desires. And let him entrust all his affairs to reason and intelligence and steer his course by them—for this was the central point, I suppose, of Diogenes' philosophy.[37]

Dio Chrysostom When the time for the Isthmian games arrived and everyone was in the Isthmus, Diogenes went down also. . . .

[He] gave his time to anyone who wished to talk with him, remarking that he was surprised by the fact that if he had claimed to be a physician for the teeth, everybody would flock to him who needed to have a tooth pulled. Yes, and by Zeus, if he had professed to treat the eyes, all who were suffering from sore eyes would present themselves. And similarly, if he had claimed to know of a medicine for diseases of the spleen or for gout or for a runny nose. But when he declared that all who followed his treatment would be relieved of ignorance, wickedness, and licentiousness, not one man would listen to him or seek to be cured by him—no matter how much richer he might become thereby. It was as though they were less inconvenienced by these spiritual complaints than by the other kind. Or as though it were worse for them to suffer from an enlarged spleen or a decayed tooth than from a soul that is foolish, ignorant, cowardly, rash, pleasure-loving, unfree, prone to anger, unkind, and wicked—in fact, utterly corrupt. . . .

When a certain man asked whether Diogenes had also come to see the contest, he responded, "No, but to take part."

Then when the man laughed and asked him who his competitors were, he said with that customary glance of his, "The toughest there are and the hardest to beat—men whom no Greek can look straight in the eye. They are not competitors, however, who sprint or wrestle or jump, or those who box and throw the spear and hurl the discus, but those that correct and chasten a man."

"Tell me, who are they?" asked the other.

"Hardships," he replied, "that are very severe and impossible to overcome for gluttonous and folly-stricken men who feast all day long and snore at night, but which yield to thin, spare men, whose waists are more pinched in than those of wasps. . . .

"But the noble and excellent man believes that his hardships are his greatest opponents, and always wants to battle with them day and night—not to win a sprig of parsley, as so many goats might do, nor for a bit of wild olive, or of pine, but to win happiness and virtue throughout all the days of his life, and not merely when the Eleans make proclamation, or the Corinthians, or the Thessalian assembly. He is afraid of none of those opponents nor does he pray to draw another, but he challenges them one after another, grappling with hunger and cold, withstanding thirst, and disclosing no weakness even though he must endure the lash or give his body to be cut or burned. Poverty, exile, loss of reputation, and the like have no terrors for him. No, he holds them as mere trifles, and while in their grip, the perfect man is often as sportive as boys with their dice and their colored balls.

"Of course," he continued, "these antagonists do seem terrible and invincible to all who are bad men. But if you treat them with contempt and meet them boldly, you will find them cowardly and unable to master strong men. In this way these opponents very much resemble dogs that pursue and bite people who run away from them, while some they seize and tear to pieces. On the other hand, they fear and slink away from men who face them and show them a fight, eventually wagging their tails when they come to know them. Most people, however, are in mortal terror of these opponents, always avoiding them by flight and never looking them in the face. It is no different from skillful boxers. They are not hit at all when they anticipate their opponents; rather, they often actually end up winning the match themselves. On the contrary, if they give ground through fear, they receive the heaviest blow. In the same way, if we accept our hardships in a spirit of contempt for them and approach them cheerfully, they avail very little against us. But if we hang back and give way, they appear altogether greater and stronger. You can see that the same thing also applies to fire. If you attack it most vigorously, you put it out; but if you do so with caution and fear, you get severely burned, just as children do when in sport, they sometimes try to put out a fire with their tongues. The adversaries of this class are a good deal like the all-fighters who engage in pankration, the ones who strike, choke, tear apart, and occasionally kill.

"And yet there is another battle even more terrible, a struggle that is no small thing, but much greater and more dangerous than the former. I mean the fight against pleasure. . . .

"Pleasure uses no open force but deceives and casts a spell with baneful drugs, just as Homer says Circe drugged the comrades of Odysseus, and some straightaway became swine, some wolves, and some other kinds of beasts. Yes, such is this thing pleasure, which hatches no single plot but all kinds of plots, and aims to undo men through sight, sound, smell, taste, and touch, with food too, and drink and sexual lust, tempting those awake and those asleep alike. It is not possible to station guards and then lie down to sleep as in ordinary warfare. No, it is just then of all times that pleasure makes her attack—at one time weakening and enslaving the soul by means of sleep itself, at another sending mischievous and insidious dreams that bring her to mind.

"Now pain and hardship come by means of touch for the most part and continue in that way, but pleasure assails a man through each and every sense that he has. And while he must face and grapple with pain and hardship, he should flee from pleasure as far as possible and only have unavoidable dealings with her. Here the strongest man is more or less the most excellent man, the one who is able to flee the greatest distance away from pleasure—for it is impossible to dwell with pleasure or even to linger with her for any length of time without being wholly conquered and enslaved. Therefore, when she gains dominion and overpowers the soul by means of her charms, her enchanted drugs, the rest of Circe's sorcery at once follows. With a stroke of her wand, pleasure coolly drives her victim into a sort of pigsty and pens him up. And now, from that time on, the man goes on living as a pig or a wolf.

"Pleasure also brings diverse and deadly vipers into being, and other crawling things that are always with her as they stand by her doors. And though yearning for pleasure and serving her, they nevertheless suffer countless hardships and suffering all in vain. For pleasure, after overpowering and taking possession of her victims, delivers them over to the most hateful and most difficult hardships.

"This is the contest which I steadfastly maintain, and in which I risk my life against pleasure and hardship, yet not a single wretched human being turns his attention to me—but only to the jumpers and runners and dancers. Neither, however, did men really look at the struggles and hardships of Heracles or have any interest in them.[38]

(Pseudo) Diogenes To Plato, the wise man, greetings. You spit on my tattered cloak and leather bag as though they were burdensome and difficult for me, and on my life as though it were useless, doing no good. *This is because you are without virtue.*

As for me, I pursued these things with virtue. What greater proof can I offer than not changing my course toward a life of pleasure and luxury, even though I could have? *Diogenes contends that his life is beneficial.* What enemy would march against one who is self-sufficient and simple? And against which king or people would those satisfied with these things carry on a war? In conformity with this, the soul has been purified of vice and has been released from empty opinion. It has cast out immoderate desires and has been taught to speak the truth and to show contempt for other false things. If you are not persuaded by this, then practice the love of pleasure and tease us for not knowing much.[39]

Apuleius Crates, the well-known disciple of Diogenes, was honored at Athens by the men of his own day as though he had been a household god. No house was ever closed to him, no head of a family ever had so close a secret as to regard Crates as an inconvenient intruder. He was always welcome. There was never a quarrel, never a grievance between family members that he was not accepted as the mediator and his word as law.

The poets tell that Hercules of old by his valor subdued all the wild monsters of legend, beast or man, and purged all the world of them. Even so our philosopher Crates was truly a Hercules in the conquest of anger, envy, avarice, lust, and all the other monstrous and shameful things that plague the human soul. He expelled all these pests from their minds, purged households, and tamed vice.

Even before he became Crates pure and simple, he was accounted one of the chief men in Thebes. His family was noble, his establishment numerous, his house had a fair and ample porch. His lands were rich and his clothing sumptuous.

But later, when he understood that the wealth that had been given to him came with no safeguard on which he might lean as on a staff in the course of his life, he realized that all was fragile and transitory—that all the wealth in all the world was no help in living well, in living virtuously.[40]

SUMMARY OF ARETĒ FOR THE CYNICS

For the Cynics, virtue is the goal of life and the substance of happiness. The one who lives virtuously is happy. Accordingly, Cynicism single-mindedly aims at virtue and rigorously pursues it, leaving aside everything else in life as "indifferent." As such, Cynicism is "a shortcut to virtue," directly heading toward it rather than moving along any other roundabout path.

Though virtue may be taught, most importantly it must be practiced. It is not enough merely to hear or read about virtue. Ongoing training is essential to its attainment. Key to this training is the shunning of pleasure and the embracing of toil and hardship. Most people, however, do not do so, and so they do not live a virtuous life.

Virtue is the means by which we become stronger. It is a weapon in the battle against everything bad.

Virtue is the same for women as it is for men. Examples of those who lived a virtuous life are the hero (and god) Heracles and the Cynics Diogenes of Sinope and Crates of Thebes.

NOTES

[1] For an introduction to Cynicism and ancient texts offering Cynic philosophy, see *The Best of the Cynics* (Sugar Land: The Classics Cave, 2021).

[2] Zeno of Citium (c. 335-263 BC) initially practiced philosophy, or a life of radical virtue, with the Cynic Crates of Thebes. He went on to found his own school, the Stoic school, named after a covered colonnade (*stoa*) in Athens where he would teach. For more on the Stoic view of aretē, see 11, "Zeno of Citium & the Early Stoics," and 12, "Epictetus the Stoic."

[3] Diogenes Laertius, *Lives* 6.103-105.

[4] Suda, *kunismos* (Cynicism), kappa 2712. The *Suda* is a tenth century AD Byzantine (Greek-Roman or Roman-Greek) historical dictionary and encyclopedia covering the ancient Greek, Roman, and Byzantine worlds. Given the similarity of their definition and description of Cynicism, it is clear the author of the *Suda* had his eye on the work of Diogenes Laertius, *Lives* 6.104, when he was writing this entry.

[5] Xenophon, *Symposium* 4.34.

[6] Diogenes Laertius, *Lives* 6.11.

[7] (Pseudo) Diogenes of Sinope, *Letter* 12 to Crates. The "pseudo" simply means the letters were not written by Diogenes himself but by later authors writing in the style and according to the ideas of Diogenes. Extant are such letters from Diogenes of Sinope, Crates of Thebes, and others. For an exploration and explanation of when these letters were written, see *The Cynic Epistles: A Study Edition*, ed. Abraham J. Malherbe (Atlanta: Society of Biblical Literature, 1977).

[8] (Pseudo) Diogenes of Sinope, *Letter* 25 to Hippon.

[9] (Pseudo) Diogenes of Sinope, *Letter* 41 to Melesippus.

[10] Ibid., 6.27.

[11] Diogenes Laertius, *Lives* 6.5.

[12] Ibid., 6.5.

[13] Diogenes Laertius, *Lives* 6.8. Phanias of Eresos was a fourth century BC Greek Peripatetic (Aristotelian) philosopher and writer, who collaborated with Theophrastus, the successor to Aristotle.

[14] (Pseudo) Diogenes of Sinope, *Letter* 50 to Charmides.

[15] (Pseudo) Crates of Thebes, *Letter* 12 To Orion.

[16] (Pseudo) Diogenes of Sinope, *Letter* 12 to Crates.

[17] (Pseudo) Diogenes of Sinope, *Letter* 51 to Epimenides.

[18] (Pseudo) Crates of Thebes, *Letter* 3 to His Students.

[19] (Pseudo) Crates of Thebes, *Letter* 15 to His Students.

[20] Julian, *Oration* 6.187.

[21] Diogenes Laertius, *Lives* 6.11.

[22] (Pseudo) Diogenes of Sinope, *Letter* 41 to Melesippus.

[23] (Pseudo) Diogenes of Sinope, *Letter* 27 To Anniceris.

[24] Diogenes Laertius, *Lives* 6.12. Diogenes Laertius tells us that the teaching was recorded by Diocles of Magnesia (second or first century BC), who was an ancient historian and writer of biography and summaries. He concentrated on the views, sayings, and lives of the earliest philosophers.

[25] Diogenes Laertius, *Lives* 6.12.

[26] (Pseudo) Crates of Thebes, *Letter* 29 To Hipparchia. The implication is that if vice is slavery, then virtue is freedom.

[27] Diogenes Laertius, *Lives* 6.105.

[28] Julian, *Oration* 6.190, 194.

[29] (Pseudo) Crates of Thebes, *Letter* 15 To His students.

[30] Diogenes Laertius, *Lives* 6.51.

[31] Ibid., 6.10.

[32] Julian, *Oration* 6.187.

[33] Diogenes Laertius, *Lives* 6.45.

[34] (Pseudo) Crates of Thebes, *Letter* 19 To Patrocles.

[35] (Pseudo) Diogenes of Sinope, *Letter* 30 To Hicetas.

[36] (Pseudo) Crates of Thebes, *Letter* 19 to Patrocles.

[37] Julian, *Oration* 6.194-195; 201.

[38] Dio Chrysostom, *Oration* 8.5-8, 11-13, 15-20, 21-27.

[39] (Pseudo) Diogenes, *Letter* 46 to Plato.

[40] Apuleius, *Florida*. Apuleius uses Hercules rather than Heracles because he wrote in Latin, and the Latin version of Heracles is Hercules.

ZENO OF CITIUM
& THE EARLY STOICS

Z ENO (c. 335-263 BC) WAS A philosopher from Citium (Cyprus). He is known as the founder of Stoicism. Inspired by the ideas and example of Socrates, he eventually learned from and practiced with the Cynic Crates of Thebes, as well as other philosophers, before setting out on his own to found his own school. Other significant early Stoics were Cleanthes of Assos (c. 331-232 BC) and Chrysippus of Soli (c. 280-207 BC).

Zeno lectured in a covered colonnade (called in Greek a *stoa* — and so the name Stoic or Stoicism) on the edge of Athens' marketplace. There he explained that the cosmos consists of matter and mind, or divine reason, which makes, orders, and governs that which is natural. What is natural, therefore, is rational (in a sense). Consequently, Zeno taught that humans should seek to be rational by means of participating in divine rationality and by judging well. Doing so they would be virtuous, thereby attaining the highest good, the virtuous and thus happy life (for a summary of the early Stoic view of aretē, see the end of the chapter).

As with the other schools of ancient philosophy, the Stoics had an enormous impact on those who later wished to pursue a life of philosophy and virtue.

Though we could have added others, all passages come from Diogenes Laertius' *Lives and Opinions of Eminent Philosophers*.[1]

IN THEIR OWN WORDS

History does not record the titles of any works by Zeno of Citium that were specifically about virtue (though he would have certainly addressed virtue in several of his works — for instance, in On Life According to Nature, *and in* On Impulse, *or On* Human Nature, *and in* On Duty*). As for other early Stoics, Cleanthes of Assos and Chrysippus of Soli, for instance, we do possess a few titles of their works about virtue—all of which are now unfortunately lost.*[2] *For examples, see the following selections.*

Diogenes Laertius Cleanthes, the son of Phanias, . . . wrote *On the Virtues* and *On the Notion that Virtue Is the Same for Men and Women.*[3]

Diogenes Laertius Chrysippus, the son of Apollonius . . . wrote *On the Difference between the Virtues* (addressed to Diodorus, in four books), *On the Kinds of Virtues* (in one book), and *On the Virtues* (addressed to Pollis, in two books).[4]

Next, we learn of the widespread reputation that Zeno of Citium had for his ability to instruct in the life of virtue and for a happiness that was tied to the same.

Letter from Antigonus to Zeno King Antigonus to Zeno the philosopher, greeting. I consider myself superior to you in glory and wealth. But in reason and education, and in the perfect happiness you have attained, I acknowledge that I am far behind you. . . . By all means, then, do your best to meet with me, understanding that you will not only be instructing me but all the Macedonians together. For he who teaches the Macedonian ruler and guides him along the path of virtue will also be training his subjects to be good men. For as the ruler is, so, for the most part, we may expect the subjects to become.[5]

Letter from Zeno to Antigonus Zeno to king Antigonus, greeting. I welcome your love of learning inasmuch as you hold to the truth that stretches out toward advantage . . . If anyone has longed for philosophy, turning away from well-known pleasure, . . . it is clear that he is inclined to nobility of life not only by nature but by deliberate choice. If any man with a nature such as yours receives a reasonable amount of training in terms of ungrudging instruction, he will easily reach perfect virtue. As for me, I am unable to join you due to old age and subsequent bodily weakness—I am eighty years old. But I send to you certain men who have studied with me. . . . If you join with these men, then you will lack nothing that is necessary for perfect happiness.[6]

Although Zeno of Citium was not from Athens, the Athenians nevertheless honored him for his life of virtue.

Diogenes Laertius The Athenians buried Zeno of Citium in the Ceramicus and honored him . . . bearing witness to his virtue.[7]

Diogenes Laertius (the text of a decree that the people of Athens passed regarding Zeno) Whereas Zeno of Citium, the son of Mnaseas, has for many years been devoted to philosophy in the city and has continued to be a good man in all other respects, exhorting to virtue and moderation those of the youth who come to him to be taught, directing them to what is most excellent, offering to all in his own manner of living a pattern for imitation in perfect conformity with his teaching, it has seemed good to the people—and may it so happen—to bestow praise on Zeno of Citium, the son of Mnaseas, and to crown him with a golden crown according to the law for his virtue and moderation.[8]

Turning to their views, the early Stoics teach that the happy life is the virtuous life. Virtue "is the only good," they say. Virtue guards "the lives of men and cities." In itself, virtue is enough for happiness.

Diogenes Laertius Happiness consists in virtue, which is the state of the soul that tends to make the whole of life harmonious.[9]

Diogenes Laertius Athenaeus the epigrammatist speaks of all the Stoics in common as follows: "You who are acquainted with the words of the Stoic Porch, you have committed to your divine books the best of teachings, that virtue of the soul is the only good. Her decrees alone protect the lives of men and cities. But those other men who declare that the goal of life is the enjoyment of the flesh are ruined by one of the Muses, the daughters of Memory."[10]

Diogenes Laertius The Stoics hold that virtue is sufficient in itself to ensure happiness.[11]

Diogenes Laertius In the second book of *On Life and Earning a Living*, while considering how a wise man should earn a living, Chrysippus says, "And yet why should he earn a living? After all, if it is for the sake of life, life is a thing indifferent. And if it is for pleasure, it is also indifferent. And if it is for virtue, it is sufficient in itself for happiness."[12]

Still, there are some Stoics who believe that, in addition to virtue, other goods are required for happiness.

Diogenes Laertius Both Panaetius and Posidonius . . . deny that virtue is sufficient for happiness. Rather, they say that health is necessary, as well as some means of living, and strength.[13]

In the next selections, we follow the general Stoic argument for why virtue is happiness.
    The first point is that the "the end or goal of life is to live in agreement with nature, which is the same as living according to virtue."
    Why is such a life virtuous and thus happy-making? It is because it is in harmony with Zeus or "the right reason that pervades all things."
    What is the significance of Zeus—reason or mind—pervading all things? In short, it is because Zeus through nature or as nature regulates all animals by means of impulse. The first impulse of any animal is toward self-preservation rather than pleasure. For human beings, Zeus (again, reason or mind) gives reason in addition to impulse so that the latter may be shaped in a skillful manner. Such a reason-based shaping or formation of impulse results in a rational life. To live in such a way means that one is living in conformity with nature and so with virtue, a life which is sufficient for happiness.

Diogenes Laertius In his treatise *On the Nature of Man*, Zeno . . . was the first to say that the end or goal of life is to live in agreement with nature, which is the same as living according to virtue since nature leads us toward virtue. Cleanthes says the same in his treatise *On Pleasure*, as do Posidonius and Hecaton in their works *On the Goal of Life*. Again, living according to virtue is equivalent to living according to the experience of nature as it actually happens—just as Chrysippus says in the first book of his *On the Goal of Life*. For our individual natures are portions of the whole of nature, which is to say the whole cosmos.[14]

Diogenes Laertius The goal of life is to live in conformity with nature—that is, with our own nature as well as with the nature of the whole cosmos. Accordingly, one holds back from every action forbidden by the law common to all things—that is to say, the right reason that pervades all things and is the same as Zeus, who leads the administration of every existing thing. This very thing is the virtue of the happy man and the good flow of life, when all actions promote the harmony of the divine power dwelling in each man with the will of the administrator of the whole cosmos.[15]

Diogenes Laertius The Stoics say that an animal's first impulse is to self-preservation since nature endears the animal to itself from the beginning, as Chrysippus affirms in the first part of his work *On the Goal of Life*. There he says that the dearest thing to every animal is its own constitution and the awareness of this. For it is not natural for any animal to be alienated from itself—or even to be brought into such a state so that it is indifferent to itself, being neither alienated from nor friendly to itself. We must assert that nature has made the animal so that it is near and dear to itself. As such, it pushes away all that is harmful and pulls near all that is suitable and fitting.

The Stoics declare false the assertion—made by some—that the first urge or impulse of animals is directed toward pleasure. By contrast they say that pleasure, if it is anything at all, is a byproduct that never comes until nature by itself has sought and taken those things suitable to the animal's constitution—a byproduct that is comparable to animals that have a cheerful expression and plants that are luxuriant or in full bloom.

The Stoics declare that nature originally made no difference between plants and animals. Nature regulates the life of plants without the use of impulse and sensation, just as certain plant-like processes go on in us. But for animals, impulse was added to this general rule of nature later on. Impulse makes animals pursue what is suitable. Nature's rule for animals is to follow the direction of impulse. Lastly, for those beings we call rational, the rational life correctly became the natural life when reason was given to them by means of a more perfect rule. Reason was added to shape impulse as a skilled craftsman. . . .

Accordingly, one holds back from every action forbidden by the law common to all things—that is to say, the right reason that pervades all things and is the same as Zeus, who leads the administration of every existing thing. This very thing is the virtue of the happy man and the good flow of life, when all actions promote the harmony of the divine power dwelling in each man with the will of the administrator of the whole cosmos.[16]

But what is the nature of virtue? The following passages give some idea. Of significance is the notion that virtue is "the perfection of anything in general," and the belief in the unity or essential relation of virtue (that "the virtues involve one another"), as well as the primacy of some virtues (practical wisdom, courage, justice, and moderation). For the Stoics, skill in dialectic is virtue. Finally, "there is no middle ground between virtue and vice."

Diogenes Laertius Virtue is in one sense the perfection of anything in general, say of a statue. Virtue may be non-intellectual, such as health, or intellectual, such as practical wisdom.[17]

Diogenes Laertius Virtue is a harmonious disposition, choiceworthy for its own sake—not from hope or fear or any external motive.[18]

Diogenes Laertius (giving the view found in several ancient authors— Chrysippus, Apollodorus, and Hecaton) The Stoics hold that the virtues involve one another. The man who has one virtue has them all inasmuch as the virtues have common principles.[19]

Diogenes Laertius Among the virtues some are primary, and some are subordinate to these. The following are the primary virtues: practical wisdom, courage, justice, and moderation. . . . Similarly, among the vices, some are primary, and some are subordinate. Folly, cowardice, injustice, and immoderation are primary. The vices are ignorance of those things of which the virtues are the knowledge.[20]

Diogenes Laertius Stoics define practical wisdom as the knowledge of good and bad things and what is neither. And courage is the knowledge of what is choiceworthy and what one must be wary of and avoid, and what is neither.[21]

Diogenes Laertius Specific virtues are magnanimity, self-control, patient endurance, ready mindedness, and good counsel. . . . They define magnanimity as the knowledge or habit that makes one superior to whatever commonly happens to both base and excellent men. Self-control is an unbeatable disposition relative to those things that are in accord with right reason or a habit that is never conquered by pleasure. Patient endurance is the knowledge or habit that suggests what we must—and what we must not—abide by and endure, and what is neither. Ready mindedness is a habit that discovers the appropriate thing to be done at any moment. Good counsel is the knowledge by which we see what to do and how to do it if we are to act in a useful and profitable manner.[22]

Diogenes Laertius The Stoics hold that dialectic itself is necessary and a virtue, and that it encompasses the other kinds of virtues.[23]

Diogenes Laertius The Stoic belief is that there is no middle ground between virtue and vice, whereas the Peripatetics say that there is the middle ground of moral progress. The Stoics declare that just as a stick must be either straight or crooked, so a man must be either just or unjust. Neither are their degrees of justice and injustice. The same is the case for the other virtues.[24]

Diogenes Laertius [The Stoic] Herillus of Carthage declared that everything that is found between virtue and vice is indifferent.[25]

Diogenes Laertius The Stoics hold that all failures or sins are equal—this according to what Chrysippus says in the fourth book of his *Ethical Inquiries*, as well as Persaeus and Zeno. For if one truth is not truer than another truth, then neither is one falsehood more false than another falsehood. In the same way, one deception is not more deceptive than another deception, nor is one failure or sin more of a failure or more sinful than another failure or sin. For the man who is one hundred stadia from Canopus and the man who is only one stadium away are equally not in Canopus. In this way, the man who commits the greater and the one who commits the smaller sin are equally behaving incorrectly. Nevertheless, Heraclides of Tarsus, the follower of Antipater of Tarsus, and Athenodorus both assert that failures or sins are not equal.[26]

Next up are several selections that explore the nature of the good (or good things) and its relation to virtue, happiness, and beauty. Relative to happiness, virtues are goods (beneficial, advantageous things) that can have either the nature of an end or a means to an end. Beauty itself is the "bloom of virtue."

Diogenes Laertius Generally speaking, good is that from which there is some advantage or benefit. More specifically, it is either what is the same as or not different from what is useful or beneficial or advantageous.[27]

Diogenes Laertius "The fulfillment or perfection of a rational being *as* a rational being following nature" is another particular definition the Stoics give for the good.[28]

Diogenes Laertius Of good things, some are related to the soul and some to external things, while some are neither related to the soul nor to externals. The goods related to the soul are the virtues and acts done according to virtue. External goods are things such as having an excellent homeland and an excellent friend and the happiness that comes from these.[29]

Diogenes Laertius Some goods have the nature of ends or goals. Some have the nature of means. Some are both ends and means at the same time. . . . The virtues are goods that have both the nature of ends and means. Inasmuch as they produce happiness, they are means to good things. On the other hand, inasmuch as the virtues are the fulfillment of happiness, being a portion of happiness itself, they are ends.[30]

Diogenes Laertius All that is good is beautiful. . . . And beauty they describe as the bloom or flower of virtue.[31]

As the following selections demonstrate, the Stoics divide all things into three categories: good things, bad things, and things that are neutral, which is to say neither good nor bad. The virtues are good things. The Stoics term neutral things "indifferent," some of which are "preferred" and some of which are "rejected," depending on a thing's value.

Diogenes Laertius Of things that are, the Stoics declare that some are good, some are bad, and some are neither.

Good things are the virtues, including practical wisdom, justice, courage, moderation, and the rest. Bad things are the opposite—folly, injustice, and the rest. Things that are neither are those things that neither benefit nor harm—things such as life, health, pleasure, beauty, strength, wealth, good reputation, and noble birth, as well as their opposites, death, disease, pain, ugliness, weakness, poverty, bad reputation, low birth, and the like. . . .

These things are not good [or bad] things, but they are "things indifferent." . . . For just as being hot, rather than being cold, is the unique property a hot thing, so too is being beneficial, rather than being harmful, the unique property of a good thing. But wealth and health do no more benefit than harm; therefore, neither wealth nor health is a good thing. Moreover, they say that what can be used well and badly is not a good thing. But wealth and health can be used well and badly; therefore, neither wealth nor health are good things. . . . To benefit is to move and maintain according to virtue, and to harm is to move and maintain according to vice.

The Stoics say that the term "indifferent" has two meanings. For one, it denotes those things that contribute neither to happiness nor to unhappiness—things such as wealth, reputation, health, strength, and similar things. It is possible to be happy apart from these things. It is the particular way that we employ these things that makes for happiness or unhappiness. Otherwise, something is indifferent if it does not excite impulse or disgust for a thing—as with the fact that the number of hairs on one's head is odd or even or whether you point or hold back your finger. By contrast, it was not in this latter sense that the former things mentioned above were called indifferent since those things do actually excite inclination or disgust for those things. That is why of those things having to do with the first kind of indifference, some are chosen, and some are not chosen, whereas of the other things having to do with the second kind, there is an equal reason for choosing or avoiding them.

Regarding indifferent things, they say that some are preferred, and some are rejected or not preferred. Those things that have worth or value are preferred, while those that do not have worth or value are rejected.

They define worth or value, firstly, as a contribution to a harmonious life. In this sense, every good has value. Secondly, value is some intermediary power or advantage that contributes toward living life according to nature. In other words, it is the assistance that wealth and health may offer in living life according to nature. . . .

Preferred things are those that have value. For example, among things of the soul, there are natural ability, skill, moral progress, and similar things. Among bodily things, there are life, health, bodily strength, vigor, wholeness, beauty, and so on. Among external things, there are wealth, reputation, noble birth, and similar things.

As for those things that are rejected, among things of the soul there are a lack of natural ability, a lack of skill, and like things. Among bodily things there are death, disease, weakness, lethargy, disability, ugliness, and like things. Among external things, there are poverty, bad reputation, low birth, and the like.

Those things that are in neither category are neither preferred nor rejected.

Yet again, of things preferred, some are preferred for their own sake, some for the sake of something else, and others are preferred both for their own sake and for the sake of something else. Those preferred for their own sake include natural ability, moral progress, and like things. Those preferred for the sake of something else include wealth, noble birth, and the like. Those preferred both for their own sake and for the sake of something else include strength, senses that work well, and wholeness.

Things are preferred for their own sake because they are in accord with nature. Things are preferred for the sake of something else because they produce more than a little of what is required or useful. The same may be said to hold for those things rejected—only the opposite.[32]

The next few selections offer the early Stoic understanding of duty, that is, acting in such a way that is fitting or appropriate. "It is always fitting to live according to virtue." Consequently, to live a rational and virtuous life, one must carry out one's duty.

Diogenes Laertius The Stoics say that duty or what is fitting or appropriate is that which, when done, may be supported by a reasonable account—for example, whatever is in conformity with living life. This is something that applies both to plant and animal life—for one may perceive, even with these, that which is fitting or appropriate.

Zeno was the first to use the word *kathēkon* for "what is fitting" or "what is appropriate." Etymologically, it is derived from *kata tinas hēkein*, that is, "belonging to something or someone." It is a fitting action or activity in relation to nature's arrangements.

Of actions done in relation to impulse, some are fitting, some are not fitting, and some are neither fitting nor not fitting. Those acts which are fitting are the ones that reason within us seizes upon and chooses to do, such as honoring one's parents, brothers, sisters, and homeland, and adapting oneself to and spending time with one's friends. Those acts which are not fitting are the ones that reason within us does not choose, such as neglecting one's parents, ignoring one's brothers and sisters, failing to be agreeable and available to one's friends, despising one's homeland, and like things. Those acts which are neither fitting nor not fitting are the ones that reason neither chooses to do nor forbids, such as picking up a twig, holding a writing utensil or a scraper, and like things.

Again, some things are duties or fitting activities regardless of the circumstances, while others depend on the circumstances. Those duties or fitting activities that do not depend on the circumstances include taking care of one's health and one's sense organs and the like. Those that depend on circumstances include, for example, maiming oneself and sacrificing or giving away one's property. The same holds analogously for those acts that are not fitting.

Once again, of those things which are fitting, some are always fitting, and some are not always fitting. It is always fitting to live according to virtue. But asking and answering questions and walking around and the like are not always fitting or appropriate. The same explanation goes for acts that are not fitting.[33]

The following selections present the early Stoic teaching regarding the soul and its parts; how error and the passions or emotions arise within the soul; what passion is (that passions are "contrary to reason and nature" and, thus, we can conclude, to virtue); and, finally, what may be considered the unhealthy or irrational versus the healthy or rational passions or emotions, which is to say those that tend toward unhappiness or happiness, respectively.

Diogenes Laertius The Stoics say the soul has eight parts. There are the five sense faculties, the vocal part, the intellectual part, which is the intellect itself, and the productive part.

From falsehood or error there arises a distortion or perversion, which extends throughout the intellect. And from this distortion grow many passions or emotions, which are responsible for much confusion and instability.

According to Zeno, a passion is itself a motion or excessive impulse of the soul that is contrary to reason and nature. . . .

The Stoics think that the passions or emotions are decisions or judgements—this according to what Chrysippus says in *On the Passions*. Avarice, for example, is the assumption that money is noble. It is similar with drunkenness and immoderation and the other passions.[34]

Diogenes Laertius According to Hecaton in the second book of his work *On the Passions*, and to Zeno in his own treatise *On the Passions*, there are four major kinds of passions or emotions: grief, fear, desire, and pleasure. . . .

Grief or pain is a contraction of the soul contrary to reason. . . .

Fear is the expectation of evil, or misfortune. . . .

Desire or longing is an appetite that is contrary to reason. . . . The state of want or lacking [which falls under the passion of desire] is the failure of desire, when desire does not reach its object but is nevertheless attracted to it in vain, stretching out to it. . . .

Pleasure is an elation that is contrary to reason that arises from getting and amassing what seems to be choiceworthy.[35]

Diogenes Laertius The Stoics say that there are three good passions or states of the soul: joy, caution, and willing. Joy, the opposite of pleasure, is sensible elation, that is, elation backed by good reason. Caution, that is, discretion or circumspection, is the opposite of fear. It is avoidance backed by good reason, or the reasonable turning of one's course. Even though the wise man will never fear anything, he will nevertheless act with caution. And they say that willing is the opposite of desire insofar as willing is reasonable appetite, that is, appetite backed by good reason.[36]

We end with the Stoic conception of the nature of the wise man—what the wise man is, what he will do, and what he will not do. The following is a compilation of such statements. Though the equation is not explicitly made, for the Stoics, the wise man is by definition virtuous.

Diogenes Laertius The wise man is . . . good and beautiful . . . without passion . . . free from vanity, for he is indifferent to good or evil report

. . . austere or harsh since he neither has dealings with pleasure nor tolerates those who have such dealings . . . earnest for and attentive to his own improvement, employing a manner of life that banishes evil out of sight and makes what good there is in things appear . . . godlike, for he has something divine within himself (whereas the thoughtless man is godless) . . . a worshipper of god . . . holy and just in what concerns the gods . . . free, whereas bad men are slaves—where freedom is the power of independent action and slavery is the opposite . . . unharmed, for he does not harm others or himself . . . not pitiful and makes no allowance for anyone; he never relaxes the penalties fixed by the laws since indulgence and pity and even equitable consideration are signs of a weak soul that substitutes kindness for chastisement.[37]

Diogenes Laertius The wise man *will* . . . take part in politics . . . marry . . . offer prayers . . . do everything well in the same way that we say Ismenias plays everything well on the flute.[38]

Diogenes Laertius The wise man *will not* . . . live in solitude since he is naturally made for a community and action . . . form mere opinions—that is, he will never assent to anything that is false.[39]

Diogenes Laertius Ariston of Chios, the Bald, who was nicknamed "the Siren," declared that the goal of life was to live in a state of indifference to everything between virtue and vice. He did not recognize variation among things indifferent but treated them all alike. Accordingly, he said that the wise man is like a good actor, who, if called on to take the part of a Thersites or of an Agamemnon, will impersonate them in a suitable manner.[40]

SUMMARY OF ARETĒ FOR ZENO OF CITIUM & THE EARLY STOICS

For Zeno of Citium and the early Stoics, virtue is, generally speaking, the perfection of a thing. More specifically, humans are virtuous when they live in conformity with nature. For human beings, the natural life is a rational life, meaning a life that allows reason "to shape impulse in a skillful manner." Impulse itself is something provided by nature, and is that which causes animals, including human beings, to "pursue what is suitable." Human beings have a duty to do what is fitting or suitable.

As indicated, for humans, the rational life itself is the same as the virtuous life. To live virtuously is to live in harmony with "the right reason that pervades all things and is the same as Zeus." Humans, however, often act in accord with passion, which is "a motion or excessive impulse of the soul that is contrary to reason and nature." Such passions are judgments or false assumptions. These drive humans to seek or flee "indifferent things" (things that are neither good nor bad, virtuous nor vicious).

In summary, the virtuous life is a life lived according to reason in agreement with nature. Such a life is a happy life.

NOTES

[1] For an introduction to early Stoicism, and for other passages related to early Stoic logic, physics (natural philosophy), and ethics (including aretē), see *The Best of Early Stoicism* (Sugar Land: The Classics Cave, 2021).

[2] For a list of Zeno of Citium's writings, see Diogenes Laertius, *Lives* 7.4.

[3] Diogenes Laertius, *Lives* 7.168, 175.

[4] Ibid., 7.179, 202.

[5] Ibid., 7.7.

[6] Ibid., 7.8-9.

[7] Ibid., 7.29.

[8] Ibid., 7.10-11.

[9] Ibid., 7.89.

[10] Ibid., 7.30.

[11] Ibid., 7.127. Diogenes Laertius further explains that this teaching is "according to what Zeno says, as well as Chrysippus in the first book of his treatise *On Virtues*, and Hecaton in the second book of his treatise *On Goods*."

[12] Ibid., 7.188-189.

[13] Ibid., 7.128. Both were later Stoics of the Middle Stoa. Panaetius of Rhodes lived from c. 185 to 109 BC. Posidonius of Apamea lived from c. 135 to c. 51 BC.

[14] Ibid., 7.87. Hecaton lived during the first century BC.

[15] Ibid., 7.88.

[16] Ibid., 7.85-86; 88. The assertion "made by some" regarding the first "impulse of animals . . . toward pleasure" refers to either the Epicureans or the Cyrenaics.

[17] Ibid., 7.90.

[18] Ibid., 7.89.

[19] Ibid., 7.125.

[20] Ibid., 7.92, 93.

[21] Ibid., 7.92. Alas, we do not know how Diogenes Laertius gave the early Stoic definition of moderation or justice because there is a gap in the text. In his *Anthology* 2, Johannes Stobaeus (fifth century AD) gives the early Stoic definition of the two this way: "Moderation is knowledge of what is to be chosen and what is to be avoided and what is neither. And justice is knowledge of the distribution of valuable things to each man." Regarding moderation and its opposite, Cicero, in the *Tusculan Disputations* 4.22, has one interlocutor, "M.," state: "The Stoics say that the fount of all disorders is immoderation or intemperance, which is a revolt from all guidance of the mind and right reason, so completely alien from the control of reason that the cravings of the soul cannot be guided or curbed. Therefore, just as moderation or temperance slays the cravings and causes them to obey right reason, and maintains the well-considered judgments of the mind, so its enemy immoderation or intemperance kindles, confounds, and agitates the whole condition of the soul, with the result that from it come distress and fear and all other disorders."

[22] Diogenes Laertius, *Lives* 7.92, 93.

[23] Ibid., 7.46. For the Stoic understanding of dialectic or skill in dialectic (*dialektikos*), see ibid., 7.42-44.

[24] Ibid., 7.127. The Peripatetics were the inheritors of Aristotle's investigations and teachings. For an explanation of the Peripatetic or Aristotelian "middle ground of moral progress," see Aristotle's ladder to virtue described above in 9, "Aristotle."

[25] Ibid., 7.165. Herillus of Carthage was a student of Zeno of Citium. Considered a heterodox Stoic, he declared that knowledge is the goal of life.

[26] Ibid., 7.120-121. Persaeus of Citium lived from c. 306 to c. 243 BC. The latter three were Stoics who lived in the second and first centuries BC.

[27] Ibid., 7.94.

[28] Ibid., 7.94.

[29] Ibid., 7.95.

[30] Ibid., 7.96-97.

[31] Ibid., 7.101, 130.

[32] Ibid., 7.101-107. A third definition of value: "Thirdly, value is the price set by an appraiser, as determined by his experience with the facts, as when an appraiser says that wheat is worth so much barley with a mule thrown in to make up the difference."

[33] Ibid., 7.107-109. "Maiming oneself" might sound like an odd example, but there are several instances from ancient history in which a man dutifully maims himself, for example, to infiltrate a city. For one, see Herodotus, *Histories* 3.153-160.

[34] Ibid., 7.110-111.

35 Ibid., 7.110-114. Diogenes adds this: "Moreover, just as we say that there are certain bodily illnesses or infirmities, for example, gout and arthritic disorders, so also there are soul illnesses, such as love of reputation and love of pleasure, and the like. By illness or infirmity is meant a disease accompanied by weakness. By disease is meant an excessive notion about something that seems choiceworthy. And just as there is a tendency toward certain maladies in the body, such as the buildup of mucus and diarrhea, so with the soul there is a tendency to enviousness, pitifulness, quarrelsomeness, and the like." (ibid., 7.115).

36 Ibid., 7.116.

37 Ibid., 7.100, 117-123.

38 Ibid., 7.121, 124-125.

39 Ibid., 7.123, 121.

40 Ibid., 7.160. In Homer's *Iliad*, Thersites is a commoner who upbraids Agamemnon, the leading man of the Achaeans (see *Iliad* 2.210-267).

EPICTETUS
THE STOIC

E PICTETUS (c. 55-135 AD) WAS a philosopher from Hierapolis in Phrygia (Turkey). Though a slave in Rome for a portion of his life, Epictetus was nevertheless allowed to study philosophy with the Stoic Musonius Rufus. At some point his master Epaphroditus (who had been the emperor Nero's slave) liberated him. When with other philosophers, he was banished from Rome around 90 AD, Epictetus travelled to and settled in Nicopolis in Epirus (Greece), where he opened a school of philosophy.

Epictetus is known for his *Discourses* and *Handbook* (*Enchiridion*), which were recorded by his student Arrian (c. 86-160 AD), a man who is known for his histories and other writings. Both works emphasize ethics. Significant points include the idea that we should act and judge based on what is up to us (such as opinions, beliefs, and desires) versus what is not up to us (such as material possessions, reputation, and status). It is oftentimes our judgment about something that is upsetting rather than the thing itself. As for how we should act, virtue is essential for the good and happy life (for a summary of Epictetus' view of aretē, see the end of the chapter).

IN THEIR OWN WORDS

We begin with a point that Epictetus returns to again and again—though here are only a few representative passages. It is that we must be virtuous, that is, do virtue rather than merely learn or talk about it.[1] Accordingly, Epictetus describes the nature of true progress in virtue, the exercise of "the powers of choice and refusal, desire and aversion" in accord with nature.

The one who is making progress—since he has learned from the philosophers that desire is for good things and aversion is for bad things, and since he has learned as well that a life that flows well and tranquility are only available to the man who gets what he desires and avoids those things for which he feels an aversion—such a one utterly gets rid of desire within himself, or he defers it to another time, and he feels aversion only toward those things that involve freedom of choice, which is to say those things that are dependent on his will. . . .

Now, if virtue promises happiness and tranquility and a life that flows well, then without a doubt progress in virtue is progress toward each of these. . . .

Why is it, then, that we grant that virtue is such as I have stated, and yet we seek progress in other things and make a show of it?

What is the point of virtue? A life that flows well.

Who is it, then, that is making progress? Is it the one who has read many books by [the Stoic philosopher] Chrysippus? But does virtue amount to the act of understanding Chrysippus? If this is the case, then progress is nothing more than knowing many of Chrysippus' works. . . .

Suppose, for example, that in talking to a boxer I said, "Show me the muscles of your arms and shoulders," and in reply he said, "Look at my weights." "No," I would say, "I want to see the effect of the weights." So, when you say, "Take the treatise *On the Active Powers* and see how I have mastered it," my response is, "Slavish fellow! I'm not asking about this treatise, but how it is that you exercise the powers of choice and refusal, desire and aversion. Do you do so in accord with nature or not? If so, then give me evidence of it and I will declare that you are making progress. But if not, then you may go on your own way and not only comment on these treatises but write some yourself. And yet what will you gain by it?"

Where, then, is progress? It is when anyone among you withdraws from external things and turns his attention to the question of his own will and moral purpose, cultivating and perfecting it so as to make it finally harmonious with nature, elevated, free, unhindered, untrammeled, faithful, and honorable. It is when one has learned that he who desires or avoids the things that are not under his control can neither be faithful nor free but must necessarily be changed and tossed about with them as in a storm. . . .

And finally, it is when one rises in the morning and keeps and observes all he has learned—he bathes as a man of fidelity, eats as a modest man, and, in like manner, he applies his chief principles in every other matter as a runner does when he applies the principles of running and the voice-trainer does when he applies the principles of voice-training. This is the one who is truly making progress.[2]

Next, Epictetus describes what it means to be and live as a human being. It is easy to talk about philosophy and things such as virtue and vice. What we must do is live and practice them.

It is no simple task, this business of living as a human being. For what is a human being? Someone says, "A human being is a rational, mortal animal." Fine, but from what other creatures are we distinguished by the rational element? "From wild animals." And from what else? "From sheep and the like."

Make sure that you never act like a wild animal, then. And if you do, you will have destroyed the human being in you, you will have missed your calling. And make sure that you never act like sheep, for in this way the human being will be destroyed in you.

"Well," you ask, "when do we act like sheep?" We do when we act for the sake of the belly, or our genitals, or at random, or in a filthy fashion, or without due consideration. "What have we destroyed?" Our reason. And when we act contentiously and injuriously and angrily and rudely, we sink to the level of wild animals. Some of us are wild animals of a larger size. Others are little animals—malignant and petty. . . .

Philosophers admonish us not to be satisfied with learning alone but to add to our learning practice and training. . . .

For who is there among us here and now that cannot give a philosophical discourse about good and evil? It will run something like this: Of things that are, some are good, others are evil, and others are indifferent. Now good things are the virtues and everything that participates in the virtues. Bad things are the opposite, while things indifferent are wealth, health, and reputation.

But if we are interrupted in the middle of our discourse by an unusually loud noise or by someone in the audience who laughs at us, we are upset.

I ask, "Where, you philosopher, are the realities you were just talking about? Where did you get what you were just now saying? From your lips—that is all. Why do you dirty the helpful principles that are not your own? And why do you go on about these most important matters? For to store away bread and wine in the pantry is one thing, but to eat and drink them is another. What is consumed is digested and distributed and it becomes sinews, flesh, bones and blood."[3]

Epictetus goes on to explain how the faculty of choice, the will, is related to virtue and vice and, therefore, to happiness and unhappiness.

What is it that has the natural power to restrain the faculty of choice? Nothing beyond choosing itself—only its own perversion. So it is that vice is in the faculty of choice alone, and that virtue is in the faculty of choice alone. . . .

If you ask me what is the highest of all things, . . . I will declare that it is the faculty of choice when it is straightened out. . . . When this has been set right, a human being becomes good. And when it fails, a human being becomes bad. It is through this, through choosing, that we are unfortunate or fortunate. . . .

In a word, when the faculty of choice is forgotten or ignored, it produces unhappiness, but when it is cared for, it produces happiness.[4]

Epictetus explains that virtue and vice are part of the nature of things in the world, the cosmos, as designed by the one who arranged and appointed all things. We should seek instruction to be at harmony with the way things are. We should "learn to wish that everything may happen as it actually does happen."

To be instructed is this: to learn to wish that everything may happen as it actually does happen. And how do things actually happen? They happen as the arranger and appointer of things has actually arranged and appointed them. And he has arranged and appointed summer and winter, and abundance and scarcity, and virtue and vice, and all such opposites for the harmony of the whole. . . .

Remembering, then, this arrangement of things, we should seek instruction, not that we may change the arrangement of things—for we do not have the power to do this, nor would we be better off if we had such a power—but so that as the things around us are what they are and exist by nature, we may maintain our minds in harmony with the things that actually happen.[5]

Epictetus discusses the example of Socrates. Socrates not only spoke about virtue in a noble manner, but he played well the role given him by the gods—to the point of death.

Socrates does not save his life by means of a shameful act—Socrates, the man who refused to call for a vote when the Athenians demanded it of him, the man who despised the tyrants, the man who held such noble discourse about virtue and moral excellence. No, it is impossible to save this man by means of a shameful act. He is saved by death, not by flight. Yes, and the good actor is saved when he stops at the right time rather than the one who acts at the wrong time.[6]

In the next three selections, we see that virtue is the right use of appearances, realizing what is and is not in our power, and judging and living accordingly. Part of living in this manner is playing the role we have been given in life, following the lead of Zeus, destiny, necessity, and the gods.

Of all the things that exist, God has put some of them in our power, that is, under our control, and some he has not. He has placed in our own power that act which is the best and the most important—the act, indeed, through which he himself is happy—the use of appearances (that is, impressions). For when the use of appearances is rightly employed, there is freedom, good flow, cheerful contentment, and stable calm. There is also justice, law, moderation, and every virtue. But all other things he has not placed in our power. Therefore, we should unite in mind with God. We should also make the following division of things: we should look after those things that are in our power and therefore under our control. As for those things that are not in our power, we should entrust them to the cosmos, willingly giving up whatever the cosmos requires—our children, our country, our body, or anything else.[7]

Remember that you are an actor in a play, and that the author of the play chooses what kind of play it will be. If he chooses short, then it will be a short play. If long, then one that is long. Moreover, if he wants you to play the part of a poor man, then you should make sure to play the part naturally. Or if the part of a disabled man, or a magistrate, or a private person, then do the same. This is your duty—to play well the part that is given to you. But to select the part—that belongs to another.[8]

Upon every occasion, we should have the following at hand:
"Lead me, O Zeus, and you O Destiny, to whatever station you have assigned me. I will follow without hesitation. And if I am not willing to follow because I have become a bad man, even so I will follow."
"Whoever nobly yields to necessity—we hold that man wise and skilled in divine things."
And a third, "Crito, if it is pleasing to the gods, then let it happen. Anytus and Meletus can kill me, but they cannot harm me."[9]

Finally, Epictetus describes the nature of true human beauty, that it consists in human virtue or excellence.

Once, when he was visited by a young student of rhetoric whose hair was somewhat too elaborately done up, and whose clothing in general was highly adorned, Epictetus said, "Tell me if you do not think that some dogs are beautiful, as well as some horses, and so on with every other creature."

"I do," said the young man.

"Is not the same also true of human beings?—some are beautiful, and some are ugly?"

"Of course.". . .

Epictetus asked, "What is it, then, that makes a dog beautiful?"

"It is the presence of a dog's virtue, its excellence."

"And what makes a horse beautiful?"

"The presence of a horse's virtue, its excellence."

"What about a human being, then? What makes a human being beautiful?"

"Is it not the presence of a human being's virtue, his excellence?"

"Very well, then, young man. If you want to be beautiful, then strive hard to be excellent with the virtue that characterizes a human being."

"And what is that?"

"Observe who it is that you yourself praise, when you praise people dispassionately. Is it the just man or the unjust?"

"The just man."

"And is it the moderate man or the licentious one who is never satisfied?"

"The moderate man."

"And is it the self-controlled man or the one who has no self-control?"

"The self-controlled man."

"In making yourself that kind of person, therefore, be confident that you will be making yourself beautiful. But as long as you neglect this, you will inevitably be ugly no matter what you do to make yourself appear beautiful."[10]

SUMMARY OF ARETĒ FOR EPICTETUS

Epictetus recognizes that it is far easier to learn and talk about virtue than it is to practice it. But in order to be free and happy, to have a life that flows well, we need to *do* virtue and thus *be* virtuous.

The practice of virtue involves choice—it *is* choice. We must choose to accept and be at harmony with the way things are in the world, the cosmos, including the good and the bad, the virtuous and the vicious. We must wish things to be as they are. We must freely accept our place and role in the great cosmic play—even if it means death (as it did for Socrates). We must choose to follow the lead of Zeus and all the other directors of life (destiny, necessity, the other gods).

If we do so, if we practice choice and choose well and therefore become virtuous, then we will display true human beauty, which consists in human virtue or excellence. If we choose well, we will be happy.

NOTES

[1] Compare Epictetus' remarks regarding the gulf between learning-talking-teaching and actual practice to the satirical criticism of Lucian of Samosata in 15, "Lucian of Samosata."

[2] Epictetus, *Discourses* 1.4.

[3] Ibid., 2.9. Epictetus makes a similar point in 2.19.

[4] Ibid., 2.23

[5] Ibid., 1.12.

[6] Ibid., 4.1.

[7] Epictetus, Fragment 4, in Stobaeus, *Anthology* 2.8.30.

[8] Epictetus, *Handbook* 17.

[9] Ibid., 53. The first is a prayer of Cleanthes of Assos, the second is a line from Euripides (a fragment), and the last is Socrates based on Plato's *Crito* 43d and the *Apology* 30c-d.

[10] Ibid., 3.1.

EPICURUS

E PICURUS (c. 341-270 BC) WAS a philosopher from the island of Samos (Greece). Even so, he was an Athenian citizen. He is known as the founder of Epicureanism, a school of philosophy that operated out of "the Garden." He taught that our understanding of things has a significant impact on our peace of mind, our happiness. Consequently, it is important to study philosophy in order to quiet any internal disturbance we may feel.

Two letters of Epicurus survive that explore various fear and anxiety-provoking matters. The *Letter to Herodotus* presents a general survey of his understanding of reality, including the reduction of everything to atoms and (the) void. The *Letter to Pythocles* offers an empirical and rational view, rather than one based on myth or pure speculation, of those sometimes-frightening things that happen in the sky and on earth—things like thunder and lightning or earthquakes.

We also have Epicurus' *Letter to Menoeceus*, which explains the blessed nature of the gods, why death "is nothing" to human beings, the truth of pleasure and pain, and what desires we should seek to satisfy. Lastly, Epicurus' *Principal Teachings* and *Vatican Sayings* summarize his views on reality and the good life in the form of pithy sayings.

Epicurus judged the topic of virtue or the virtues important enough that he wrote a work on it called, *On Justice and the Other Virtues*. Unfortunately, this work is no longer extant. Nevertheless, it is to Epicurus' view of virtue that we now turn (for a summary of Epicurus' view of aretē, see the end of the chapter).

Unless otherwise noted, the following passages are all attributed to Epicurus himself and his writings. That said, most of them, aside from the Vatican Sayings, are found in Diogenes Laertius' *Lives*.[1]

IN THEIR OWN WORDS

For Epicurus, the summary significance of virtue is that it is a key which unlocks the door to a pleasant life. And that—the pleasant life—is, in turn, happiness, which is the goal of life. To restate the point, virtuous behavior is chosen for the sake of pleasure, with the understanding that pleasure is sought for the sake of happiness. That said, Epicurus holds that pleasure cannot be had without virtue. To be virtuous, therefore, is to experience the pleasant life. Virtuous qualities such as wisdom, moral nobility or fineness, and justice are essential to living with pleasure.

In the following selections, we see the tie between virtue, living pleasantly, and happiness.

Epicurus The virtues have become one with living pleasantly. Living pleasantly is inseparable from the virtues.[2]

Epicurus We say that pleasure is the beginning point and goal of living happily.[3]

Epicurus We must practice those things which produce happiness since if happiness is present, we possess everything, and if it is not, we do everything to acquire it.[4]

Diogenes Laertius Epicurus believes that . . . we choose the virtues for the sake of pleasure and not on their own account, even as we take medicine for the sake of health.[5]

Diogenes Laertius Epicurus declares that virtue is the only thing that is inseparable from pleasure. Everything else—things like food, for example—may be separated from pleasure.[6]

Athenaeus of Naucratis In his work, *On the Goal of Life*, Epicurus says, "You should therefore honor that which is morally noble and the virtues and everything like that if they produce pleasure. But if they do not produce pleasure, then we should have nothing to do with them."[7]

Epicurus It is impossible to live pleasantly without living wisely, nobly, and justly—just as it is impossible to live wisely, nobly, and justly without living pleasantly. The person who fails to inaugurate a wise, noble, and just life is the person who does not have a pleasant life.[8]

If for Epicurus virtue is so closely associated or identified with pleasure and the happy life, then to understand virtue we must seek answers to a number of questions: What is pleasure? What pleasures should we seek? All? Some? How is pleasure related to pain? How is pleasure linked with desire?

Perusing his writings, we'll discover that by pleasure, Epicurus is really only referring to a small subset of all possible pleasures. They are not the pleasures of "decadent men," he asserts, but, we may conclude, those of the opposite kind of men—the noble, the moral, the virtuous. These are simple pleasures, those that exist, we might say, just on this side of the dividing line that separates pleasure from pain, the pursuit of which allows for a self-sufficient, independent life.

Since desire is that which moves us toward pleasure and away from pain, it is necessary to understand desire's many manifestations in order to determine which desires to satisfy and which to leave unsatisfied.

All of this—knowing what desires to fulfill and, therefore, what pleasures to seek—requires "sober reasoning," Epicurus observes. The source or foundation of virtue, and so of living pleasantly and happily, is practical wisdom (itself a virtue), which allows us to live in a thoughtful and intentional manner. Consequently, pleasant living begins in the mind, springing from the careful use of reason and the practice of virtue. It is not a "lucky" life, whether for good or ill. It is one that listens to and follows the natural and necessary of life rather than their opposites.

Epicurus We must consider that of the desires, some are natural, and some are groundless. Of the natural desires, some are necessary, and some are merely natural. And of the necessary desires, some are necessary for happiness, some for freeing the body from disturbance, and some for living itself.

He who has a firm understanding of these things knows how to direct every choice and every avoidance toward securing bodily health and mental tranquility since this is the goal of a blessedly happy life. Everything we do is for the sake of being free from pain and from fear. The soul's storm scatters as soon as we achieve this condition. Then we have no need to go around looking for anything that is lacking or seeking something else by which the good of the soul and the good of the body will be fulfilled.

We have the need for pleasure only when we feel pain due to the absence of pleasure. When we feel no pain, however, there is no need for pleasure. For this reason, we say that pleasure is the beginning point and goal of living happily. We recognize that pleasure is our first good, present at birth, and that it is the beginning point of every choice and avoidance. We resort to pleasure when we use feeling as the measure for judging every good.

Even though pleasure is our first and inborn good, we nevertheless do not choose every pleasure. Rather, we oftentimes forgo many pleasures when a greater annoyance will follow from choosing them. And oftentimes we acknowledge that many pains are better than many pleasures when an even greater pleasure follows from patiently enduring these pains for a long period of time. And so, even though every pleasure is naturally good and fitting, not every pleasure is to be chosen. In the same way, even though every pain is bad, not every pain is always to be avoided. To be sure, we may aptly judge every case by measuring one feeling in comparison with the other and taking a look at the advantages and disadvantages of both sides. Sometimes we treat a good thing as though it is bad. On the other hand, sometimes we treat a bad thing as though it is good.

We regard self-sufficiency as a great good. This is not so that we may enjoy just a little in every case, but so that when things are scarce, we may nevertheless be satisfied with little, genuinely persuaded that the ones who derive the greatest pleasure from luxury are the ones who need it the least, and that everything natural is easy to get, but whatever is groundless is hard.

Simple food gives just as much pleasure as rich food does, as soon as the hunger pains are gone. A barley cake and water offer the highest possible pleasure when they are given to a hungry man. Getting used to simple and inexpensive food, therefore, aids the

health of a man and enables him to perform the necessary requirements of life with resolution. Not only that, but such a habit better
disposes us for when we encounter extravagant fare now and
again, and it makes us fearless in the face of fortune.

So then, when we say that pleasure is the beginning point and
goal of life, we do not mean the pleasures of decadent men or the
pleasures of sensuality, as some ignorant persons believe, or those
who do not agree with us, or those who have willfully misrepre-
sented our position. Rather, by pleasure we mean the absence of
pain in the body and of trouble in the soul. A pleasant life is not
produced by stringing together one drinking party after another, or
by having sex with young boys or women, or by enjoying fish and
other delicacies set on a luxurious table. Instead, it is produced by
sober reasoning that examines what is responsible for every choice
and avoidance, and expels those beliefs by which the greatest confusion lays hold of the soul.

Practical wisdom is the foundation of all these things and the
greatest good. For this reason, we value practical wisdom even
more than philosophy. Every other virtue is produced from practical wisdom, teaching us that we cannot live pleasantly without living wisely, nobly, and justly—just as we cannot live wisely, nobly,
and justly without living pleasantly. The virtues have become one
with living pleasantly. Living pleasantly is inseparable from the virtues.[9]

Epicurus Pleasure in the flesh will not increase after need-based
pain is removed. After that, pleasure may only be varied. And the
limit of pleasure in the mind is reached in thinking about these and
like things that used to cause the greatest fears in the mind.[10]

Epicurus While the flesh behaves as though the limits of pleasure
are unlimited and thus it would take an unlimited amount of time
to furnish these pleasures, the mind—having reasoned out the purpose and limits of the flesh, and having banished fears having to do
with eternity—provides a complete life that does not require an unlimited amount of time. Nevertheless, the mind does not avoid

pleasure. And even when circumstances cause one to leave life, the mind enjoys the best life.[11]

Epicurus Luck rarely interferes with the wise man. Rather, it is reason that has managed, does manage, and will manage the greatest and most essential things throughout the course of a wise man's life.[12]

Epicurus If at any moment you do not direct each of your actions to the goal of life indicated by nature, but, instead, you turn aside to some other goal in the act of pursuing some object or avoiding it, your activity will not be consistent with the conclusions drawn from reason.[13]

Epicurus We must obey nature rather than doing violence to her. We will obey nature by satisfying the necessary desires and the natural desires, too, as long as they do no harm, but sharply rejecting the harmful desires.[14]

Epicurus The wise man who has measured himself with necessary things knows better how to give than to take, so large a treasury of self-sufficiency has he found.[15]

Epicurus Let us completely get rid of thoughtless habits, even as we would worthless men who have done us great harm for a long time.[16]

Diogenes Laertius (citing "the views of Epicurus and his school") Once a man has become wise, he will not assume the opposite disposition—not of his own free will, anyway.[17]

Although Epicurus wrote the book, On Justice and Other Virtues, *(which is no longer extant) and mentions various virtues in the writings we still possess, he does not often go into the nature of any of the virtues in detail. Of those he explores in any detail, they are wisdom, practical wisdom, courage, justice, and friendship—assuming he, like Aristotle, believed friendship was a virtue or at least closely allied to the virtues and a virtuous life.*

The following selections offer a smattering of what Epicurus has to say about courage, justice, and friendship (these three since we have already noted the significance of wisdom or practical wisdom for virtue above). Notice how each virtue is the means to some beneficial end rather than existing as an end in itself—a point Epicurus explicitly makes regarding virtue's tie to pleasure and happiness.

Diogenes Laertius (citing "the views of Epicurus and his school") The wise man believes that courage does not spring up naturally, but by means of rationally figuring out what is expedient.[18]

Epicurus Natural justice is a pledge of reciprocal advantage neither to harm one another nor to be harmed.

There is no such thing as justice in itself. Rather, justice is an agreement neither to harm nor be harmed that is made when men gather together from time to time in various places.

Injustice is not something evil in itself. Rather the evil coincides with the worry and worming fear that one will not escape the notice of those who are responsible for punishing injustice.

It is impossible for the man who secretly violates the agreement to neither harm one another nor be harmed to feel confident that he will remain undiscovered, even if up to the present moment he has already escaped ten thousand times. No, to the end of his life such a man is never sure he will remain undetected.

Taken generally, justice is the same for all because of its reciprocal advantage when men associate with one another. But in its specific application to places and conditions, justice is different depending on the circumstances.[19]

Epicurus Of all the means that are procured by wisdom to ensure blessed happiness throughout the whole of life, by far the most important is the acquisition of friendship.[20]

Epicurus Every friendship is desirable in itself, even though it begins because of its utility.[21]

Epicurus Our need is not so much for the advantage that comes from our friends as it is for the confidence that comes from that advantage.[22]

Epicurus The true friend is neither the one who always seeks some advantage, nor the one who never links advantage with friendship. The one trades goodwill for compensation, while the other cuts off hope for the future.[23]

Epicurus Friendship dances around the world of men calling out to all of us, "Rise up to happiness!"[24]

We've seen that pleasure and happiness require virtue, and that the source of each is wisdom. This wisdom in turn requires ongoing study and reflection, which is to say, the pursuit of philosophy. Epicurus' call, then, for everyone and at every time of life is to study philosophy in order to pursue a thoughtful and virtuous life. For if we have this, he declares, we have happiness. And "if happiness is present, we possess everything." In fact, the virtuous man is received by the gods, who are, by common definition, "blessed living beings."[25]

Epicurus Let no one put off studying philosophy when he is young, nor become weary of it when he is old, for no age is too early or too late for the health of the soul. To suggest that the time for studying philosophy has not yet come or that it is long gone is like saying that it is too early or too late for happiness. Therefore, both the young and the old should seek wisdom by doing philosophy. . . . We must practice those things which produce happiness since if happiness is present, we possess everything, and if it is not, we do everything to acquire it.[26]

Epicurus The gods always receive those men who are like them since they make every virtue their own, while rejecting everything that does not belong to them.[27]

.　.　.

Summary of Aretē for Epicurus

For Epicurus and Epicureanism, virtue plays a central role in securing both a pleasant and happy life, so much so that Epicurus equates living virtuously with living pleasantly, and the latter with happiness. Epicurus contends that we humans cannot live well or happily without living pleasantly, and, furthermore, that we cannot live pleasantly without living virtuously.

Since reason in the mind manages this virtuous, pleasant, and happy life, we must practice philosophy, which is the pursuit of wisdom. This wisdom—namely, practical wisdom—is the source and foundation of every virtue.

By practicing philosophy, we become wise. By being wise, we grow in virtue. By being virtuous we satisfy natural and necessary desires and, therefore, experience true, simple, and necessary pleasures. By living a truly pleasant life, we possess happiness. For Epicurus, there is nothing more.

Notes

[1] For an introduction to Epicurus' philosophy and his life, as well as a collection of his writings and sayings and other ancient writing on Epicureanism, see *The Best of Epicurus* (Sugar Land: The Classics Cave, 2021).

[2] Diogenes Laertius, *Lives* 10.132 (*Letter to Menoeceus*).

[3] Ibid., 10.128 (*Letter to Menoeceus*).

[4] Ibid., 10.122 (*Letter to Menoeceus*).

[5] Diogenes Laertius, *Lives*, 10.137, 138. One must keep in mind that, for Epicurus, happiness is, in a sense, the unspoken analogue of health since for him the right sort of pleasure is the same as happiness.

[6] Ibid., 10.138.

[7] Athenaeus of Naucratis, *Deipnosophists* 12.67. The same lines are repeated in *Deipnosophists* 7.11.

[8] Diogenes Laertius, *Lives* 10.140 (*Principal Teaching* 5).

[9] Ibid., 10.127-132 (*Letter to Menoeceus*).

[10] Ibid., 10.144 (*Principal Teaching* 18).

[11] Ibid., 10.145 (*Principal Teaching* 20).

[12] Ibid., 10.144 (*Principal Teaching* 16).

[13] Ibid., 10.148 (*Principal Teaching* 25).

[14] Epicurus, *Vatican Sayings* 21.

[15] Ibid., 44.

[16] Ibid., 46.

[17] Diogenes Laertius, *Lives* 10.117. With this remark, Epicurus (and his school) seems to be proposing the ongoing or habitual nature of wisdom and thus, possibly, of virtue in a manner similar to Aristotle.

[18] Ibid., 10.120.

[19] Ibid., 10.150 (*Principal Teaching* 31, 33-36).

[20] Ibid., 10.148 (*Principal Teaching* 27).

[21] Epicurus, *Vatican Sayings* 23.

[22] Ibid., 34.

[23] Ibid., 39.

[24] Ibid., 52.

[25] For Epicurus on the "blessed" nature of the gods, see Diogenes Laertius, *Lives* 10.123 (*Letter to Menoeceus*): "You should acknowledge that the god is an indestructible and blessed living being. This is the commonly held understanding of the god, the common epithet in writing."

[26] Ibid., 10.122 (*Letter to Menoeceus*).

[27] Ibid., 10.124 (*Letter to Menoeceus*).

PLOTINUS

P LOTINUS (c. 205-270 AD) WAS a philosopher from Lycopolis (Egypt). After studying with the Alexandrian philosopher Ammonius Sacca, and after attempting a journey to Mesopotamia with the Roman emperor Gordian, Plotinus eventually made his way to Rome, where he set up a school and gave talks and held conferences.

Plotinus is known for what historians call Neoplatonism (a development of Plato's philosophy), the system of philosophy that appears in the *Enneads*, a work written by Plotinus but gathered and arranged by his student Porphyry of Tyre (c. 234-305 AD).

Significant ideas include the absolutely transcendent One beyond all speech and distinctions. From the One emanates Thought or Mind; from Mind proceeds Soul; and from Soul come individual human souls. These souls plunge into the material world of bodies and matter. The ultimate goal for humans is to return to the One by means of a number of stages that pass beyond sense-perception and discursive thought to mystical union with the One. The wise and virtuous man, therefore, will orient himself to the Supreme and thus toward happiness, which is fullness of life. Consequently, virtue is crucial to Plotinus' philosophical program of life (for a summary of Plotinus' view of aretē, see the end of the chapter).

The following lengthy selection comes from Plotinus' treatise *On the Virtues* (found in *Enneads* 1.2). It presents Plotinus' major thinking about virtue and its significance in moving toward happiness and the Supreme.

Note: this is the only passage we present from Plotinus. Consequently, there is no explanatory commentary as Plotinus' own train of thought, however obscure at times, is sufficient.

. . .

IN THEIR OWN WORDS

Since evils are here in this realm, and since these evils "prowl about this realm by necessity," and since the soul wishes to flee these evils, then "we must flee from this realm."

But what is the nature of this flight we must take? Plato says that it is in becoming like god—like the divinity. And this, he says, is found if one "is becoming just and holy, and in one who is beginning to live by means of practical wisdom"—which is to say the whole of virtue.

But does not likeness in virtue imply likeness to some being that possesses virtue? What god, or divine being, then, would we be like? Presumably, we would be like the being who, above all, possesses such virtue—that is, the soul of the cosmos, the world soul, and the ruling principle within it, the principle endowed with a most wonderful practical wisdom. What could be more fitting than that we, living in this world, should become like its ruler?

Nevertheless, to begin with, we are confronted with the question of whether virtues are even to be found in this divine being—moderation of desires, for instance, or courage. As for courage, nothing can truly harm this being, and so it has nothing to fear. And as for moderation, no pleasant thing could possibly exist that would stir up longing desire when present or absent.

If, in fact, the desire for the intelligibles that is in our nature also exists in this being, then we do not need to look anywhere else for the source of order and of the virtues within ourselves.

But the question remains: does this being possess the virtues?

We cannot expect to find within this being what are spoken of as the virtues related to the social order—the practical wisdom that has to do with the rational part of our nature; the courage that has to do with the spirited, passionate part of our nature; the moderation that has to do with a certain agreement, a concord between the desiring part of our nature and the reasoning part; or the justice that has to do with the due application of all the other virtues as each in turn should command or obey. . . .

Now, if we admit that likeness is possible—even though by a

varying use of different virtues, and even though the virtues related to the social order are not sufficient—then there is no reason why we should not, by virtues that are still our own, achieve likeness to a being in which virtue has no place. But how?

Here's a way to understand it. When anything is warmed by the presence of fire, the fire itself does not need to be heated by the presence of another fire. It might be argued that there is heat in the fire—but it is a heat that is inherent. Reasoning by analogy, then, virtue in the soul comes from the outside, whereas the virtue of the being by which we are virtuous is inherent, an essential aspect of the being.

Against this illustration drawn from fire, it may be urged that the analogy would make this being identical with virtue, whereas we hold it to be something higher.

The objection would be valid if what the soul takes in were one and the same with the source. But in fact virtue is one thing, and the source of virtue is another. The house that is in the material, sense-realm is not identical with the idea of the house conceived in the intellect. Even so it stands in its likeness. The material, sense-realm house has proportion and order, while the pure idea is not constituted of any such elements. Proportion, order, and symmetry are not parts of an idea.

So it is with us. It is from the supreme being that we derive order and proportion and harmony, which are virtues in this realm. But since the Supreme is not lacking harmony, order, or proportion, it has no need for virtue. Nevertheless, it is by our possession of virtue that we become like the Supreme. Such is our demonstration that human assimilation to the Supreme by means of virtue does not necessarily involve the presence of virtue in the Supreme itself. Even so, we need more than a formal demonstration. We must persuade as well as demonstrate.

Let us first examine the virtues by which we say likeness comes. And let us discover what the nature of this thing is, which, as we possess it—as image or copy—is virtue, but as the Supreme possesses it—as model or archetype—is not virtue.

We must first distinguish two modes of likeness or assimilation.

The first entails such identity of nature as exists when both like things proceed from the same principle. The second is that of one thing to another that precedes it as its principle. In the latter case, there is no reciprocity. The principle does not resemble that which comes after it; rather, the resemblance must be thought about in an entirely different manner. It does not require that similar objects be of the same kind. Instead, it implies that they are of different kinds inasmuch as they resemble each other differently.

What, then, is virtue—both the whole of virtue and each one? The clearest way forward will be to look at a particular virtue first. Then it will be easy to determine the common essence underlying them all.

The above-mentioned virtues related to the social order lend our souls order and beauty as long as we live. They improve our souls by limiting and regulating our desires and regulating every feeling. They dispel false judgment, deliver us from incorrect views—and this by sheer efficacy of the better, by the very setting of the bounds, by the fact that the regulated or measured is lifted outside of the sphere of the unmeasured and lawless.

This measure given to our souls resembles the form given to matter, and the proportion of intelligible things. It is, as it were, a trace of what is most perfect above. What is unmeasured— since it is no more than measureless matter—cannot in any way resemble divinity. The greater the participation in form, the greater the likeness or assimilation to the formless divinity. The closer we get to form, the greater the participation therein. So it is that the soul, whose nature is closer to the divinity and more alike it than the body is, participates more in the divine and increases that resemblance enough to make it seem that the divinity is all that the soul itself is. This is how the deception comes about that represents the soul itself as the divinity, falsely holding that the soul is the whole of the divine.

So then, this is how virtues related to the social order become like the divine.

We come now to another mode of likeness that is, we read in Plato, the fruit of the higher virtues. In discussing this, we will better understand the nature of the virtues related to the social order, and the higher virtues, and the difference between them.

Plato is evidently making a distinction between two kinds of virtue when he states that "assimilation to the divinity" consists in "a divine flight" from this realm, and when he adds the qualification "for the citizen" to the virtues related to the social order, and when, in another place, he asserts that all the virtues are processes of purification. It is clear from this that he is distinguishing two kinds of virtue and that assimilation to the divine does not follow from the virtues related to the social order.

But in what sense can we call the virtues purifications? And how does purification result in likeness or assimilation to the divine?

It is in this sense: the soul is evil to the extent that it is confused with the body—when it shares in the body's feelings and experiences and thinks the body's thoughts. By contrast, the soul possesses good and virtue if it does its work alone and does not think the body's thoughts (for the soul, this is thinking and living according to practical wisdom); and if it does not share in the body's feelings and experiences (for the soul, this is being moderate, showing self-control); and if it does not fear separation from the body (for the soul, this is being courageous); and if reason and intelligence lead the way without opposition (for the soul, this is justice or rectitude). When the soul is disposed in this manner, it thinks dispassionately. This disposition of the soul may be called likeness or assimilation to the divinity since the divinity is pure as is its work. The one who imitates it in this manner, then, possesses practical wisdom.

But it is not the divinity that possesses such a disposition, for dispositions are only the property of souls. Moreover, the soul thinks in one way, and the divine being in another. . . . The divinity's thought is a primary principle from which our thought is derived and differs. As a spoken word is an image of a thought in the soul, so is a thought in the soul an image of the divinity's thought. . . . In the same way, then, virtue is in the soul. Virtue does not belong to the supreme mind or to that which is beyond.

But now we must investigate whether this purification is the same as virtue, or whether, purification leading the way, virtue comes after it. Does virtue consist in being pure or in the process of becoming pure?

The process itself is incomplete relative to being pure, which is at present the goal. Being pure is the removal of everything alien to the soul. But the good itself is something else—something more.

If one was good before one was impure, then purification would suffice. But if purification suffices in this manner, then what remains is the good and not the purification. We must, therefore, investigate what it is that remains.

The good cannot have the same nature of whatever it is that remains. This is so because the good cannot come to be with an evil thing.

Should we say, then, that what remains is that which is like the good, that which *seems* good? Yes, for it is unable to remain in the good since it goes both ways—both toward good and toward evil.

Coming together with what is like it is the good itself, whereas coming together with its opposite is evil. So then, it must purify itself and come together with what is like it. This coming together is a turning around, a conversion.

So then, does this conversion occur after the purification? No. The turning around happens at the same time as the purification.

Is virtue, then, a conversion? No, virtue is the result of the conversion.

So then, what is this turning? That it sees. That it receives the impression of the thing perceived just as the eye receives the impression of the thing seen.

But wasn't this always there? Wasn't it merely forgotten? Yes—what it now sees it most definitely always possessed, yet it possessed it as though it was lying in the dark, inactive. Light was required to drive away the darkness and come to know it was there. Thus, it must be thrown into the light. . . .

We must now speak about the extent of the purification. With this, the nature of likeness to the divine being will become clear.

The question is substantially this: how far is purification able to go to dispel desire and longing and every other thing like this, as well as grief and everything like it? And to what degree is the soul able to separate itself from the body?

Separation simply means that the soul withdraws to its own place. It will be without feeling. It will make use of necessary pleasures and all the activity of the senses only for the restoration and health of the body, and to be released from bodily distress, so that it may not be troubled, but the suffering is removed. If such is not possible, then the soul gently endures the suffering and makes it smaller by not giving in to it—by not feeling with it. Desire, whether for or against, is removed. If possible, all passionate desire. But if not, at least it does not allow these desires to run wild. Rather, it regulates the involuntary to the body where it becomes small and weak.

The soul has nothing to fear, though doubtlessly there will be an occasional involuntary feeling of fear. Sometimes, though, fear serves as a warning, an admonition. And what about longing? Whatever there is, it is clear that it is never for anything bad. It won't even hold within itself the longing for the food and drink that restores—nor for those things belonging to Aphrodite. And if it does desire, it has desire only for natural things, I suppose, and not without deliberation or purpose. And if any indeliberate desire does take place, it'll go no further than the imagination and will be no more than a fleeting thing.

But the soul itself is spotless when it comes to all of these and wishes to purify the irrational so that it will not be confused—or at least to make the incidence of confusion smaller and infrequent given the proximity of that which is straight, just as a man who is neighbors with a wise man will benefit from the proximity of the wise man and becomes like him. At the very least he feels shame, daring to do nothing that the good man does not wish to do.

So then, there is no battle in the soul since it is enough that the reasoning part is present. The inferior part of the soul stands in awe of and respects the reasoning part—so much so, that for any movement contrary to the reasoning part, the inferior part is vexed and censures its own weakness for not having remained quiet in the presence of its master.

So then, not one of these things are failures—not one is a sin since the human being has been set straight, he's reformed. But the object of attention is not merely to flee from failures, but it is to be divine, god. . . .

What form, then, does each virtue take in such a one? Wisdom and practical wisdom consist in the contemplation of all that exists in the Intelligence, the divine Mind—that which the Intelligence knows by direct contact, without mediation.

Each virtue is twofold—one in the Intelligence and one in the soul. That which is in the Intelligence is not virtue, but that which is in the soul is virtue.

So then, what is it in the Intelligence? It is its act and its essence. The act and essence of the Supreme, manifested in a new way in this realm, is virtue. The Supreme is not justice itself or the absolute of each virtue. Rather, it is the exemplar—the pattern, model, the blueprint—the source of what is virtue in the soul. . . .

But if justice is really taking care of one's own affairs, that is, carrying out one's own proper function, then does justice always involve many parts? The justice appropriate to what involves many parts does, but not justice in itself. It can be one. Justice that is true, justice revealed, justice in itself is one to itself—a unity in which there is no this, that, or the other.

In this way, the higher justice in the soul is to act in a way that is oriented toward the Supreme, to the Intelligence; the higher moderation is that internal turning toward the Supreme; the higher courage is a freedom from emotion that is similar to the characteristic lack of feeling of the Supreme toward which the soul looks—but which the soul must gain by means of virtue so that it will not suffer along with the inferior part dwelling within. . . .

In the soul, wisdom and practical wisdom are the seeing, the vision, of the Intelligence. . . .

Plotinus recognizes the need for adaptation and that one improves. . . .

And as one reaches to higher principles and other standards, these in turn will serve as the measure for what he does. From this point on, he does not limit moderation to the regulation of things desired, but, insofar as he is able, he is separated from the whole of life, even the life of a conventionally good human being that is directed by the virtues related to the social order. He lets go of all this, choosing another life in its place, the life of the gods. He advances toward the gods, not toward good human beings or toward the likeness of them. Likeness to good human beings is similar to the likeness one image has to another image . . . But likeness to the other is likeness to the model itself.[1]

SUMMARY OF ARETĒ FOR PLOTINUS

For Plotinus, virtue is the means by which we humans are assimilated to the Supreme, the divine; it is the path by which we "flee from this realm," this material, sensible realm, which is full of evils, and make our way to the divine realm. Though virtue is not in the Supreme (as the Supreme does not long for things or fear things, for instance, and therefore there is no need for moderation or courage), the Supreme nevertheless serves as the archetype or model of virtue. Virtue itself is an image or copy. Consequently, in being virtuous, we reflect and thus manifest the Supreme.

Traveling along the path of virtue first requires a conversion or turning around that involves seeing in a new manner that is facilitated by abundant light. Conversion occurs simultaneously with purification, which dispels various desires and feelings, and separates the soul from the body, allowing the soul to withdraw "to its own place."

In terms of virtue, which Plotinus calls "the result of conversion," the path is twofold, corresponding to two goals or goods. One is the goal of becoming a "conventionally good human being." The virtues that aim at and achieve this goal are what Plotinus calls "the virtues related to the social order" (what some give as "civic virtues"). These virtues "improve our souls by limiting and regulating our desires and regulating every feeling." The higher virtues, by contrast, aim at and directly achieve assimilation to the divine. With them we become godlike, the other goal.

As for specific virtues, Plotinus names and describes practical wisdom, courage, moderation, and justice.

NOTES

[1] Plotinus, *Enneads* 1.2.1-7.

PART 3

Comic Interlude

Lucian of Samosata

L UCIAN (c. 120-c. 180 AD) WAS A writer from Samosata in Armenian Commagene. Initially a travelling sophist and rhetorician
(he was educated following the typical Greek curriculum), he began to write satires (a relatively new form of humorous, critical dialogue) after a mid-life move to Athens.

The selections that follow all come from a handful of Lucian's
works. Utilizing a range of voices, including those of the gods Zeus,
Pan, and Momus or Mōmos (the god of blame or satire), and various men, Lucian humorously criticizes philosophy, or, rather, philosophers, and their approach to virtue — an approach that sounds
loud and obnoxious, seems meaningless, and frequently does not
practice what it preaches. Accordingly, rather than offering a positive or systematic presentation of aretē, he lampoons what others
thought and how they failed to live the good life.

IN THEIR OWN WORDS[1]

*First off, in a thinly veiled roast of philosophy or philosophers, Lucian, in his
own voice (in* A Literary Prometheus*), explains how Comedy has treated
Dialogue — Dialogue, who deeply speculates about Nature and Virtue.*

There was no great original connection or friendship between Dialogue and Comedy. The former stayed at home, spending his time
in solitude, or at most he took a stroll with a few intimates. By contrast, Comedy put herself in the hands of Dionysus, haunted the
theatre, frolicked in company, laughed and mocked and rhythmi-
cally stepped to the flute at times.

More. Comedy would scale her poetic anapests, as likely as not,
and pelt the friends of Dialogue with nicknames — theoretical

hairsplitters, airy metaphysicians, and the like. The thing she loved more than anything was to make fun of them, showering them in Dionysian freedom, portraying them as walking along upon the air and arguing with the clouds, or measuring the jump of a flea—all examples of their ethereal refinements.[2] Nevertheless, Dialogue kept up his deep speculations about nature and virtue, until, as the musicians say, the interval between them was two full octaves, from the highest to the lowest note.

It is this incompatible pair that we have dared to unite and harmonize—reluctant as they are and disinclined to reconciliation.[3]

In the next set of selections, various speakers question the philosophers and their proclivity to speak about things like virtue and nature. Do these words actually mean anything? they wonder.

In The Double Indictment, *Zeus explains how philosophy went from being the practice of a few to that of the many. They all sing virtue's praises.*

Zeus: But in those days during Socrates' life, philosophy was not generally known and had but few advocates. It is not surprising that the scale then fell against Socrates in favor of Anytus and Meletus. But now it is different! Look at the number of tattered cloaks and staffs and leather bags that one sees around. Philosophers everywhere—long-bearded, book in hand—defend your cause, the cause of justice. The public walks are filled with their contending hosts, and every single one of them calls virtue his nursemaid. Many have abandoned their former professions, eagerly turning to the leather bag and the tattered cloak—the outfit of the Cynic. These ready-made philosophers—once carpenters or cobblers, now duly tanned by the sun to the true Ethiopian hue—are singing the praises of virtue high and low.[4]

From The Gods in Council, *Momus, the god of blame or satire, questions the existence of things such as virtue, nature, destiny, and luck (realities that were frequently personified in Greek literature—and thus the capitalization below). Perhaps they are merely words—names—that point to no reality at all.*

Momus: I have also heard with considerable amusement the introduction of various strange names, denoting persons who neither have nor could conceivably have any existence among us. Show me this Virtue about whom we hear so much. Show me Nature, and Destiny, and Luck—if they are anything more than unsubstantial names, the vain imaginings of some philosopher's empty head.

Yet these flimsy personifications have so far prevailed upon the unintelligent . . . I would appreciate it if you would tell me whether you have ever seen Virtue or Nature or Destiny anywhere. I know that you must have heard of them often enough from the philosophers, unless your ears are deaf enough to be proof against their bawling.

I might say much more, but I'll stop myself. I gather that public indignation has already risen to a boiling point—especially in those quarters in which my plain truths have hit home.[5]

From Timon the Misanthrope, *we hear Zeus admitting to Hermes that he has not paid attention to Timon and others in Attica (a region including Athens) since the arrival of the philosophers there, the very ones who give long speeches "about some virtue and incorporeal things and other nonsense."*

Zeus: This is a case we must take up and see to, Hermes. No wonder Timon is down on his luck. Well, we would be placing ourselves on the level of his despicable sycophants if we forgot all the fat ox and goat thighs he has burned on our altars—the savor of them is still in my nostrils. But I have been so busy, there is such a din of perjury, assault, and burglary. I am so frightened of the temple robbers. They swarm now! You cannot keep them out or take a nap with any safety. And so, because of one thing or another, it has been forever since I had a look at Attica. I have hardly been there since philosophy and contentious argumentation came into fashion. Indeed, with their shouting matches going on, prayers are quite inaudible. One must sit with one's ears plugged if one wishes to avoid burst eardrums. Such are the long speeches that go on and on and on about some virtue and incorporeal things and other nonsense.[6]

In The Double Indictment, *the god Pan laments his own simple-mind-edness and inability to understand what the philosophers are so urgently talking about, including "some virtue, and forms, and nature, and things without a body—things unknown to me with strange names."*

Pan: I can't understand a word they say—their wisdom is too much for me. I am mountain-bred. I tell you, Justice, smart city-language is not in my line. Sophists and philosophers are not known in Arcadia. I'm good at the flute or pipe. I can mind goats. I can dance. I can fight at a pinch—and that is all.

But I hear them all day long, going through all this, croaking like frogs about some virtue, and forms, and nature, and things without a body—things unknown to me with strange names. They are good enough friends when the argument begins, but their voices climb higher and higher as they go on, ending in a scream. They get more and more excited and all try to speak at once. They grow red in the face, their necks swell, and their veins pop out like a flute-player hitting a high note. Then the argument is turned upside down, and they forget what they are trying to prove. Finally, they go off abusing one another and brushing the sweat from their brows.

Victory goes to the man who can show the boldest front and speak in the loudest voice and hold his ground the longest. The people—particularly those with nothing better to do—adore them and stand bewitched by their confident shouting. To me they seemed no better than swaggering braggarts, and it grieved me to see them copying my beard.[7]

The next set of selections point out the gap between what philosophers say about virtue and the good life and how they actually behave.

The first comes from Lucian's Icaromenippus, an Aerial Expedition. *In it the interlocutor Menippus is speaking to his friend, reporting the speech of Zeus, who points out the oft-observed gap between what cranky and quarrelsome philosophers espouse in public and how they behave in private. The implied call is for a quiet integrity.*

When all the gods were gathered, Zeus commenced: The immediate occasion of my summoning you is the arrival of this stranger yesterday. But I have long intended to take counsel with you regarding the philosophers, and now, urged by Selene and her complaints, I have resolved to put off the consideration of the question no longer.

There is a group of men that has recently become conspicuous. They are idle, quarrelsome, vain, irritable, dainty, silly, puffed up, arrogant, and, in Homeric phrase, 'a pointless weight upon earth.' These men have divided themselves into bands, each dwelling in a separate word-maze of its own construction. They call themselves Stoics, Epicureans, Peripatetics, and more laughable names yet. Then they take to themselves the holy name of virtue, and with uplifted brows and flowing beards exhibit the deceitful semblance that hides immoral lives. Their model is the tragic actor, from whom if you strip off the mask and the gold-spangled robe, there is nothing left but a paltry fellow hired for a few coins to play a part.

Nevertheless, quite undeterred by their own characters, they look down on the human and mock the divine. They gather a company of guileless youths and feed them with solemn chatter about virtue and quibbling word puzzles. To their students, they sing the praises of patient endurance and moderation and self-sufficiency and spit upon wealth and pleasure. When they are by themselves, however, there is no limit to their gluttony or their indulgence of lust . . . But the greatest offense is this: they themselves neither work nor do they help others in their work. They are useless drones.[8]

In the second selection from Timon the Misanthrope, *Timon performs the same task as Zeus above regarding the philosopher Thrasycles—a man who "turns his morning maxims inside out," speaking about virtue in the morning and practicing pleasure in the evening.*

Timon: But who is this? Is this Thrasycles the philosopher? Sure enough it is. A halo of beard, eyebrows an inch above their place, superiority in his manner, a look that might storm heaven, locks waving to the wind . . . This hero of the careful getup, the solemn gait, the plain attire. In the morning he will utter a thousand maxims expounding virtue, speak with gladness against pleasure, and laud the one who is content with little. Yet then, when he comes to dine after his bath, his servant fills his drinking cup to the edge. He rejoices most when his wine is straight up, no added water. And draining this Lethe-sized portion, he proceeds to turn his morning maxims inside out. He swoops like a hawk on dainty dishes, elbows his neighbor aside, fouls his beard with trickling sauce, and laps like a dog with his nose in his plate—all as if he expected to find virtue there. And he runs his finger all around the bowl, not to lose any of the gooey goods.[9]

Next, in conversation with Tuchiadēs in The Parasite, *a Demonstration that Sponging Is a Profession, Simon points out that although the philosophers talk about virtue and courage, when it comes to actual fighting in battle and dying, they are conspicuously absent—all but for Socrates.*

Tuchiadēs: Yes, I know all that. But then these are orators, trained to speak, not to fight. But the philosophers—you cannot say the same of them.

Simon: Oh, yes, Tuchiadēs. They discuss courage every day, and they do a great deal more toward wearing out the word virtue than the orators. But you will find them still greater cowards and shirkers. How do I know? In the first place, can anyone name a philosopher who has been killed in battle? No, they either do not serve, or else they run away. Antisthenes, Diogenes, Crates, Zeno, Plato, Aeschines, Aristotle, and all their company—they never so much as set eyes on a battle. The wise man Socrates was the only one who dared to go out. And in the Battle of Delium he ran away from Mount Parnes, fleeing safely to the wrestling school in Taureas. It was far more civilized, in his view, to sit there chatting with lads, tossing them sophisms, than to fight with a Spartan man.[10]

We end with extended selections from Hermotimus, *or the Rival Philosophies. Therein, the non-philosopher Lycinus queries his friend Hermotimus about the value of studying philosophy—whether it actually brings one closer to virtue and happiness, as all the philosophers claim. For Hermotimus, who has been studying philosophy for some twenty years, it is an exceptionally good question—one he should have asked earlier on.*

Lycinus: Good morning, Hermotimus. I guess by your book and your quick pace that you are on your way to a lecture—and a little late. You were going over something as you walked, your lips working and muttering, your hand flung out this way and that as you got a speech into order in your mind. You were doubtless inventing one of your crooked questions or pondering some tricky problem. Never a vacant mind, that's you, even in the streets. Always on the stretch and in earnest, bent on advancing in your studies.

Hermotimus: Yes, by Zeus, Lycinus, I admit the charge. I was going over the details of what the speaker said in yesterday's lecture. One must lose no chance, you know. The healing doctor from the island of Cos spoke so truly—"Life is short but art is long." And what the speaker referred to was only the medical arts—a simpler matter. As for philosophy, you will never grasp the whole, however long you study, unless you are wide awake all the time, contemplating it with intense and eager gaze. The stake is so great, too—whether you will miserably waste away with the many or be counted among philosophers and reach happiness.

Lycinus: It is a glorious prize, indeed! Nonetheless, you cannot be far off from the goal now if one may judge by the time you have given to philosophy and the extraordinary vigor of your long pursuit. For twenty years now, I'd say, I have watched you perpetually going to your teachers, generally bent over a book and taking notes of past lectures, pale with thought and emaciated in body. I suspect you find no release even in your dreams, you are so wrapped up in the thing. With all this you will surely get hold of happiness soon—if, in fact, you have not found it long ago without telling us.

Hermotimus: Alas, Lycinus, I am only just beginning to get an inkling of the right way. Very far off dwells virtue, as Hesiod says. And long and steep and rough is the way there. And travelers must walk on, sweating all the while.[11]

Lycinus: And you have not yet sweated and travelled enough, Hermotimus?

Hermotimus: Surely not—otherwise I would have made it to the summit, and I would be happy in every way. As it is, I'm only setting out, Lycinus.

Lycinus: Ah, but Hesiod, your own authority, tells us, "Well begun is half done." So, we may safely say you're halfway there by now.

Hermotimus: Nope. Not even there yet. That would be a huge accomplishment!

Lycinus: Where *should* we place you, then?

Hermotimus: Still on the lower slopes—just trying to get on. But it is slippery and rough, and one needs a helping hand.

Lycinus: Well, your teacher can give you that from his perch on the summit—just like Zeus in Homer with his golden cord. He can lower down to you his discourse, and with it, he can haul and heave you up to himself and to the virtue that he himself has possessed for so long.

Hermotimus: That's exactly what he's doing! If it depended on him alone, I would have been hauled up long ago. It's my own part that's lacking.

Lycinus: You must be of good cheer and maintain a stout heart. Gaze at the end of your climb and the happiness at the top and remember that he is working with you. What's his expectation? When will you make it to the top? Does he think you'll be there next year—say by the Great Mysteries or the Panathenaea?

Hermotimus: Too soon, Lycinus.

Lycinus: By next Olympiad, then?

Hermotimus: No, that's not even enough time for the practice of virtue and the attainment of happiness.

Lycinus: Okay, well, let's say two Olympiads, then, to give an outside estimate. If you can't get the job done by then, you may fairly be judged guilty of laziness. That amount of time would allow you three roundtrips from the Pillars of Heracles[12] to India, with time for exploring the tribes on the way instead of sailing straight and never stopping. Tell me—how much higher and more slippery is the peak on which your virtue dwells than that birdless crag that Alexander stormed in a few days?

Hermotimus: There's no resemblance, Lycinus. This is not a thing, as you imagine it, to be achieved and taken quickly. . . . As it is, a good number begin the climb with great confidence, and they do make progress—some very little indeed, others more. But when they get halfway up, they find endless difficulties and discomforts. So it is that they lose heart and turn back, panting, dripping, and exhausted. But those who endure to the end reach the top. And from that point on, they live a happy life, looking down from the heights upon the ants that are the rest of us.

Lycinus: Wow, Hermotimus! What tiny things you make us out to be—not even as big as the Pygmies but positively groveling on the face of the earth. I understand it, though. Your thoughts are already up there, and we, the common men who walk upon the earth, should count you in with the gods in our prayers—for you've been transported above the clouds, you've gone up to that place you've worked so hard for.

Hermotimus: Ah! If only that ascent may yet be, Lycinus! But it is a long way off.

Lycinus: But you've never told me *how* long—in terms of time.

Hermotimus: No, I haven't since I myself do not know with any precision. My guess is that it will not be more than twenty years. By that time, I will surely be on the summit.

Lycinus: By Heracles! You speak about an exceptionally long time!

Hermotimus: Great as the reward is, Lycinus, so is the toil.

Lycinus: That may be the truth. But about these twenty years—do you have your teacher's promise that you will live so long? Is he a prophet as well as a philosopher? Or is it a soothsayer or a Chaldean expert that you trust? Such things are known to them, I understand. You would never slave away and toil night and day like this if there were any uncertainty of your life lasting to the highpoint of virtue. I mean your fate may spring on you just as you were close to the top, lay hold of you by the heel, and drag you down with your hopes unfulfilled.

Hermotimus: Hands off, then! These are words of ill omen, Lycinus. May life be granted me so that I may grow wise and be happy—even if only for a single day!

Lycinus: Will one day of happiness be enough for you even with all this trouble?

Hermotimus: Even the briefest moment of it will be enough.

Lycinus: But is there even happiness up there? . . . How can you tell? You've never been up there yourself.

Hermotimus: I trust my teacher's word. And he knows well since he's already reached the highest point.

Lycinus: Oh, do tell me what he says about it. What is happiness like?—wealth, glory, and pleasures incomparable?

Hermotimus: Hush, friend! All these have nothing to do with the virtuous life!

Lycinus: Well, if these will not do, what *are* the good things he offers to those who reach the end of the exercise?

Hermotimus: Wisdom, courage, true nobility, justice, full and firm knowledge of all things as they are. But wealth and glory and pleasure and all bodily things—these a man strips off and abandons before he makes the final ascent, like Heracles burning on Mount Oeta before his deification. He too cast off whatever of the human he had from his mother and soared up to the gods with his divine part pure and unalloyed, sifted by the fire. Even so those I speak of are purged by the philosophic fire of all that deluded men count admirable. And reaching the summit, they possess happiness with never a thought about wealth and glory and pleasure—except to smile at any who count them more than phantoms.

Lycinus: By Heracles, Hermotimus, and his death on Oeta— these behave like men and have their reward, it seems. But there is one thing I would like to know. Are they allowed to come down from their elevation, sometimes, and have a taste of what they left behind them? Or once they've gone up, must they remain there attending to Virtue, jeering at wealth and glory and pleasure?

Hermotimus: The latter—definitely. More than that, though. Once a man has come into Virtue's presence, he will never be subject to wrath or fear or desire. No—nor will he be able to feel pain or any such sensation. . . .

Lycinus: Answer this, friend. When you first went in pursuit of philosophy, you found many gates wide open. What led you to pass by the others and go in at the Stoic gate? Why did you assume that that portal was the only true one that would set you on the straight road to virtue, while the rest all opened on blind alleys? What was the test you applied *then*? . . .

But now . . . let us assume that the Stoic philosophy, and no other, is correct. Then we can examine whether it is practicable and possible, or its disciples are squandering all their toil. It makes wonderful promises, I am told, about the happiness in store for those who reach the summit—for only they will enter into full possession of the true good. The next point you must help me with is this. Have you ever encountered such a Stoic, one who has reached the heights of Stoicism—one who is unconscious of pain, not tempted by pleasure, free from wrath, superior to envy, contemptuous of wealth, and, in a word, happy? Such a man would be the measure and judge of the life of virtue. As for anyone else, including the man who falls short in the slightest degree, even though he is better than other men at all points, he is nevertheless incomplete, uninitiated. And in that case, he is not yet happy. . . .

There is another thing I do not think you have observed. Virtue is manifested, of course, in action, in doing what is just and wise and courageous. But you—and when I say you, I mean the most advanced philosophers—you do not seek these things and do them, but you spend the greater part of your life considering miserable sentences and demonstrations and problems. It is the man who does best at these that you hail a glorious victor. And I believe that is why you admire this experienced old teacher of yours. He puzzles his partners in conversation. He knows how to ask crafty questions and trick you into pitfalls. So it is that you pay no attention to the fruit, which consists in action, but you are extremely busy with the husks, and you smother one another with the leaves in your debates. Come now, Hermotimus, what else are you busy with from morning to night?

Hermotimus: Nothing; that is what it comes to. . . . *Later:* Oh! I could cry like a baby! It cuts me to the heart—it is all so true. It is too much for me when I think about all those wretched, wasted years! Paying all that money, too, for my own labor! Now I am sober once again after having had far too much to drink. I see the true nature of my desire and what it has brought on me.

Lycinus: No need for tears, dear fellow. There is a very sensible fable of Aesop's. A man sat on the shore and counted the waves breaking. Missing count, he was excessively annoyed. But the fox came up and said to him, "Why vex yourself, good sir, over the past ones? You should let them go and begin counting anew."

So you—since this is your new expectation—you had better reconcile yourself now to living like an ordinary man. You will give up your strange and delusional hopes, and without shame and with a friendly mind, even in your old age, you'll unlearn what you've come to know and alter your course for the better.

Now, friend, I beg you not to imagine that I have said all this as an anti-Stoic, moved by any special dislike for your school. My arguments hold against all schools. I would have said exactly the same thing if you had chosen Plato or Aristotle. . . . But since Stoicism was your choice, the argument appears to have been aimed at that school—though it really wasn't.

Hermotimus: You are quite right. And now I am off to transform myself. When we next meet, there will be no long and shaggy beard, and no artificial composure. I will be natural, as a gentleman should be. I may go so far as a fashionable tunic in order to announce my renunciation of nonsense. I only wish there were an emetic that would purge out every doctrine they have put into me. I assure you, if I could reverse Chrysippus' plan with hellebore, and drink forgetfulness—not of the world but of Stoicism—I would not think twice about it.

Well, Lycinus, I owe you a debt indeed. I was being swept along in a rough and muddled torrent, unresisting, drifting with the stream, when you stood there and fished me out. I have good enough reason, I think, to shave my head like those people who are saved from shipwreck. And I will go to make votive offerings today for the dispersion of that thick cloud that was over my eyes. From now on if I meet a philosopher on my walks—and this will be contrary to my will—I will turn aside and avoid him as I would a mad dog.[13]

NOTES

[1] The translations presented in this chapter are modified versions of those of H.W. Fowler and F.G. Fowler (1905).

[2] The reference is to Aristophanes' comedy the *Clouds* 144-145, wherein Socrates queries how many flea feet a flea can jump.

[3] Lucian of Samosata, *A Literary Prometheus* 6.

[4] Ibid., *The Double Indictment* 6.

[5] Ibid., *The Gods in Council* 13.

[6] Ibid., *Timon the Misanthrope* 9.

[7] Ibid., *The Double Indictment* 11.

[8] Ibid., *Icaromenippus, an Aerial Expedition* 29-30.

[9] Ibid., *Timon the Misanthrope* 54-55.

[10] Ibid., *The Parasite, a Demonstration that Sponging Is a Profession* 43. We encountered six of the seven in Part 2—Plato and Aristotle, as well as Antisthenes of Athens, Diogenes of Sinope, and Crates of Thebes (Cynic philosophers), and Zeno of Citium (the founder of Stoicism). Given the fact that the list consists of philosophers, Lucian is doubtlessly referring to the author of Socratic dialogues Aeschines (sometimes called Aeschines Socraticus) (fourth century BC) rather than the Athenian orator of the same name and time. For Socrates' flight in the Battle of Delium, see Plato's *Symposium* 220e-221c. Interestingly, Alcibiades tells the story of Socrates' retreat in order to praise him. "It was Socrates, out of all the other men of the army, who saved me [Alcibiades]. I was wounded and he would not leave me behind. Instead, he helped me save both my armor and my own life. . . . Moreover, gentlemen, Socrates was a worthy sight to behold when the army was fleeing after the battle of Delium. . . . He was retreating with Laches. . . . I first noticed how sensible Socrates was in comparison to Laches—how calm and collected he was. And next, when I looked again, he appeared like that line of yours, Aristophanes, as he walked along. Just as it is his habit to do in our own streets, he was 'strutting like a proud bird with a sidelong glance' calmly looking at friends and enemies alike, and making it clear to anyone—even from a distance—that whoever attacked him would encounter a strong resistance. The result? Both he and his comrade safely got away—since, generally speaking, men who appear calm like that are left alone whereas the enemy pursues those in flight."

[11] See Hesiod, *Works and Days* 286-292.

[12] The Pillars of Heracles are the headlands of the Strait of Gibraltar.

[13] Ibid., *Hermotimus, or the Rival Philosophies* 1-8, 15, 76, 79, 83-86.

PART 4

Talking about *Aretē*—the Orators

ISOCRATES

I SOCRATES (436-338 BC) WAS an orator and teacher from Athens. Thanks to shyness and a certain weakness of voice, he wrote, rather than presented, most of his speeches. He also taught composition. He had a school in Chios that specialized in rhetoric, and later a school in Athens devoted to philosophy and the education of the whole person—the development of the mind, character, and judgment, as well as the ability to speak well.

As we will see, Isocrates often mentions aretē in his speeches and stresses its significance. One must train in aretē, he admonishes, as it is truly advantageous. One may do so with maxims (as one may use exercises to train the body) and by following the example of virtuous individuals. Friends and other companions who are willing to exhort one to virtue are also important. Literature plays a key role in an education toward virtue, particularly the poetry of Homer. True delight comes from a virtuous life, whereas pain follows the opposite. It is vital for a city-state to form its citizens in virtue, and for those in a position of influence to turn a king toward the same, as a king will in turn cultivate his subjects.[1]

All the following selections come from Isocrates' speeches.

IN THEIR OWN WORDS

The first passages come from Isocrates' speech (or written treatise) To Demonicus. *Isocrates begins the speech by making the straightforward point that the thoughts and opinions of good and noble men vary from those of bad and base men. He explains that he is writing Demonicus a moral treatise because Demonicus is his friend Hipponicus' son, and it is beneficial to point out to the young how they might improve their way of life and character. He goes on to compare beauty, riches, bodily strength, and a noble birth to excellence or virtue. While the former things may or may not be advantageous, virtue is always helpful. It is "that possession which is most holy and secure."*

I intend to counsel you on the things which young men should reach out for and grasp and on what actions they should keep away from, as well as what kind of men they should associate with and how they should manage their own lives. For only those who have passed over this road in life have been able truly to reach virtue—that possession which is most holy and secure.

For beauty is spent by time or wasted away by disease. Riches are better at serving vice than the noble and good man. They make it possible to live a lazy life, summoning young men to pleasure. Bodily strength accompanied with practical wisdom is, indeed, an advantage, but without this ally it harms those who possess it more than it helps. And while it adorns the bodies of those who exercise, bodily strength gets in the way of the care of the soul.

But virtue, when it authentically increases in our thoughts and purposes, is the one possession that remains with us in old age. It is better than riches and more useful than a noble birth. It makes possible that which is for others impossible. It endures with confidence that which is fearful to most people. It holds that being sluggish is blameworthy, and that engaging in hard work is praiseworthy.[2]

Next, Isocrates presents a number of examples or models of the virtuous life — the heroes Heracles and Theseus and, most importantly, Demonicus' own father, Hipponicus. Demonicus should imitate his father. More, he should "vie with [his] father in his ways of life." But to do so, he must train with "noble maxims," as these are able to develop the soul in the way that various exercises develop the body. (Some of these maxims will be given next.)

It is easy to learn the virtuous life from the labors of Heracles and the deeds of Theseus, whose excellence of character has impressed upon their deeds so clear a stamp of glory that not even endless time can cast oblivion upon their achievements.

No—if you will but also recall your father's principles, you will have from your own house a noble illustration of what I am telling you. For he did not belittle virtue nor pass his life in laziness. On the contrary, he trained his body by means of toil and hardship, and endured dangers by means of his soul. Nor did he love wealth inordinately. Instead, although he enjoyed the good things available to him as is fitting for a mortal, he nevertheless cared for his possessions as if he had been immortal. Neither did he order his life in a base manner, but he was a lover of beauty and goodness. He was magnificent, sharing things in common with his friends. He prized more those who were devoted to him than those who were related to him by blood—for he considered that in the matter of companionship, nature is a much better guide than convention, character than kinship, and freedom of choice than necessity.

But all time would fail us if we should try to recount all his activities. On another occasion I will give them to you in detail. For now, I have produced a sample of the nature of Hipponicus, after whom you should pattern your life as after an example. You should regard his character and manner of life as your law. Strive to imitate and rival your father's virtue. I say this because it would be a shame . . . for children not to imitate those who were excellent among their ancestors.

You must consider that no athlete is so duty-bound to train against his competitors as are you to consider how you may vie with your father in his ways of life. But it is not possible for the mind to be so disposed unless one is filled up with many noble maxims. For as it is the nature of the body to be strengthened by appropriate toils and hardships, so it is the nature of the soul to be developed by serious and excellent sayings. Consequently, I will try to set before you in brief form those practices by which I think you can make the most progress toward virtue and be honored most by all other human beings.[3]

Isocrates offers many "noble maxims" or "serious and excellent sayings" to Demonicus. Included are the following.[4]

Show devotion to the gods.

Conduct yourself toward your parents as you would have your children conduct themselves toward you.

Train your body with exercises that lead not to bodily strength but to health.

Consider that no adornment is more appropriate for you than a sense of shame, justice, and moderation. For as all men believe, the character of the young is ruled by these virtues.

Fear the gods, honor your parents, respect your friends, obey the laws.

Hunt after pleasures that enjoy a good reputation. For enjoyment with honor is the best thing—but without it, enjoyment is absolutely worthless.

Guard yourself against accusations—even if they are false.

If you love learning, then you will learn much.

Be affable in your manner and courteous in the way you speak.

Train yourself in self-imposed toils and hardships so that you may be able to endure those that are contrary to your choosing.

Practice self-control in all the things by which it is shameful for the soul to be controlled—namely, in those things related to gain, impulse, pleasure, and pain.

Faithfully guard the secret that is given to you.

Make no man your friend before looking into how he has used his former friends.

Be slow to give your friendship, but when you have given it, strive to make it long-lasting.

You will best serve your friends if you do not wait for them to ask for your assistance but willingly go at the crucial moment of need to offer them your help.

In matters of clothing, be a man who loves beauty but not one who puts all his faith in looking good.

Do not be fond of the excessive acquisition of goods but enjoy your possessions with measure.

Be satisfied with present circumstances—still, seek improvement.

Do well to good men.

Hate flatterers as you would deceivers.

Be affable in your relations with those who approach you—never haughty.

Beware of drinking parties. But if there is a time you must be present, then stand up from your seat and depart before you get drunk.

Cultivate the thoughts of an immortal by being great in soul, but of a mortal by enjoying in due measure your possessions.

Consider education and culture to be a good far superior to the lack of education and culture.

Praise is the foundation of friendship, just as blame is that of enmity.

In your deliberations, let the past be a pattern for the future, for the unknown may be discerned by reference to the known.

Be slow in deliberation but quick to carry out your resolutions.

The best thing we have in ourselves is good judgement.

Whenever you consult someone about your own affairs, first observe how he has managed his own.

When you are placed in authority, do not employ any base or unworthy person in your administration.

Neither stand by a base deed nor plead for a base man in court.

Prefer honest poverty to unjust riches; justice is better than wealth.

Give careful consideration to all that concerns your life. But above all, exercise yourself in practical wisdom. For the greatest thing in the smallest place is a good mind in a human body.[5]

When you are about to say anything, always first consider it in your mind—for with many the tongue outruns the understanding. Let there be only two occasions when you speak: one, when the subject is one that you know clearly and well, and, two, when the subject is one about which you are compelled to speak. Speech on these occasions alone is better than silence. At all other times it is better to be silent than to speak.

Consider that nothing in human life is certain or secure. That way you will neither feel too joyous when there is good luck nor too sad when luck turns bad.

Moving on from his presentation of maxims and precepts, Isocrates counsels Demonicus to surround himself with others who exhort him to virtue. Further, he should realize that true delight follows from the toil of virtue and self-control, whereas pain follows from laziness and the pursuit of excessive pleasure.

Just as the majority prefer the tastiest to the healthiest food, we find that most other men associate with friends who err along with them, sharing in their faults, those who do not admonish them. You, I think, are minded otherwise. . . .

When one sets for himself the highest standard of conduct, it is probable that in his relation to others he will approve only of those who exhort him to virtue.

Most of all, you'll be urged on to strive for noble deeds if you realize that it is from them most of all that we derive pleasure in the truest sense. For while the result of laziness and a love of being filled is that pain follows from pleasure, on the other hand, the love of toil and hardship in the pursuit of virtue, and self-control in managing one's life always yield enjoyments that are pure and more abiding. In the former case we experience pain following upon pleasure. In the latter we enjoy pleasure after pain.[6]

While the base are not always criticized for their poor behavior, the excellent and noble and those who claim virtue are. Not only that, but it is also clear the gods reward good men and punish bad men. We should learn whatever is good and noble from any source that offers it.

Bear in mind that while base men may be pardoned for acting without principle, since it is on such a foundation that from the first their lives have been built, yet excellent and noble men may not neglect virtue without subjecting themselves to criticism from many sides. This is so because all men hate less those who miss the mark and do wrong than those who have claimed to be respectable and yet are in fact no better than a common man. . . .

And if a mortal may guess at the thoughts of the gods, I think that they also have revealed very clearly in their treatment of their nearest relations how they are disposed to the base and excellent among human beings. For Zeus, who, as the myths relate and all men believe, was the father of Heracles and Tantalus, made the one immortal because of his virtue, and inflicted on the other the severest punishments because of his vice.

With these examples before you, then, you should strive for the character and conduct of one who is noble and good. And you should not only abide by what I have said, but also learn about the best things from the poets and acknowledge them from the other wise men—if they have said anything useful. For just as we see the bee settling on all the flowers and sipping the best from each, so also those who strive for education and culture should not leave anything untasted, but they should collect useful knowledge from every source. For hardly even with these pains can they overcome the failures of nature.[7]

The second set of selections come from Isocrates' speech To Nicocles. *Nicocles was the king of Salamis, an ancient Greek city-state on the island of Cyprus. We have included those selections related to virtue, along with brief summaries.*

In the first, Isocrates observes that educating a ruler in virtue will benefit the ruler and the ruled.

Those who educate individuals in private stations benefit those men alone, but if an educator can turn those who rule over the people toward virtue, he will help both those who hold positions of authority and their subjects in that he will give to rulers a greater security in office and to the people a gentler government.[8]

The great task of the king is soul care and the pursuit of virtue.

No athlete is so called on to train his body as a king is to train his soul—for not all the public festivals in the world offer a prize comparable to those for which you who are kings struggle every day of your lives. Hold this thought in your spirit, and see to it that in proportion as you are above the others in rank so shall you excel them in virtue.[9]

Education and diligence are essential in the project of self-improvement and benefit in terms of virtue.

Do not hold the view that while diligence is useful in all other matters, it is not so in making us better and wiser. And do not judge us—humankind—so unfortunate that, although in dealing with wild beasts we have discovered arts by which we tame their souls and increase their worth, yet in our own case we are powerless to help ourselves in the pursuit of virtue. On the contrary, be convinced that education and diligence are very much able to benefit our nature.[10]

Kings benefit from the virtue of their friends, the loyalty of their citizens, and their own wisdom.

Believe that your safest bodyguard is found in the virtue of your friends, the loyalty of your citizens, and your own practical wisdom—for it is through these that one is best able to acquire and preserve absolute power.[11]

Virtue, rather than luck, is something to orient yourself to and take pride in, something for people to talk about with genuine admiration.

Do not show yourself ambitious for those things that are within the power of vicious men also to achieve but show that you are oriented to and pride yourself on virtue, in which base men have no part. Consider that the truest honor is shown to you not in public demonstrations that are inspired by fear but when people in the privacy of their homes speak with admiration of your judgment rather than of your luck.[12]

Seek memorials attesting your virtue. Risk your life if necessary.

Consider that as long as there are private individuals who are ready to lay down their lives in order to be praised after they have reached their end, it is terrible for kings not to dare to pursue a course of action from which they will be highly esteemed during their lives. As a memorial, prefer to leave behind images of your virtue rather than of your body. Make every effort to preserve your own and your state's security, but if you are compelled to risk your life, choose to die with honor rather than to live in shame.[13]

Next up are selections emphasizing virtue (with brief summaries) from the Nicocles, or the Cyprians.

In the first, Isocrates judges that virtue is the greatest good. It is best not only to be inclined to virtue by nature but also from conviction in accord with reason.

Now men who are orderly and well-behaved by nature deserve our praise and admiration, but still more do those deserve it who are so in accord with reason. For those who are moderate by chance and not by judgment may possibly be persuaded to change, but those who, besides being so inclined by nature, have formed the conviction that virtue is the greatest of goods, will, it is clear, stand firm in this position all their lives.[14]

Shoot for virtue rather than riches since virtue leads to all good things. Both making and spending one's wealth can be beneficial if done with virtue.

Do not strive to gain riches rather than a good reputation, knowing that both among the Greeks and the barbarians those who have the greatest reputation for virtue have at their command the greatest number of good things. Consider that the making of money unjustly will produce not riches but danger. Do not suppose that getting is gain or spending is loss—for neither the one nor the other always has the same significance, but either, when done in season and with virtue, benefits the doer.[15]

One should exhort the young to virtue in both word and deed.

Urge the young on to virtue not only with advice but also by demonstrating to them with actions how good men should be.[16]

Imitate the virtuous not the vicious.

Vie not with those who have the most possessions but with those who know no vice within themselves—for with such a soul a man is able to live out his life most pleasantly. Do not suppose that vice can benefit more than virtue, and that it is only its name which is offensive. No, consider that even as are the names which things have received, so also are their properties.[17]

Selections from the Panegyricus *are next.*

Isocrates starts by wondering why the wise in mind are not celebrated in a similar manner to the strong and successful in body.

I have often wondered at those who first called together the all-Greek assemblies and established the athletic games. I have been amazed because they judged that the success of bodies deserved a great reward, while they apportioned no honor prize to those who had toiled in private for the common good and had trained their own minds and souls in order to benefit others. In truth they should have made provision for the latter. For if every athlete acquires twice the bodily strength he now possesses, the rest of the world will not be better off. But let a single man be well-off in terms of practical wisdom, and all men who are willing to share in his understanding will enjoy its benefits.[18]

It is important for rulers to turn those in their care toward virtue or battle excellence (aretē). The Greeks, led by Athens and Sparta, could not have defeated the "barbarian" Persians without a training in virtue. Indeed, maybe the gods gave the Greeks this war just to highlight their virtue. It is virtue that wins wars both on land and sea.

Now the men who are responsible for our greatest blessings and deserve our highest praise are, I believe, those who risked their bodies in defense of Hellas. Nevertheless, we cannot in justice fail to recall those who lived before this war and were the ruling power in each of the two states—for it was those who trained the coming generation and turned the majority of people toward virtue and made of them stern enemies of the barbarians. . . .

I suppose that some god out of admiration for their virtue brought about this war so that men endowed by nature with such virtue should not remain unsung or end their lives without renown but should be judged worthy of the same honors as are given to those who have sprung from the gods and are called demigods. For while the gods surrendered the bodies of these to the necessary end of nature, even so they have made immortal the memory of their virtue. . . .

Our ancestors . . . desired above all to maintain the reputation they had won, and to prove to the world that in the former battle they had conquered by means of virtue and not luck. Further, they hoped to induce the Greeks to carry on the war with their ships, by showing that in fighting on the sea—no less than on the land—virtue prevails over numbers.[19]

Education and literature, particularly Homer, and recalling the virtue of others is key to cultivating a similar virtue—here, doubtlessly battle excellence and courage.

I think that even the poetry of Homer has won a greater reputation because he has nobly praised the men who fought against the barbarians. For this reason, our ancestors resolved to give his art a place of honor in our musical contests and in the education of our youth, so that we, hearing his verses often, may thoroughly learn about the enmity that exists between us and them, and that we, admiring the virtue of those who were in the war against Troy, may desire similar deeds.[20]

In the Archidamus, *Isocrates argues that life is preserved by virtue, particularly by justice—that "right" wins out in the end over "might."*

No man could ever persuade me that one should ever judge anything to be of greater significance than justice. I say this because I see that our laws have been made to secure it, that noble and good men are ambitious to practice it, and that well-governed states are quite busy with it. Moreover, I observe that the wars of the past have in the end been decided not according to might but according to right—and that, generally speaking, human life is destroyed by vice and preserved by virtue.[21]

Honor is all-important to the Spartans (Lacedaemonians) since they lay claim to virtue.

No one, for example, would reproach the Epidaurians or Corinthians or Phliasians if they thought of nothing else than escaping destruction and saving their own lives. The Lacedaemonians, however, cannot seek their deliverance at all costs—rather if to "safety" they cannot add "with honor," then for them death with good repute is preferable. This is so because those who lay claim to virtue must make it the supreme object of their lives never to be found doing a shameful thing.[22]

In the Areopagiticus, *the source of the next set of selections, Isocrates suggests that the virtuous conduct of one group can positively influence the wayward behavior of another group.*

The Athenians of that day were not watched over by many preceptors during their boyhood only to be allowed to do what they liked when they attained to manhood. On the contrary, they were subjected to greater supervision in their prime than when they were boys. For our forefathers emphasized moderation so much that they gave the supervision of orderly behavior to the Council of the Areopagus—a body that was composed exclusively of men who were of noble birth and had displayed in their lives great virtue and moderation, and which, therefore, surpassed all the other Greek councils.

And we may judge what this institution was like at that time even by what happens today. For even now, when everything connected with the choice and the examination of magistrates has fallen into neglect, we find that when those who are intolerable in everything else enter the Areopagus, they shrink from giving in to their true nature. Instead, they are governed by its traditions rather than their own vicious instincts. So great was the fear that the Areopagus' members inspired in base men, and such was the memorial of their own virtue and moderation that they left behind them in this place.[23]

Far more than laws, humans learn virtue (or not) from the example of those around them.

The men of the Areopagus thought that virtue is not increased by written laws but by everyday practices. For the majority of men end up resembling the behaviors around them when they were brought up and educated. Furthermore, they held that where there is a multitude of specific laws, it is a sign that the city-state is poorly managed—for it is in the attempt to build up obstacles to the spread of faults and crimes that men in such a city-state feel compelled to multiply the laws.[24]

Those from Athens should feel upset if they do not measure up to their ancestors in terms of virtue since those from Athens are particularly virtuous.

We should feel aggrieved and resentful if we end up being worse than our ancestors—for it is their virtue . . . we should strive zealously to imitate, particularly since it is fitting for Athenians to be the best among humankind.

This is not the first time that I have expressed this sentiment—I have done so many times and before many people. For I know that while other regions produce varieties of fruits and trees and animals, each peculiar to its locality and much better than those of other lands, our own land is able to produce and nurture men who are not only the most gifted in the world in the arts and in the powers of action and of speech but are also above all others in courage and in virtue.[25]

Next come selections from On the Peace.
First, Isocrates states that virtue is the most important ingredient for happiness.

Nothing can contribute so powerfully to making money, or to reputation, or to suitable action, or, generally speaking, to happiness and prosperity, as virtue and the parts of virtue. For we also acquire the other benefits we need by means of the good qualities we have in the soul. . . .

I mentioned a moment ago the qualities that we must possess as a foundation if we are to be happy and prosperous—namely, piety, moderation, justice, and every other virtue. As for the means by which we may most speedily be formed with such a character, what I am going to say will probably seem repellent to you when you have heard it. It is also far removed from the opinions held by the rest of the world. . . .

The means? Isocrates advises the Athenians to stop pursuing an empire. An empire is actually harmful to good character, he says.

Our ancestors, proving themselves to be men of this character, handed on the city to their descendants in a most happy and prosperous condition and left behind them an immortal memorial of their virtue. And from this we may easily learn a double lesson: that our land is able to rear better men than other lands, and that what we call empire, though it is profitable, is of a nature to deprave all who have anything to do with it.[26]

It is important for a city-state to cultivate the virtues of the public, its citizens. The cultivation of virtue benefits those who love wisdom.

While you commend moderation in individual men and believe that those who practice it enjoy the most secure existence and are the best among your fellow citizens, you do not think it fit to make the public practice it. And yet it is fitting for the public much more than individuals to cultivate the virtues and to shun vices. For a man who is godless and base may die before paying the penalty for his faults, but city-states, since they are immortal, must sooner or later submit to punishment at the hands both of men and of the gods. You should bear these considerations in mind and should not pay attention to those who gratify you for the moment, while caring nothing for the future.[27]

I recommend and exhort those who are younger and more vigorous than I to speak and write the kind of discourses by which they will turn the greatest city-states—those which have oppressed the rest—into the paths of virtue and justice, since when the affairs of Hellas are well, it follows that the affairs of those who love wisdom are much better.[28]

In the Evagoras, *Isocrates admonishes Nicocles, the king of Salamis on Cyprus we encountered above, to be as virtuous as his father, Evagoras. He should strive to be a better man than those around him.*

You must not be content if you happen to be already better than those around you. But you should be vexed if—endowed as you are by nature and distantly descended from Zeus and in our own time from a man of such distinguished virtue—you do not far surpass not only all others but also those who possess the same high station as yourself.

It is up to you not to fail in this. For if you persevere in the study of philosophy and make as great a progress as you have so far, you will quickly become the man that it is fitting you should be.[29]

The next passage comes from Isocrates' Busiris. *Well into the speech, Isocrates explains that the gods are by nature virtuous as are their offspring— and this contrary to how humans often speak of them.*

Now I, for my part, think that not only the gods but also their offspring have no share in any vice. Rather, they themselves are by nature endowed with all the virtues and have become for all mankind guides and teachers of the most honorable conduct. For it is foolish that we should attribute to the gods the responsibility for the good of our children, and yet suppose them not to worry about the good of their own. No—if anyone of us had the power to regulate human nature, he would not even allow his household slaves to be base.[30]

In the final selection from the Panathenaicus, *Isocrates describes the nature of the truly virtuous man.*

What man, then, do I call cultivated and educated since I exclude the arts and skills and sciences and natural capacities?

First, I include those who manage well the circumstances they encounter each day, and who possess a judgement that is accurate in meeting occasions as they arise and rarely misses the expedient course of action.

Next, I include those who are graceful and just in their interaction with all whom they associate, calmly and readily bearing with what is unpleasant or disagreeable in others and being themselves as easygoing and measured to their associates as it is possible to be.

Furthermore, I include those who always control their pleasures, and are not unduly overcome by their misfortunes, enduring them with courage and in a manner worthy of our common nature.

Finally, and most important of all, I include those who are not spoiled by success, deserting their true selves and becoming arrogant. Rather, they hold their ground steadfastly as intelligent men, not rejoicing in the good things that have come to them by means of luck but in those that through their own nature and intelligence are theirs from their birth.

Those who have a character that is in accord not with one of these things but with all of them, these, I contend, are wise and complete men—men who possess all the virtues.[31]

NOTES

[1] Note that aside from brief characterizations about what each orator thought and taught about aretē in the introduction to each at the beginning of the chapter, we do not offer summaries as we did with the philosophers since their presentation was far less systematic.

[2] Isocrates, *To Demonicus* 1.5-7.

[3] Ibid., 1.8-12.

[4] The maxims are found in ibid., 1.13-43. They have been offered here in the order they appear in the text. That said, we have not included all the maxims. The reader should be aware that, even though we have not employed ellipses, some text is missing.

[5] Compare the Roman satirist Juvenal's later (first or second century AD) recommendation that Romans ought to pray for "a sound mind in a sound body" (*mens sana in corpore sano*) rather than other desiderata (see *Satire* 10.356 ff.).

[6] Ibid., 1.45-46.

[7] Ibid., 1.48, 50-52.

[8] Isocrates, *To Nicocles* 2.8.

[9] Ibid., 2.11.

[10] Ibid., 2.12. "Wiser" here is related to practical wisdom.

[11] Ibid., 2.21.

[12] Ibid., 2.30.

[13] Ibid., 2.36

[14] Isocrates, *Nicocles, or the Cyprians* 3.46-47.

[15] Ibid., 3.50.

[16] Ibid., 3.57.

[17] Ibid., 3.59. The name or word for "vice" in Greek is *kakia*, a word that comes from *kakos*, a term that ranges in meaning from "bad" to "ugly" to "ignoble" and "base." As such, *kakia* is not only apparently bad, but, following from its name, it is truly or actually bad.

[18] Isocrates, *Panegyricus* 4.1-2.

[19] Ibid., 4.75, 84, 91.

[20] Ibid., 4.159.

[21] Isocrates, *Archidamus* 6.35-36.

[22] Ibid., 6.91.

[23] Isocrates, *Areopagiticus* 7.37-38.

[24] Ibid., 7.40. "Behaviors" (*ēthos*) could have also been given as manners, customs, habits, character.

[25] Ibid., 7.73-74.

[26] Isocrates, *On the Peace* 8.32, 63, 94.

[27] Ibid., 8.119-120.

[28] Ibid., 8.145.

[29] Isocrates, *Evagoras* 9.81.

[30] Isocrates, *Busiris* 11.41-42.

[31] Isocrates, *Panathenaicus* 12.30-32.

DEMOSTHENES

D EMOSTHENES (384-322 BC) WAS an orator and statesman from Athens. He wrote many speeches as an advocate in the law courts and as an Athenian statesman. He is most known for his "philippics" against the king of Macedon, Philip—against Philip's aggression in Thrace and northern Greece, and his ultimate invasion into central Greece, where he decisively defeated a coalition of Greeks headed by Athens and Thebes at the Battle of Chaeronea (338 BC).

For Demosthenes, "intelligence or understanding" is "the beginning of all virtue" and its "fulfillment is courage." He explains that "by the one it is judged what ought to be done, and by the other this judgment is preserved and carried to success." As such, aretē ranges from knowing what to do, to doing it. Courage is particularly important as the virtue that aids one in the ongoing battle to preserve freedom. In the end, courage and the many other "qualities that constitute virtue" lay claim to "ageless honors," and so to a reputation for excellence and an eventual memorial for the same. Other significant virtues are moderation and self-control. As for how one becomes virtuous, philosophy is essential in the process of educating "thought and understanding." Otherwise, it is worthwhile to be and study with great and noble men.

The following selections sample two of Demosthenes' epideictic orations, speeches that point out or demonstrate why one should be praised or blamed.[1]

IN THEIR OWN WORDS

The first set of passages comes from Demosthenes' Funeral Speech, *which was given after the Battle of Chaeronea.*

After the city-state decreed that those who repose in this tomb, having acquitted themselves as good and brave men in the war, should have a public funeral, and appointed me to the duty of delivering over them the customary speech, I began straightaway to study how they might receive their due tribute of praise.

But as I studied and searched my mind, the conclusion forced itself upon me that to speak as these dead deserve was one of those things that cannot be done. For since they scorned the love of life that is inborn in all men and chose rather to die nobly than to live and look upon Greece in misfortune, how can they have failed to leave behind them a record of virtue surpassing all power of words to express? Nevertheless, I propose to treat the theme in the same vein as those who have previously spoken in this place from time to time.

It is possible to infer that the city-state seriously concerns itself with those who die in battle both from these rites in general and, in particular, from this law in accordance with which it chooses the speaker at our public funerals. For knowing that among good men the acquisition of wealth and the enjoyment of the pleasures that go with living are scorned, and that their whole desire is for virtue and words of praise, the citizens believed we ought to honor them with such eulogies as would most certainly secure them in death the glory they had won while living.

Now, if it were my view that, of those qualities that constitute virtue, courage alone was their possession, I might praise this and be done with the speaking. But since it fell to their lot also to have been nobly born and strictly brought up and to have lived with lofty ideals so that they had every reason to be good men, I would be ashamed if someone discovered that I had passed over any of these topics. I shall begin, therefore, from the origins of their people and family.

The nobility of birth of these men has been acknowledged from time immemorial by all mankind. . . . Such is the pride of birth that belongs to the ancestors of these men throughout the ages.

As for courage and the other elements of virtue, I shrink from rehearsing the whole story, being on my guard for fear an untimely length will attach to my speech. Nevertheless, those facts as it is worthwhile even for those who are familiar with them to recall to mind and most profitable for the inexperienced to hear—events of great power to inspire and calling for no tedious length of speech—these I will try to rehearse in summary fashion.

For the ancestors of this present generation—both their fathers and those who bore the names of these men in the past, by which they are recognized by those of our people—never at any time wronged any man, whether Greek or barbarian. Instead, it was their pride, in addition to all their other good qualities, to be noble and good men, and to be supremely just, and in defending themselves to accomplish a long list of noble deeds. . . .

Moving on, Demosthenes recounts a variety of virtuous deeds, both mythical and historical, including most importantly the epic wars against the Persians.

Let no one think I have enumerated this list of achievements because I am at a loss regarding what to say about each of them. For even if I were the most helpless of all men in discovering what is fitting for me to say, the sheer virtue of the dead reveals what sentiments lie to hand and are easy to rehearse.

After calling to mind their noble birth and the magnificent things done by their ancestors, however, it is my intention with all speed to link my speech with the deeds of the dead, to the end that, just as their ancestors and the dead were akin in the flesh, so I may make the words of praise spoken over them to apply to both alike. . . .

From the beginning, these men were outstanding in all the activities that formed their schooling, engaging in the exercises that were appropriate for each stage of life, causing gratification to all who had claim to it—their parents, friends, and relations. Therefore, just as if recognizing footprints, the memory of those who were near and dear to them now turns to these men every hour in fond recollection, finding many a reminder of occasions when they knew in their hearts that these were young men of surpassing worth. Arrived at manhood they rendered their innate nobility known, not only to their fellow-citizens but to all men.

For of all virtue, I say, and I repeat it, the beginning is intelligence or understanding and the fulfillment is courage. By the one it is judged what ought to be done, and by the other this judgement is preserved and carried to success.

In both these qualities, these men were distinctly superior—for if there were ever a rising danger that touched all the Greeks, these men were the first to detect it. And time and again they challenged the rest to save the situation. This action is a demonstration of sound judgement joined with practical wisdom. . . .

Of necessity it happens, when a battle takes place, that the one side is beaten and the other victorious. But I would not hesitate to assert that in my judgement the men who die at the post of duty on either side do not share the defeat but are both alike victors. For the mastery among the survivors is decided as the deity disposes, but that which each was duty-bound to contribute to this end, every man who has kept his post in battle has done. But if, as a mortal being, he meets his doom, what he has suffered is an incident caused by chance, but in soul he remains unconquered by his opponents. It is my judgement, therefore, that we must thank the virtue of these men, along with the folly of our opponents, that our enemies did not set foot upon our land. . . .

I believe also that if someone were to ask those in the opposite ranks whether they thought they had won by their own deeds of virtue or by a startling and cruel turn of fortune and by the skill and daring of their own commander, not one of them would be so shameless or audacious as to claim credit for what happened. . . .

As for the other questions touching this campaign, everyone is at liberty to draw conclusions according to his judgement. Nonetheless, what has become manifest to all living men alike is this—that, in effect, the freedom of the whole Greek world was being preserved upon the souls of these men. At any rate, since fate removed them, not one of those remaining has made a stand against the foe. And while I desire that my words may be free from offence, it seems to me that if one should declare that the virtue of these men was the very life of Greece, he would speak the truth. . . .

With excellent reason one might declare them to be now seated beside the gods below, possessing the same rank as the brave men who have preceded them in the Islands of the Blessed. For though no man has been there to see or has brought back this report concerning them, yet those whom the living have assumed to be worthy of honors in the world above, these, we believe, basing our assumption on their fame, receive the same honors also in the world beyond.

After challenging the parents and others to endure bravely their grief as the fallen would have done, Demosthenes declares the excellence of what they have left behind—a memorial to virtue.

It is a grievous thing for fathers and mothers to be deprived of their children and in their old age to lack the care of those who are nearest and dearest to them. Yes—but it is a proud privilege to see them as the possessors of ageless honors, and to behold the memorial of their virtue erected by the people, and to hear them judged deserving of sacrifices and games for all future time. It is painful for children to be orphaned. Yes—but it is a beautiful thing to be the heir of a father's good reputation and honor. And of this pain we shall find the deity to be the cause, to whom human beings must naturally yield. But of the honor and moral excellence, the source is found in the choice of those who willed to die nobly.[2]

The second set of passages come from Demosthenes' Erotic Essay —which is nothing like what it may sound. Rather, in it Demosthenes praises Epicrates, the young man who is dear to him and whom he especially cherishes in terms of eros.

Well, since you wish to hear the essay, I will bring it out and read it aloud. But first you must understand its purpose.

The writer's wish is to praise Epicrates, whom he thought to be the most charming young man in the city, though there were many fine gentlemen among those of his own age, and to surpass him more in understanding than in beauty of person. Observing also that, generally speaking, most erotic compositions attach shame rather than honor to those about whom they are written, he has taken precautions that this would not happen in his case, and he has written only what he says he is convinced of by his judgement, believing that an honest lover would neither do anything shameful nor request it.

Now, that part of my essay which you may find to be the most erotic, so to speak, is on this topic, but the rest of it in part praises the young man himself and in part counsels him about his education and his plan for life. . . .

When I have described the good qualities you possess, I hope that at one and the same time I will prove you to be worthy of admiration and myself not senseless if I love you, being what you are. Also, in offering you the advice that is most urgently needed, I believe I will demonstrate proof of my own goodwill and furnish a basis for mutual friendship. . . .

Cherishing such hopes, I enter upon my theme. All men would agree with me, I believe, that it is of the utmost importance for young men of your age to possess beauty relative to appearance, moderation relative to the soul, and courage relative to both, and consistently to possess grace relative to speech. As for these two kinds of qualities, natural and acquired, good fortune has so generously endowed you with nature's gifts that you consistently enjoy distinction and admiration, and the other kind you are bringing to such perfection through your own diligence that no fair-minded person could have fault to find with you.

And yet what should he possess who is worthy of the greatest praise? Must he not manifestly be loved by the gods and among men be admired for some qualities on his own account, for others because of his good fortune? Now the longer list of your virtuous qualities it will perhaps be fitting to describe summarily later on, but the praise I have to utter for each of the gifts of fortune I will now try to declare with truthfulness.

Demosthenes describes Epicrates' bodily beauty. His skin. His face. The gods missed nothing, he says. And one can detect his virtue merely by his glance.

As for his moderation and self-control, it is my privilege to pass the finest of compliments—namely, that though such youthfulness readily invites scandal, it has been your lot to be praised instead. For so far from overstepping the mark, you have chosen to live more sensibly than is expected of your years. . . .

Personally, I think you deserve to be eulogized even more for this reason, that, while other young men think it one of the impossible things to please men of every type, you have so surpassed these as to have risen superior to all the difficult and troublesome people, allowing the others no reason even for suspecting faulty relations with any and overcoming your annoyance with them by the adaptability of your manners. . . . And this is a most unmistakable proof of your virtue. For no one finds himself disappointed regarding favors from you which it is just and fair to ask. But no one is permitted even to hope for such liberties that would lead to shame. . . .

Turning now to courage—for it will not do to omit this either.

Demosthenes describes Epicrates' courage in various athletic games, particularly in chariot racing or "dismounting," an event that was only open to citizens.

Certainly, your father and mother and the rest of your kinsmen are rightly envied because you so far surpass those of your own age in virtue. But still more enviable are those whom you . . . select to be your friends, judging them worthy of your companionship.

I do not know whether to call these young men admirers or unique for their sound judgement. For, as it seems to me, fortune, scorning base men and wishing to arouse the minds of the noble, at the very beginning made your nature beautiful—not for a life of pleasure, to be deceived thereby, but for a life of service toward virtue in order to be happy.

Accordingly, I shall leave this topic and now endeavor to counsel you on the means of rendering your life still more worthy of esteem. . . .

Now you must . . . seek to discover what is of supreme consequence in human affairs, and why it is that turning out well would do us the most good, but turning out badly would hurt us most along life's pathway. For it requires no proof that upon this factor we must expend the greatest care, which more than anything else possesses the power to tip the scale to one side or the other.

Now of the powers residing in human beings, we will find that intelligence or understanding leads all the rest, and that philosophy alone can correctly educate and train it. I think you should participate in this study and not balk at or flee from the labors involved in it. You should do so reflecting that through idleness and laziness even quite superficial things become difficult, while through persistence and diligence none of the worthwhile things is unattainable. And consider that of all things the most irrational is to be ambitious for wealth, bodily strength, and such things, and for their sake to submit to many hardships, all prizes that are perishable. . . . [It is also irrational] not to aim at the improvement of the mind, which has supervision over all other powers, abides continually with those who possess it, and guides the whole of life. . . .

Demosthenes explains how being and studying with a great man improves one in terms of virtue.

You may infer this [*rule of association*] to be true . . . particularly by examining those men who have been notable before your time. You will hear first that Pericles, who is thought to have far surpassed all men of his age in intellectual grasp, associated with Anaxagoras of Clazomenae, and only after being his student, he acquired this power of judgement. You will next discover that Alcibiades, though his natural disposition was far inferior in respect to virtue, and it was his pleasure to behave himself now arrogantly, now obsequiously, now licentiously, yet, as a fruit of his association with Socrates, he corrected many errors of his life and over the rest drew a veil of oblivion by the greatness of his later achievements.

But not to spend our time rehearsing old examples while others are available closer to our own times, you will discover that Timotheus was judged worthy of the greatest reputation and numerous honors, not because of his pursuits as a younger man but because of his achievements after he had studied with Isocrates. You will discover also that Archytas of Tarentum became ruler of his city and managed its affairs so admirably and so considerately as to spread the record of that achievement to all mankind—yet at first, he was despised, and he owed his remarkable progress to studying with Plato. . . .

So, then, I have eagerly exhorted you so that our city may enjoy virtue such as yours, and so that you may enjoy the honors that this deserves.

I do not think that it will be in your power to live as fortune decrees, but that the city-state will appoint you to oversee some department of her business. And in proportion as your natural gifts are the more conspicuous, she will judge you worthy of greater responsibilities and will all the sooner desire to test your abilities. The wise plan, therefore, is to train your mind and judgment so that you may not go wrong when that day comes.[3]

NOTES

[1] The translations that follow are largely those of Norman W. Dewitt (1949), though with significant modifications relative to this book.

[2] *Funeral Speech* 1-7, 12, 16-21, 23, 34, 36-37.

[3] *Erotic Essay* 1-2, 6, 8-9, 17, 19-20, 22, 31-32, 34, 36-38, 45-46, 55.

DIO CHRYSOSTOM

D IO CHRYSOSTOM (C. 40-112 AD) WAS an orator and philosopher from Prusa (Bursa, Turkey). Known as Dio "the Golden-Mouthed" (Chrysostom), he originally practiced rhetoric in Rome until he was banished in 82 AD for his opposition to the emperor Domitian. Thereafter, Dio lived and taught as a Cynic, wandering throughout the Roman Empire and even beyond. When the exile was lifted, he focused once again on writing and speech making.

As with other Cynics, aretē was important to Dio's way of thinking and plan of life. For most people, he suggests, there is a gap between what is praised (virtue) and what is actually preferred (other things). The truth is that happiness is not pleasant things but "excellence of character" and virtue. Such excellence and virtue may be cultivated by enduring hardship (something that the person of noble character welcomes), or with the help of teaching and the encouragement of sensible and wise individuals. Virtuous men and women should both care for themselves and for others, including urging others on to virtue. For kings (though the same is true for everyone), virtue is absolutely necessary—particularly the four cardinal virtues of practical wisdom, courage, moderation, and justice. Good reputation and wealth, Dio says, typically accompany virtue.

The following selections come from a handful of Dio Chrysostom's many discourses.[1]

IN THEIR OWN WORDS

We begin with the first discourse, On Kingship, *in which Dio states that virtue is helped along with the spoken encouragement of the sensible and wise person.*

Unfortunately, skill and proficiency in music cannot provide perfect healing and complete relief for defect of character. No indeed! To quote the poet: "God did not even grant this boon to Asclepius' sons." No, it is only the spoken word of the sensible and wise man, such as were most men of earlier times, that can prove a competent and perfect guide for and helper of a man endowed with a ready to obey and good nature, and can lead him toward all excellence by fitting encouragement and direction.[2]

From the second discourse, On Kingship, *Dio counsels one to always be thinking about or pursuing virtue and great achievements.*

Whether he is drinking or singing, the high-minded and kingly man should never utterly forget virtue and glorious deeds, but he himself should always be engaged in some great and some admirable action or recalling deeds of that kind.[3]

In his third discourse, On Kingship, *Dio declares that virtue is "an absolute necessity" for a king—particularly, practical wisdom, justice, moderation, and courage. Happiness is not pleasantries but "excellence of character" and virtue.*

This, it seems to me, is exactly Homer's view as well. For, after speaking of the ideal king, he concludes by saying, "And the people beneath him flourish with excellence." Such a king considers excellence or virtue a fair possession for others but an absolute necessity for himself.

Who, in fact, must exercise greater practical wisdom than he who is concerned with the weightiest matters? Who a keener sense of justice than he who is above the law? Who a more rigorous moderation than he to whom all things are permissible? Who a stouter courage than he upon whom the safety of everything depends? And who takes greater delight in the works of virtue than he who has all men as spectators and witnesses of his own soul, so that nothing he may do can ever be hidden any more than the sun can run its course in darkness (for, in bringing all other things to light, it reveals itself first)?[4]

The good ruler alone holds that happiness consists not in pleasant feelings or living but much rather in noble goodness. It is found with virtue and freewill instead of necessity. To him patient endurance does not mean hardship but safety. He increases his pleasures by toil, thereby getting more enjoyment out of them, while habit lightens his toil. To him "useful" and "pleasurable" are interchangeable terms.[5]

The good ruler regards virtue as holiness and vice as utter impiety, being firmly persuaded that not only those who rob temples or blaspheme the gods are sinners and accursed but, much more so, the cowardly, the unjust, the licentious, the fools, and, in general, those who act contrary to the power and will of the gods.[6]

In his eighth discourse, Diogenes, or on Virtue, *Dio observes that men of noble character welcome the challenges of hardships as the occasion for winning "happiness and virtue." In it, Diogenes the Cynic is speaking.*

"But the noble man holds his hardships to be his greatest antagonists. And with them he is ever accustomed to battle day and night—not to win a sprig of parsley as so many goats might do, nor for a bit of wild olive, or of pine, but to win happiness and virtue throughout all the days of his life. And not merely when the Eleans make proclamation, or the Corinthians, or the Thessalian assembly. He is afraid of none of those opponents, nor does he pray to draw another antagonist, but he challenges them one after another, grappling with hunger and cold, withstanding thirst, and revealing no weakness even though he must endure the lash or give his body to be cut or burned. Hunger, exile, loss of reputation, and the like have no terrors for him. No—he holds them as mere trifles, and while in their very grip, the perfect man is often as sportive as boys are with their dice and their colored balls."[7]

In the Olympic Discourse, or On Man's First Conception of God, *Dio makes the following general observation about the relationship between wealth, reputation, and virtue.*

Not only do virtue and reputation accompany wealth, as we are told, but wealth likewise, and of necessity, accompanies virtue.[8]

In the thirteenth oration, In Athens, about His Banishment, *Dio contends that it is a great thing to find someone who will teach the ways of virtue—far better than any wealth or delightful thing.*

And so it came about that I too endeavored to talk to the Romans when they had summoned me and invited me to speak. But I did not take them by twos and threes in wrestling schools and cloistered walks—for it was not possible to meet them in this manner in that city. Rather, when a great number had gathered in one place, I would tell them that they needed a better and more carefully planned education if they were ever to be genuinely happy—and not merely in the opinion of the majority, as was now the case.

I told them that if anyone should win them to this view and take them in charge and teach them that not even one of those things is a good to which they devoted themselves and for which they strove with all their zeal to acquire, in the belief that, the more they acquired, the better and happier their life would be. I said, rather, that they would be better off if they wholeheartedly practiced moderation, courage, and justice, and took them into their souls—if they secured from somewhere teachers who taught these things and all the other things too, not caring whether the men were Greeks or Romans, or, for that matter, if there is among the Scythians or the Indians a man who teaches the things of which I have spoken . . . a teacher, I mean, who would be able to rid them of licentiousness and greediness and all such infirmities. . . .

They should lead that teacher to their homes. . . . And after establishing him on their acropolis, they should issue an edict commanding all the young men to meet with him regularly and associate with him, and equally the older men too. They should do this until all of them—having come to long for justice eagerly and having learned to despise gold and silver and ivory, and rich food, too, and perfume and those things belonging to Aphrodite—will thereafter live happy lives, being masters first and foremost of themselves and then of other human beings.

For only then, I continued, will your city be great and strong and truly imperial, since at present its greatness arouses distrust and is not very secure. For, I said, in proportion as courage, justice, and moderation increase among you, in that degree there will be less silver and gold and furniture of ivory and of amber. And fewer things of crystal and citron-wood and ebony. And a smaller number of women's adornments and embroideries and dyes of many hues. In short, all the things that are now considered in your city precious and worth fighting for, you will need in smaller quantities. And when you have reached the summit of virtue, you won't need them at all. The houses in which you live will be smaller and better, and you will not have and support so great a throng of idle and utterly useless slaves. The most paradoxical thing of all is that the more god-fearing and pious you become, the less frankincense and fragrant offerings and garlands there will be among you. And you will offer fewer sacrifices and at less expense. And the whole multitude that is now being supported in your city will be much smaller, while the entire city, like a ship that has been lightened, will ride higher and be much more buoyant and safer.[9]

In the Rhodian Discourse, *Dio offers an interesting analogy relative to how citizens should behave for the well-being of their city-state.*

You Rhodians should be even more jealous about your city and to be indifferent to nothing that takes place here. And if you have this spirit in everything you do, perhaps men will think that you are in no way worse than your ancestors. For that you do preserve your character in your present situation, and hold fast to your role of virtue is, in my opinion at least, an admirable thing.

An apt illustration is found, I think, in the conduct of men on board a ship at sea: when a storm strikes them or a hurricane, not even the most licentious of them is to be seen doing anything shameful. Instead, they are all giving their undivided attention to the sailing. By contrast, in fair weather recklessness prevails among both the sailors and the passengers—even if they do not indulge in immoderation. In the same way, I believe that war usually rouses and sways even the more pathetic of men. But in such peaceful and quiet times as these, it is the part of the best men not to drift into any shameful or disorderly practices.[10]

In his address To the People of Alexandria, *Dio explains the difference between being praised for one's virtue versus what one possesses or what one lives near.*

Perhaps these words of mine are pleasing to your ears and you imagine that you are being praised by me, as you are by all the rest who are always flattering you. But I was praising water and soil and harbors and place—and everything except yourselves.

For where have I said that you are sensible and moderate and just? Was it not quite the opposite? For when we praise human beings, it should be for their good order, gentleness, concord, constitutional order, for following those who give good counsel, and for not being always in search of pleasures.

But arrivals and departures of vessels, and superiority in size of population, in merchandise, and in ships—these are appropriate subjects for praise in the case of a fair, a harbor, or a marketplace, but not of a city. No—if a man speaks in praise of water, he is not praising men but wells. If he talks about a good climate, he does not mean that the people are good but the land. If he speaks of fish, he is not praising the city—how absurd!—but a sea, a lake, or a stream. Yet if someone eulogizes the Nile, you Alexandrians are as elated as if you yourselves were rivers flowing from Ethiopia.

Indeed, it is safe to say that most other people also are delighted by such things and count themselves blessed if they dwell, as Homer puts it, "on a tree-clad isle" or one that is "deep-soiled" or on a mainland "of abundant pasture, rich in sheep" or nearby "shadowy mountains" or "fountains of translucent waters,"—none of which is a personal attribute of those men themselves.

That said, when it comes to human virtue, they care not at all, not even in their dreams![11]

In the Second Tarsic, *Dio states that competition in virtue—justice, friendship, goodwill, humane kindness—is good.*

To compete with the whole world on behalf of justice and virtue, and to take the initiative in friendship and harmony, and in these ways to surpass and prevail over all others—this is the noblest of all victories, as well as the safest and most secure.

But to seek to outdo everyone by any and every means in a fight is suitable to blooded gamecocks rather than men. . . .

On the other hand, goodwill and a reputation for superiority in virtue and humane kindness—those are true goods; those are the objects worthy of competition and serious regard.[12]

In On Concord in Nicaea upon the Cessation of Civil Strife, *Dio proposes that the founders of a city desire the inhabitants to possess various virtues, as well as other good things.*

It is fitting that those whose city was founded by gods should maintain peace and concord and friendship toward one another. For it is disgraceful if they do not prove to be extremely happy and dear to the gods and to some extent superior to the others in good fortune, desiring, as they must, to show birth to be something reflecting truth and not just a false and empty term. For founders, kinsmen, and progenitors who are gods wish for their own people to possess nothing—neither beauty of land nor abundance of crops nor multitude of inhabitants—so much as moderation, virtue, lawful government, and honor for the good citizens and dishonor for the bad.[13]

Dio explores what we may call the "preference gap" in his discourse On Virtue, *presented here nearly in its entirety. It is that gap which exists between what one praises and celebrates and what one actually prefers. He goes on to explore the value of living virtuously.*

It seems to me a fact hard to explain that people praise and admire one set of things yet aim at and have seriously pursued a different set. For virtually everyone praises and calls "divine" and "august" such things as courage and justice and practical wisdom and, in short, every virtue. Moreover, whomever they believe to be, or to have been, characterized by such virtues, or nearly so, him they admire and celebrate in song. And certain ones they represent as gods and others as heroes—Heracles, for example, the Dioscuri, Theseus, Achilles, and all the demigods, as they are called. And whomever they assume to be like those beings, they one and all are ready to obey and to serve, no matter what orders he may give, and they are ready to appoint as their king and ruler and to make the guardian of their possessions any man whom they supposed to be really prudent and righteous and wise and, in a word, a good man.

Therefore, in this respect no one could censure them as not perceiving that virtue is something august and precious and all-important.

Even so, they really desire any and everything in preference to becoming good. And they busy themselves with everything rather than with the problem of becoming moderate and sensible and just and excellent men—able to direct themselves well, to manage a household well, to rule a city well, to bear well either wealth or poverty, to behave well toward friends and kinsmen, to care for parents according to custom and with justice, and to serve the gods with piety.

But some busy themselves with farming, some with trading. Some are devoted to military affairs, some to the medical profession. Some acquire a thorough knowledge of carpentry or of shipbuilding, some of playing the lyre or the flute or of shoemaking or wrestling. Some devote their whole attention to gaining a reputation as clever speakers in the assembly or in the law court, some to becoming strong in body. And yet the traders, farmers, soldiers, physicians, builders, lyre players, flutists, athletic trainers, yes, and even the orators, as they are called, and those who have great strength of body—all these one would find to be wretched and unfortunate in many, or indeed in almost all, instances.

On the other hand, if their soul becomes sensible or rational and their mind really good, and if they are able to manage successfully their own affairs and those of their neighbours too, these men will necessarily also lead happy lives, having shown themselves to be lawful, having obtained a good spirit to guard them, and being dear to the gods. . . .

Why, then, do not those who desire to be happy do their best to make themselves happy instead of devoting their entire attention to things that allow for bad and wretched lives?

Yet without flute and lyre players and shoemakers and athletic trainers and orators and physicians it is not impossible for men to live very noble and lawful lives—and, I suppose, even without farmers and builders. At any rate the Scythians, who are nomads, even though they neither have houses nor sow seed nor plant trees and vines, they are by no means prevented from playing their part as citizens with justice and in accord with law. Yet without law and justice men cannot avoid living badly and in much more savage fashion than the wild beasts. Moreover, where shoemakers and farmers and builders are of inferior quality, no serious harm results on that account—it is merely that the shoes are inferior and the wheat and barley scarcer. On the other hand, where rulers and judges and laws are inferior, the affairs of those people are in poor shape and their life is more unfortunate, and factions, injustices, deeds of arrogance, and impiety flourish in abundance with them.

And there is this point. When one is not himself a shoemaker it is profitable to purchase shoes from another person, and when one does not understand building, to hire another person for that work, and when one is not a farmer, to purchase grain and pulse. Even so, when one is himself unjust, it is not profitable to get his justice from another, nor, when one lacks wisdom and does not know what he ought to do and what he ought to refrain from doing, to be constantly regretting every single act and counting on another person for knowledge.

In addition to all the other considerations, he who needs money or clothing or housing or anything else not only knows that fact but also seeks to get these things from those who have them. By contrast, he who has no sense does not even know this very fact—that he has no sense. Instead, he claims to be sufficient, competent, and he obstinately persists in his senseless folly. Everything he does or says is thoughtless, and he denies that he is unjust or foolish or licentious. Rather, he insists that he is ever so competent in these matters, even though he has never paid any attention to them or learned anything as far as those things are concerned.

In fact, these men do not even believe in the existence of a knowledge according to which they will know what they should do or what they should not do and how they will live correctly. No, they believe that the laws are sufficient for them for that purpose, the laws on the statute books. But how they are to obey the laws and voluntarily do what those laws prescribe is a matter to which they give no serious thought.

And yet how is he any less a thief—the one who refrains from thieving out of fear yet nevertheless approves and does not despise and condemn the business—how is he any less a thief than those who actually commit theft? . . . Besides, such persons require the presence of many to threaten and restrain them since they are not able by themselves to refrain from their misdeeds. But even when at home, they are men of thievish disposition. Still, even though they are of such character, they choose the lawgivers and punish the lawless—just as if unmusical people were put in the position to choose the musicians, or as if those who know nothing of surveying and geometry were to choose those who survey land.

And here is an indication of the poor condition of humankind. If men were to do away with the laws, and immunity were to be granted to strike one another, to commit murder, to steal the property of one's neighbours, to commit adultery, and to plunder others, then who would refrain from these deeds, and who would, without the slightest scruple or hesitation, be willing to commit all manner of crimes? For even now we are no less living

unwittingly with thieves and kidnappers and adulterers and joining with them in the activities of citizenship. And in this respect,
we are no better than the wild beasts—for they too, if they are
frightened by men or dogs set to guard against them, refrain from
thieving.[14]

Finally, in On Envy, *Dio suggests that the virtuous man will not only
take care of himself, but he will also care for others and urge them on to
virtue.*

The man about whom I speak will strive to watch over himself with
dignity and with steadfastness, never deserting his post of duty but
always honoring and promoting virtue and moderation and trying
to lead all men thereto. He does so partly by persuasion and exhortation, and partly by issuing abuse and reproach in the hope that he
may thereby rescue someone from senseless folly and from base desires and from a lack of self-discipline and soft living. Privately, he
takes them aside one by one, and he also admonishes them in
groups every time he finds the opportunity—"With gentle words
at times, at others, harsh"—until, I imagine, he ends up spending
his life in caring for human beings.[15]

NOTES

[1] The translations that follow, though with occasional modifications, are
largely those of J.W. Cohoon (1932, 1939), H. Lamar Crosby (1946, 1951), and
Cohoon and Crosby together (1940).

[2] Dio Chrysostom, *On Kingship, Oration* 1.8.

[3] Dio Chrysostom, *On Kingship, Oration* 2.31.

[4] Dio Chrysostom, *On Kingship, Oration* 3.9-11.

[5] Ibid 3.123-124.

[6] Ibid 3.53.

[7] Dio Chrysostom, *Diogenes, or on Virtue* 8.15-16.

[8] Dio Chrysostom, *Olympic Discourse, or On Man's First Conception of God* 12.11.

[9] Dio Chrysostom, *In Athens, about His Banishment* 13.31-35.

[10] Dio Chrysostom, *Rhodian Discourse* 31.164-165.

[11] Dio Chrysostom, *To the People of Alexandria* 32.37-38.

[12] Dio Chrysostom, *Second Tarsic* 34.45; 48.

[13] Dio Chrysostom, *On Concord in Nicaea upon the Cessation of Civil Strife* 22 (or 39).2-3.

[14] Dio Chrysostom, *On Virtue* 52 (or 69) 1-9.

[15] Dio Chrysostom, *On Envy* 61 (or 77-78).38.

JULIAN THE EMPEROR

J ULIAN (C. 332-363 AD) WAS THE emperor of the Roman Empire from 361 AD to the year of his death. Dear to his heart from an early age, however, was the study of literature and philosophy in which he was educated by some of the best minds of the day. In time, he used his wide-ranging knowledge to author a variety of writings, some of which appear below (the source of the selections[1]).

Though he was brought up in the Christian religion, he eventually left the Church to return to Rome's (and Greece's) traditional religion. It is for this reason that his name is often given as "Julian the Apostate." Significantly for him, this traditional religion was part of an all-encompassing philosophical system, Neoplatonism, which, he believed, was incompatible with Christianity.

In agreement with Plotinus, the man primarily responsible for Neoplatonism, aretē plays a leading role in Julian's approach to the good life. For him virtue is the most beautiful thing. The goal of virtue is to "tend to what is noble." It is that which all the philosophers have pursued, he observes. To be virtuous is to be well-born and wealthy. It is the basis of friendship. We learn about virtue by means of experience. Moreover, one who wishes to cultivate virtue must submit to God and perform the traditional forms of worship.

IN THEIR OWN WORDS

The first selection is from Julian's letter to Alypius, the brother of Caesarius. In it he declares that the goal of all virtue is that which is fine and noble.

Regarding your administration of affairs, inasmuch as you study to act in all cases both energetically and humanely, I am well pleased with it. For to blend mildness and moderation with courage and force, and to exercise the former toward the most reasonable men and the latter implacably in the case of the wicked for their regeneration, is, I am convinced, a task that calls for no slight natural endowment and virtue.

I pray that you may ever hold fast to these objectives, and that you may combine them both so that they tend to what is noble. Not without reason did the most eloquent of the ancient writers believe that this is the goal set for all the virtues.

May you continue in health and happiness as long as possible, my well-beloved and most dear brother![2]

The next selections come from The Heroic Deeds of the Emperor Constantius, or On Kingship. *Julian urges the one who wishes to cultivate virtue to submit to God.*

To this God, I say every man, whether he is a private citizen or a king, should entrust the reins of his life . . . For it is senseless and arrogant indeed for those who cultivate virtue not to submit to God once and for all, as far as possible. For we must believe that this above all else is what God approves. Again, no man must neglect the traditional form of worship or lightly regard this method of paying honor to the higher power, but rather consider that to be virtuous is to be scrupulously devout. For piety is the child of justice, and that justice is a characteristic of the more divine type of soul is obvious to all who discuss such matters.[3]

Julian goes on to observe that Socrates would only praise those rulers who delighted in virtue. All wise men praise virtue.

For I have observed that Socrates the Athenian — you know the man by hearsay and that his reputation for wisdom was proclaimed aloud by the Pythian oracle — I say I have observed that he did not praise that sort of thing, nor would he admit that they are happy and blessed who are masters of a great territory and many nations, with many Greeks too among them, and still more numerous and powerful barbarians. . . . Therefore, he never praised Xerxes or any other king of Persia or Lydia or Macedonia, and not even a Greek general, except for only a very few, whomsoever he knew to delight in virtue, and to cherish courage with moderation, and to love practical wisdom with justice. But those whom he observed to be cunning, or merely clever, or generals and nothing more, or ingenious, or able, though each one could lay claim to only one small part of virtue . . . these too he would not praise without reserve. . . .

The sum and substance of all the speeches of wise and inspired men is the praise of virtue. And virtue, they say, is implanted in the soul and makes it happy and kingly, yes, by Zeus, and statesman-like and gifted with true generalship, and generous and truly wealthy.[4]

Julian further explains that when one shares his goodness with another, one's virtue is not diminished, just as the sun's light is not less when the sun shines.

No one ever takes away the light of the sun from the sun—not even the moon when in their meetings she oversteps his wheeling body, nor when she takes his rays to herself, and often, as the saying goes, turns midday into night. Nor is he deprived of his light when he illumines the moon in her station opposite to himself and shares with her his own nature. Nor when he fills with light and day this great and wonderful universe. Just so, a good man who gives a share of his goodness to another never appears to have less virtue relative to the amount shared.[5]

Agreeing with the Athenian from Plato's Laws, *Julian suggests that he who has virtue is well-born and wealthy.*

So divine and all-noble is that possession, and most true is the saying of the Athenian stranger, whoever that inspired man may have been: "All the gold beneath the earth and above ground is too little to give in exchange for virtue." Let us, therefore, now boldly call virtue's possessor wealthy—yes, and I would say well-born also, and the only king among them all, if anyone would assent to this.

For as noble birth is better than a lowly ancestry, so virtue is better than a character not in every way admirable.[6]

The next selections come from the Consolation upon the Departure of Sallust. *In the first, Julian recognizes the virtue that formed the basis of his friendship with Sallust.*

I constantly feel the lack of your company and call to mind the friendship that we pledged to each other, that friendship that we ever cemented afresh—based as it was, first and foremost, on virtue, and secondly on the obligations that you continually conferred on me and I on you. Not by oaths or by any such ties did we ratify it, like Theseus and Peirithous, but by being of the same mind and purpose.[7]

If we do not also imitate them, it is not right to praise the Homeric heroes. Nor is it right to suppose that whereas God was always ready to assist them, he will disregard the men of our day if he sees that they are striving to achieve that virtue for which he favored the others.[8]

The next selections come from Julian's Letter to Themistius the Philosopher. *In the first, he recognizes that happiness requires more than virtue—at least for one engaged in public affairs.*

For in public life, it is neither virtue alone nor a wise policy that is paramount, but to a far greater degree Fortune holds sway throughout and compels events to go as she wills.

Indeed Chrysippus, though in other ways he seems a wise man and to have been honored rightly as such, yet in ignoring Fortune and Chance and all other such external causes that happen to block the path of men of affairs, he uttered paradoxes wholly at variance with facts about which the past teaches us clearly by countless examples. For instance, shall we call Cato a fortunate and blessed man? Or shall we say that Dio of Sicily was happy? It is true that they probably did not worry about death. Even so, they did care a lot about not leaving unfinished the undertakings that they had begun, and to secure their objectives there is nothing they would not have endured.

In that they were disappointed. And I admit that they endured their lot with grace and dignity, as we learn, and derived no small consolation from their virtue. But no one could call them happy, observing that they had failed in all those noble enterprises—unless, perhaps, according to the Stoic conception of happiness.

And regarding that same Stoic conception, we must admit that to be applauded and to be counted blessed are two quite different things. And that if every living thing naturally reaches out for happiness, it is better to make it our aim to be congratulated for being blessed than to be applauded for being virtuous.

Still, happiness that trusts in Fortune is very rarely secure. And yet men who are engaged in public life cannot, as the saying goes, so much as breath unless she is on their side.[9]

Julian goes on to emphasize the fact that knowing God requires virtue.

Who, I ask, ever found salvation through the conquests of Alexander? What city was ever more wisely governed because of them, what individual improved? Many indeed you might find whom those conquests enriched—but not one whom they made wiser or more moderate than he was by nature, if indeed they have not made him more insolent and arrogant. By contrast, all who now find their salvation in philosophy owe it to Socrates. And I am not the only person to perceive this fact and to express it, for Aristotle, it seems, did so before me when he said that he had just as much right to be proud of his treatise on the gods as the conqueror of the Persian empire. And I think he was perfectly correct in that conclusion. For military success is due to courage and good fortune more than anything else or, let us say, if you wish, to intelligence as well, though of the common everyday sort. But to conceive true opinions about God is an achievement that not only requires perfect virtue, but one might well hesitate whether it be proper to call one who attains to this a man or a god. For if the saying is true that it is the nature of everything to become known to those who have an affinity with it, then he who comes to know the essential nature of God would naturally be considered divine.[10]

In his oration To the Uneducated Cynics, *Julian recognizes the essential unity of those philosophers who pursue truth and virtue.*

Now it has become evident that Plato was not pursuing one aim and Diogenes [of Sinope, the Cynic] another, but their end was one and the same . . . And now are we to ignore all this evidence and without further question fence off from one another and force apart men whom the passion for truth, the scorn of opinion, and unanimity in zeal for virtue have joined together?[11]

In the Hymn to the Mother of the Gods, *Julian points out the beauty of virtue and piety by way of comparison with a ceremonial practice (the cutting of the tree). He prays for virtue and good fortune, among other goods.*

Thereupon, in their proper order, all the other ceremonies take place. Some of them are celebrated with the secret ritual of the mysteries, but others by a ritual that can be told to all.

For instance, the cutting of the tree belongs to the story of Gallus and not to the mysteries at all. But it has been taken over by them, I think, because the gods wished to teach us in symbolic fashion that we must pluck the fairest fruits from the earth—namely, virtue and piety—and offer them to the goddess to be the symbol of our well-ordered constitution here on earth. For the tree grows from the soil, but it strives upward as though to reach the upper air, and it is beautiful to behold and gives us shade in the heat, and casts before us and bestows on us its fruits as a boon. Such is its superabundance of generative life. Accordingly, the ritual enjoins on us, who by nature belong to the heavens but have fallen to earth, to reap the harvest of our constitution here on earth—namely, virtue and piety—and then to strive upward to the goddess of our forefathers, to her who is the principle of all life.[12]

But how shall I conclude my discourse? Surely with this hymn to the Great Goddess:

O Mother of gods and men, you who are . . . enthroned with Zeus. . . . O life-giving goddess who are the counsel and the

providence and the creator of our souls. . . . O you who give all good
things to the intellectual gods and fill this sensible world with all
things, and with all the rest, you give us all things good!

Grant to all men happiness, and that chief happiness of all, the
knowledge of the gods. . . . And for myself, as fruit of my worship
of you, grant that I may have true knowledge regarding the dogmas
about the gods. Make me perfect in theurgy, the divine work. And
in all that I undertake, in the affairs of the state and the army, grant
me virtue and good fortune, and that the close of my life may be
painless and glorious in the good hope that it is to you, the gods,
that I journey![13]

In the Misopogon, *Julian suggests that a people's morals—virtue and
other good qualities—are passed down even as plants transmit their own
qualities to their descendants. The Greeks have many good qualities, but
the Athenians among them are remarkable for them.*

Now since this was the conduct of Antiochus, I have no right to be
angry with his descendants when they emulate their founder or
him who gave his name to the city.

For just as in the case of plants it is natural that their qualities
should be transmitted for a long time, or rather that, in general, the
succeeding generation should resemble its ancestors, so too in the
case of human beings it is natural that the morals of descendants
should resemble those of their ancestors.

I myself, for instance, have found that the Athenians are the
most ambitious for honor and the most humane of all the Greeks.
And indeed, I have observed that these qualities exist in an admirable degree among all the Greeks, and I can say for them that more
than all others, they love the gods and are hospitable to strangers. I
mean all the Greeks generally—but among them the Athenians
above all, as I can testify.

And if they still preserve in their characters the image of their
ancient virtue, surely it is natural that the same thing should be true
of the Syrians also—and the Arabs and Celts and Thracians and
Paeonians and those who dwell between the Thracians and the

Paeonians, I mean the Mysians on the very banks of the Danube, from whom my own family is derived, a people wholly uncultivated, austere, awkward, without charm, and immovable in their judgments (qualities all of which are proofs of a terrible lack of cultivation).[14]

In his seventh oration, To the Cynic Heracleios, Julian acknowledges the virtue of Dionysus and Heracles. Later he suggests that, thanks to his teachers, he has truly taken a shorter path to virtue, whereas the aspiring (though somewhat false) Cynic Heracleios' "short path" was no path at all.

I have heard many people say that Dionysus was a human being because he was born of Semele, and that he became a god through his knowledge of theurgy and the mysteries, and like our lord Heracles for his kingly virtue, he was taken up to Olympus by his father Zeus.[15]

For you, Heracleios, have neither been well educated, nor did fate bestow on you such a guide to the poets as I had—I mean this philosopher now present, Maximus of Ephesus.

And later, I arrived at the threshold of philosophy to be initiated therein by the teaching of Iamblichus, whom I consider superior to all the men of my own time. He used to teach me to practice virtue before all else, and to regard the gods as my guides to all that is good. Now whether he accomplished anything of real profit he himself must determine or, rather, the ruling gods. But at least he purged me of such infatuate folly and insolence as yours, and tried to make me more moderate than I was by nature. And though, as you know, I was armed with great external advantages, nevertheless, I submitted myself to my preceptor and to his friends and colleagues and the philosophers of his school. And I was eager to be instructed by all whose praises I heard uttered by him, and I read all the books that he approved.

Consequently, I was then initiated by those guides—in the first place by a philosopher who trained me in the preparatory discipline, and next by that most perfect philosopher who revealed to me the entrance to philosophy.

And though I achieved but little on account of the engrossing affairs that overwhelmed me from without, still for all that I have had the benefit of right training and have not travelled by the short road, as you say you have, but have gone all the way around. Though indeed I call the gods to witness, I believe that the road I took was really a shorter road to virtue than yours. For I, at any rate, if I may say so without bad taste, am standing at the entrance, whereas you are a long way off.[16]

Finally, in the Panegyric in Honor of the Emperor Constantius, *Julian declares that, of all things, virtue is the most beautiful and noble thing.*

There is an ancient rule taught by him who first introduced philosophy to mankind, and it is as follows. All who aspire to virtue and moral nobility must make it their business in their words, deeds, conversation, and, in short, in all the affairs of life, great and small, to aim in every way at what is noble. Now what sensible man would deny that virtue is the most beautiful thing of all?[17]

We not only learn about virtue in lectures but by means of experience. For instance, we learn virtue in battle by actually going into battle.

Your mind, meanwhile, was trained by practice in public speaking and other studies suitable to your years. But it was not wholly without the discipline of experience, nor was it for you merely to listen to lectures on the virtues as though they were songs or stories, and so wait all that time without actual acquaintance with brave works and undertakings. Plato, that noble philosopher, advised that boys should be furnished, as it were, with wings for flight by being mounted on horseback and taken into battle so that they could be spectators of the warfare in which they would soon be combatants.[18]

Finally, Julian catalogues the virtues of a ruler.

It is your conviction that the affection of his subjects is the surest defense of an emperor. Now it is the height of absurdity to try to win that affection by giving orders and levying it as though it were a tax or tribute. The only alternative is the policy that you have yourself pursued, I mean of doing good to all men and imitating the divine nature on earth. To show mercy even in anger, to take away harshness from acts of vengeance, to display kindness and toleration to your fallen enemies—this was your practice, this you always commended and enjoined on others to imitate. . . .

I maintain that your conduct has not only been humane and just, but prudent in a still higher degree. ... To such a degree does every act of yours incline toward clemency and is stamped with the mintmark of perfect virtue.[19]

Notes

[1] The translations that follow, though with occasional modifications, are largely those of W.C. Wright (1913, 1923).

[2] Julian the emperor, *Letter 7 to the same (to Alypius, brother of Caesarius)*.

[3] Julian the emperor, *The Heroic Deeds of the Emperor Constantius, or On Kingship, Oration II* 70.

[4] Ibid., 79, 80.

[5] Ibid., 80-81.

[6] Ibid., 81.

[7] Julian the emperor, *Consolation on the Departure of Sallust* 242.

[8] Ibid., 250.

[9] Julian the emperor, *Letter to Themistius the Philosopher* 255-256.

[10] Ibid., 264-265.

[11] Julian the emperor, *To the Uneducated Cynics, Oration VI* 188-189.

[12] Julian the emperor, *Hymn to the Mother of the Gods, Oration V* 169.

[13] Ibid., 179-180.

[14] Julian the emperor, *Misopogon* 348.

[15] Julian the emperor, *To the Cynic Heracleios, Oration VII* 219.

[16] Ibid., 235.

[17] Julian the emperor, *Panegyric in Honor of the Emperor Constantius, Oration I* 3.

[18] Ibid., 11. The "your" in "your mind" refers to Constantius.

[19] Ibid., 48, 49.

CONCLUSION
WHAT THE ANCIENT GREEKS
THOUGHT AND SAID ABOUT *ARETĒ*

A RETĒ, AS WE have seen, "is in one sense the perfection of anything." In this sense, and keeping the aretē spectrum of Chapter
2 in mind, we observe that soil or land may be excellent for growing
things. Or a statue may be excellent in its representation of a god. Or
a dog may be excellent in terms of its ability to run and hunt. Or a
human may be excellent as a sprinter, warrior, farmer, faithful
spouse, or relative to some other ability or function. Or in a more integral manner, a human may be virtuous in a way that follows general human nature, body and soul—that innermost part of being
human, including its cardinal virtues of wisdom, courage, moderation, and justice. Or a human may be virtuous in a way that follows
an individual's specific nature and situation—including talents, relationships, roles, duties, healthy inclinations, and like things.

To repeat: aretē is "the perfection" of a thing. Looking at the
Greek term for perfection here,—the word is *teleiōsis*, a term that
contains the Greek word *telos* (end, goal, target)—, we note that it
signifies the "development" of a thing toward an end.[1] As such, it
is an *activity* or *action*, a *movement toward* something, one in or during which the end or goal is always kept steadily in sight. In this
way, aretē as perfection (*teleiōsis*) is that (activity) which is moving
toward an end. This kind of perfection assumes an active and ongoing imperative: "Be excellent; be the best"—which is to say, "Seek
and move toward excellence; seek and move toward being the
best." This imperative is the one we hear and see from Homer on.
"Old Peleus enjoined his child Achilles to always be the best and to
stand out among other men."

Yet there's more. Perfection (*teleiōsis*) is also a *resting* in the sense
that it is the completion or fulfillment of a thing. The thing or person perfected *arrives* or *has arrived* at the end, goal, or target (*telos*);

the thing or person *is*.[2] The emphasis here is on the nature of a thing and its natural *telos* or *teleiōsis*—that is, what it is meant and able to do and be at its fullest. A flower in bloom, right at the point where it has finished blooming and just before it begins to wilt, has reached this perfection. For a moment it rests in a kind of stability. It is fully developed—fully unfolded as itself, a flower. In this way, it is fullness, complete in itself, in its own *flower being* or *flower nature* (both general and specific, as a flower and as *this* particular flower). It is perfect. It is beautiful.[3]

It is in these two ways that the Greeks viewed aretē as the *teleiōsis* of a thing. Indeed, aretē is the perfection of a thing, the "bestness" of a thing relative to itself (its own nature, general and specific) or to the intelligent or rational uses of another (and thus the nature that such an intelligence assigns to a thing).

But one may ask: Why should anyone seek aretē for oneself or in anything that one possesses or does? Why the imperative? Is aretē desired for the sake of itself, as a self-evident and intrinsic good, or for the sake of something else? Is it an end or the means to an end?

In Homer, Hesiod, and other early poets and writers, aretē seems to be aimed at something other than aretē itself, at external goods such as the defense of oneself and one's people, victory in battle, the accumulation of wealth, the garnering of success, and the approval of others manifested by a good reputation, honor, and glory, both now and in the memory of those to come (in the form of songs and stories). In Homer, for example, aretē wins for the hero social status, a high standing among others, and so the ability to satisfy desire, an ability that amounts to happiness.[4] In Hesiod, aretē is success in terms of securing the means of survival, as well as some measure of comfort and respect. In other writers, aretē achieves a position of leadership for an individual or an empire for a whole people, not to mention other desiderata.

Following this more external mode, that is, the aim of aretē at something other than aretē itself, we early on see aretē expressed in the body and the mind, in words, and relative to others. It is prowess, strength, athleticism, and beauty in the body. Within the mind, it is thinking for oneself, wisdom, cunning, and understanding in the art of war and other matters. In words, it is the ability to advise, to influence and convince. In human relations, it is justice and hospitality. Acting against others, it is manliness, speed, might, battle excellence, and courage or valor. Acting with others, it is combined strength and loyalty. However it is expressed, aretē is used to compete with others at times and to cooperate at others. Either way, the goal is similar in that one wishes to possess excellence in order to reach some level of greater satisfaction, which is to say, some level of happiness. As such, although aretē is certainly appreciated for itself, in the end it is valued for what it can obtain—a "what" that consists mostly of desired external things.[5]

The problem? Aretē does not secure these longed-for goods in a permanent manner. Rather, there is much to say and do. In Homer, for instance, the hero must constantly prove his aretē by what he says and does. Hence the imperative: "Always be the best!" In this way, the hero's aretē is always a moving toward and demonstration of perfection. He must regularly prove his excellence, that he is the best, that he stands out from the rest, even if such a demonstration results in his death.[6] The struggle for excellence is similar in Hesiod. But instead of the heroic words and deeds of the warrior, the poet counsels the ongoing hard work of—what we may call—the heroic farmer that results in aretē or "success" —in food, survival, material wealth, and the admiration of his neighbors. "The immortal gods have put sweat in front of Excellence (Aretē)," or "Success," sings Hesiod. "The path to her is long and steep." The path is work and more work. Later writers say much the same. The poet Simonides of Ceos reports that "excellence (aretē) dwells upon rocky peaks that are hard to climb." Theognis of Megara expresses the imperative this way: "Wear yourself out for the sake of excellence (aretē)." For the Spartan Tyrtaeus, excellence is "never relaxing from war." Herodotus reports that the Athenians achieved their objective (success in battle) "by excellence (aretē) and constant effort."

With Socrates and the philosophers, there is a significant, even revolutionary, shift. Though great effort is still required, that movement toward, now aretē is aimed at what we may call an internal good (or goods), a happiness (*eudaimonia*) that has its source in the person, existing within the person's innermost self, the soul. Being both integral and internal to the person, this aretē and the good it aims at is under a person's control rather than coming from or existing as some external thing such as wealth or honor or even bodily goods such as health or strength.[7] This internal aretē or good is happiness as inner harmony (what Plato calls "justice") or tranquility, where the now-measured desires and the now-pacified and well-ordered emotions or passions are obedient to reason, which rationally apprehends the (moral) good or end (*telos*) and acts accordingly, with the help of the spirited part of the soul. Aretē is no longer *merely* or *only* the means to happiness (though it is that too[8]), but it is one and the same with happiness. "Happiness is," as Aristotle put it, "an activity of the soul that accords with perfect virtue." The early Stoics concurred: "Happiness consists in virtue."

We see here that aretē is both the *movement toward* and *resting in* the good or goal. Aretē is not only how a flower blooms, whatever contributes to and is the process of that blooming, but it is the blooming of the flower itself, its flourishing, the very condition of being in bloom.

Since for human beings aretē *is* happiness, since it *is* human flourishing, the old external things won by earlier Greeks by means of aretē are no longer truly necessary. Accordingly, Socrates declares he can walk through the Athenian market and happily exclaim, "O the many things I do not need!" Similarly, the Cynics can extol a life of absolute simplicity or frugality, so much so that a later author, one influenced by the Cynics, speculates that "God seems to be [the virtue of] self-control (*enkrateia*) because he desires nothing but has everything in himself." Why would one need external things if the one thing necessary, happiness, were carried within, the flowering or fruit of aretē—or, better put, aretē itself?[9]

How does this happiness or inner harmony come about? The simple answer is that it does so through the various virtues (*aretai*) that serve as the perfection of one aspect or the whole of human nature—what we may term integral human being. In Plato's highly influential formulation: "Aretē is the means by which a thing performs its function well," where a thing's function is "that which it alone can do, or what it does better, than anything else." The idea: aretē corresponds to function, and function corresponds to nature, something given by the creator (even as a human craftsman assigns the cutting function to what *was* a lump of iron and *is now* a pruning knife). Accordingly, one must understand a thing's nature and corresponding function(s) to grasp its excellence(s) or virtue(s). For most of the philosophers, the key aspect of human nature is reason, something that other non-human animals do not possess—or at least, we moderns would add, they do not possess it in the same degree as we humans do. Non-human animals live by impulse, the Stoics would say, whereas we humans live by—or we humans are at least *capable* of living by—reason, following the rational order of the world given by the creator or divine Mind.[10]

It is the excellence of a rational life, of a life that participates in reason, that allows some of the philosophers to proclaim that the excellent or virtuous life is a divine life, or at least a participation in the divine. Looked at from one perspective, aretē is *human* flourishing; looked at from another, it is deification, the transformation of (a) human being into (a) more divine being or even into divinity itself. "When this man has produced true virtue," declares the prophetess Diotima to Socrates in Plato's *Symposium*, "nourishing it and letting it grow, he becomes dear to the gods. And if ever immortality is granted to humans, that man, above all others, will be immortal."[11] Plotinus similarly affirms that the one who is on the path of virtue is ultimately on the way to divinity. "He advances toward the gods." By being virtuous, he explains, by "improving our souls by limiting and regulating our desires and regulating every feeling," we rationally participate in measure and form. And "the greater the participation in form, the greater the likeness or assimilation to the formless divinity." The emperor Julian expresses the hope that "it is to you, the gods, that I journey." His quest for virtue is an expedition to the divine. In many ways, early Christianity took on this goal—that of *theosis* or deification—as its very own.[12]

Others, of course, do not see things in such grand terms. For Aristotle, aretē is very much a human thing. "The human good," he says ". . . is the activity of the soul that accords with virtue." Sure, "the opposite of brutishness" may be "virtue that is above or beyond [*hyper*] us," that is, above or beyond human nature (what Aristotle calls "a heroic or divine aretē"). And so the excellent and virtuous life may be aimed in the direction of divinity. Nevertheless, a divine man is beyond or *super* human and, accordingly, very rare, he says.[13]

Regardless of the precise nature of the human beings who possess aretē, and whether aretē was aimed at something external or something internal, the constant call from Homer on was to be the best, to be excellent, to be virtuous. Over the past few millennia, men and women have heard that call and have responded with their own attempts to be virtuous. We may look at the founding generation of the United States of America as an example. For instance, when Thomas Jefferson summarized the (Epicurean) beliefs that guided him in life and doubtlessly in penning the *Declaration of Independence*, he wrote: "Happiness is the aim of life. Virtue is the foundation of happiness. . . . Virtue consists in 1. Prudence, 2. Temperance, 3. Fortitude, 4. Justice."[14] He was not the only American founder focused on virtue. In *First Principles: What America's Founders Learned from the Greeks and Romans and How that Shaped Our Country*, Thomas E. Ricks reveals that "the word 'virtue' appears about six thousand times in the collected correspondence and other writings of the Revolutionary generation." He tacks on: "That's more often than 'freedom'."[15] It was George Washington's goal to be a man of "public virtue." John Adams wished to prove himself "a Lawyer of distinguished Genius, Learning, and Virtue."[16]

What about us? We who are surveying the thoughts and words of the ancient Greeks regarding aretē would do well to heed the call to be excellent or virtuous. As Glaucus puts it in Homer: "My father sent me . . . and insistently ordered me to always be the best." Or as the poet Phocylides recommends to all: "Seek after excellence." Our ancestors the Greeks are calling on us to do likewise and to be the same—to be the best, or, as the former First Lady had it, "Be best."[17]

Why should we listen and act? Because, as Aristotle observes, "Happiness is an activity of the soul that accords with perfect virtue." Because, as Epicurus puts it, "Living pleasantly is inseparable

from the virtues." Because, as Epictetus assures us, "Virtue promises happiness and tranquility and a life that flows well." And finally, because, as Socrates says, "He who lives well is blessed and
happy."

Let's give the final words to Socrates, who was, according to
Xenophon of Athens, "the best of men, a truly happy man . . . the
most helpful man in the pursuit of virtue." During his trial before
the assembly of Athens, Socrates said the following:

> Men of Athens, I greet and love you, but I will obey the god rather than
> you. And while I live and can continue, I will never give up philosophy.
> Nor will I stop exhorting you and pointing out the truth to any one of
> you whom I happen to encounter. Rather, in my accustomed way, I will
> say, "Best of men, you who are a citizen of Athens, the greatest of cities
> and the most famous for wisdom and power—are you not ashamed to
> care for the acquisition of the most wealth possible, and for reputation
> and honor, when you neither care for nor worry about practical wisdom
> and truth and your soul, that it may be in the best possible condition?
> And if any of you disagrees, saying that he *does* care, then I will not let
> him go, nor will I go. But I will question him. I will examine and cross-
> examine him. And if it appears to me that he does not possess virtue, but
> he says he does, I will upbraid him for devaluing the highest things and
> valuing the lowest. I will do this with anyone I meet—young or old, for-
> eigner or citizen. . . . I believe that no greater good ever came to pass in
> the city than my service to the god. For I go about doing nothing else than
> urging you, young and old, not to care for your bodies or your wealth
> more than for your soul, how it may be the best. And I tell you that virtue
> is not born from wealth, but from virtue come wealth and all other good
> things to human beings, both to an individual and to a state.[18]

NOTES

[1] "Development" is one meaning of *teleiōsis*. To develop (development) etymologically means to unfold—toward a thing's potential, toward fullness of existence.

[2] *Teleiōsis* also means "completion" or "fulfillment" or "accomplishment." Etymologically, completion means "with fullness." Thus, "fulfillment" or "filling
full" is the same thing as "completion." Filling full of what? It is a full sharing
or participation in the general or specific being that is the thing itself—whether
soil being or *plant being* or *dog* (or general *animal*) *being* or *human being* or *divine*

being. The same is true for "accomplishment" (which, incidentally, has both the *moving toward* and *resting* elements—"toward" and "with").

[3] Recall the Stoic statement: "All that is good is beautiful. . . . And beauty they describe as the bloom or flower of virtue."

[4] Aretē, here, is to be the best, to excel, to be outstanding (excellent). For more on Homer's conception of happiness and how aretē secures status and the ability to satisfy desire, see Tim J. Young, *A Hero's Wish: What Homer Believed about Happiness and the Good Life* (EuZōn Media: Sugar Land, 2015).

[5] In *A Hero's Wish: What Homer Believed about Happiness and the Good Life*, Tim J. Young presents the goods that humans, and particularly Homeric heroes, desire in terms of a "Pyramid of Desire," which includes "lower desires" and "higher desires." At the base of the pyramid, the lower desires include the desire "to avoid displeasure and satisfy desire"; "to be alive and have health"; "to satisfy the basic desires for food, sex, and sleep"; "to live a life of ease, comfort, pleasure and delight—including the experience of good weather, feasting, drinking, music, song, and dancing, along with finding diversion in games and contests." The higher desires include the desire "to be attached to a household for both security and identity"; "to have loyal friends and allies"; "to be free"; "to be wealthy"; "to be superior, the best, to have power, rule, and status"; "to avoid shame and humiliation"; "and at the top of the pyramid . . . to have glory, honor, a name and song" (109). Aretē—being best and having power—secures for the hero (at least for a time) all the things desired on the Pyramid of Desire.

[6] So it is, for instance, that we see the Lycian hero Sarpedon urging on his righthand man Glaucus to march into battle so they may prove that they are *actually* glorious and god-like (that is, men with aretē)—this, even though, as Sarpedon observes, "the countless fates of death are at hand." See Homer, *Iliad* 12.310-330.

[7] The language representing the shift from "external" to "internal" comes from the Greeks themselves, who recognized goods of the soul (internal things such as virtue and moral progress), goods of the body (such as beauty, health, and strength), and external goods (such as wealth, glory, reputation, and noble birth). See, for instance, Diogenes Laertius, *Lives* 5.30.

[8] Recall the statement of the early Stoics: "The virtues are goods that have both the nature of ends and means. Inasmuch as they produce happiness, they are means to good things. On the other hand, inasmuch as the virtues are the fulfillment of happiness, being a portion of happiness itself, they are ends."

[9] For Socrates, see Diogenes Laertius, *Lives* 2.25. For the "later author," see Basil of Caesarea, *Letter* 366 (though the actual author, some scholars speculate, may be someone else). His remark doubtlessly stems from the Cynic tradition. The Cynics, Diogenes Laertius (*Lives* 6.104) reports, "used to say that it was characteristic of the gods to need nothing, and that, consequently, when a man desires very little or nothing at all, he is like the gods." Otherwise, compare the difference (*moving toward* versus *resting in*; an external versus an internal goal or good) to the Christian distinction between Martha and Mary as found in Luke 10.38-42

(Martha, who is frantically running around *getting things done* versus Mary, who is centered on "the one thing necessary," God) and the later Christian tradition that contrasted an "active" life with a "contemplative" life. See, for example, Thomas Merton, *The Seven Story Mountain* (San Diego: Harcourt Brace Jovanovich, 1948), 414. Relative to education, we see the distinction between those who believe that education should primarily be a moving toward something practical (various external goods—"knowledge" and "progress," wealth, information, innovation, technology, and other things that always seem out of reach no matter how often we reach them) versus a more traditional view that values education for itself, not only as the movement toward liberation (in wisdom and virtue—and thus a "liberal education") but a very part of that liberation itself.

[10] Whatever one makes of evolutionary theory relative to human beings (whether random as many contend or somehow designed and guided by God or Intelligence, as argued for in the intelligent design movement), we humans nevertheless have a nature that has been, so far as we can tell, relatively stable for at least two hundred thousand years. Therefore, it still makes sense to ascertain human nature and describe aretē relative to this relatively stable nature and its various natural functions and ends. This may be upheld in contrast to those who deny human nature altogether and suggest that *what* we humans are, what our nature is, is up to us to decide—which is to say that human nature does not actually exist (outside of "choice" or "identification"), and, therefore, neither human function(s) nor corresponding human virtue(s) exist.

[11] For Plato, as for all ancient Greeks, "immortal" is shorthand for "divine," as the gods are always counted "immortal and ageless."

[12] Eastern Orthodox Christianity (as well as Roman Catholic Christianity) understands a similar goal for (a) human being in terms of *theosis* or deification, participation in the nature and life of God (i.e., union with God). One undergoes a process of purification (*katharsis*), illumination (*theoria*), and, finally, *theosis*. Jesus himself cites the Psalms, where the psalmist refers to those "to whom the word of God came," that is, human beings, as gods (*theoi* or s. *theos*)—this by participation (see John 10.34-35 and Psalm 82.6). The author of 2 Peter gives "fellowship or participation in the divine nature" as the goal of human life. Moving on to the Church Fathers, most famously, St. Athanasius declared that "God became man [Jesus Christ] so that men might become gods." St. Gregory of Nazianzus said, "Man has been ordered to become God." And St. Basil the Great: "From the Holy Spirit is the likeness of God, and the highest thing to be desired, to become God." Finally, St. Irenaeus: "If the Word is made man, it is that man might become gods." For these statements, see Mark Shuttleworth's booklet, "Theosis: Partaking of the Divine Nature" (Ben Lomond: Conciliar Press, 2005). In *St. Gregory Palamas and Orthodox Spirituality* (Crestwood: St. Vladimir's Seminary Press, 1974), the Orthodox theologian Fr. John Meyendorff observes that "Gregory of Nyssa [Basil's brother] and Maximus the Confessor both belong to the great line of Christian mystics who have succeeded in expressing the fundamental realities

of Christian spirituality in the framework of Neoplatonic philosophy"—i.e., that of Plotinus and other Neoplatonists. He goes on to say, "To express this New Testament doctrine of union with God"—found in John 17:22-23—"a union that alone can deliver men from death and sin, union that is the very essence of Christ's work, . . . the Greek Fathers use the concept of 'deification' (*theosis*)" (35). As we see in St. John Climacus' seventh century *The Ladder of Divine Ascent*, the life of the Christian, and particularly that of the monk, is one of growing in virtue or the virtues—with, of course, the vital help of God (without which such a growth cannot occur).

[13] For the contention that "it is rare for a man to be divine," see Aristotle, *Nicomachean Ethics* 7.1. By the way, Aristotle also says that it is rare to find a beast-like or brutish man among human beings. Therefore, Aristotle's ladder to virtue mostly consists of the movement from moral viciousness to virtue along the rungs of moral weakness and moral strength.

[14] Cited in Thomas E. Ricks, *First Principles: What America's Founders Learned from the Greeks and Romans and How that Shaped Our Country* (New York: Harper Collins, 2020), 84. In the terms used in *Aretē*, "prudence" is the same as practical wisdom, "temperance" as moderation, and "fortitude" as courage.

[15] Ibid., 6. That said, and even though James Madison also practiced virtue in both his public and personal lives, he nevertheless realized, even as Aristotle did, that most humans (and thus most citizens) would not actually *be* virtuous. And so there was the need for a founding charter or constitution that would not rely on human virtue (the rational taming of impulse) in making for a prosperous nation, but would rather cleverly balance impulse, we might say, against impulse, or vice and moral weakness against the same. See ibid., 206 ff.

[16] Ibid., 61. We should note that Benjamin Franklin, as he presents himself in his *Autobiography*, is famous for his program of delineating and practicing virtue. Realizing that " the mere speculative conviction that it was our interest to be completely virtuous was not sufficient to prevent our slipping, and that the contrary habits must be broken, and good ones acquired and established before we can have any dependence on a steady, uniform rectitude of conduct," he identified and defined thirteen virtues (with corresponding precepts) that he would cultivate: temperance, silence, order, resolution, frugality, industry, sincerity, justice, moderation, cleanliness, tranquility, chastity, humility.

[17] In order to facilitate a personal practice of aretē, of being the best, you may wish to carry, consult, and train with the sayings found in The Classic Cave's *The Wisdom & Way of Greek Virtue (Aretē)*—Pocket Edition (Sugar Land: The Classics Cave, 2021) or work through the prompts and exercises found in the *Aretē (Excellence or Virtue) Workbook & Journal* (Sugar Land: The Classics Cave, 2021). For conversation starters centered on aretē intended to kindle discussion and ignite practice, use *Aretē (Excellence or Virtue) Cave Sparks* (Sugar Land: The Classics Cave, 2021)— employ them with a friend or within a group, classroom, or your family.

[18] Plato, *Apology* 29d-30b.

PART 5

Points of Wisdom & Ways of Practice

- A Plan of Life Aimed at *Aretē*

- Points of Wisdom Related to *Aretē*

- Ways of Practice Following *Aretē*

A PLAN OF LIFE
AIMED AT *ARETĒ*

The following presents a plan of life aimed at aretē—*a plan representing ancient Greek wisdom and practice from the course of a thousand years.*

1. **Follow the *eudaimonia* (happiness) imperative: Be happy!** According, realize and be convinced that happiness, the goal of life, is tied to virtue—that to *be* happy one must *practice* virtue.

2. **Abide by the *aretē* imperative: Be the best! Be outstanding!** Hear the hero Glaucus: "My father insistently ordered me to always be the best and to stand out among other men." And wise Nestor: "Old Peleus enjoined Achilles to always be the best and to stand out among other men." Do *the* best—*your* best. Be your most outstanding self.

3. **Discover and internalize the general nature of aretē.** Know the various meanings of *aretē*—that *aretē* is excellence or virtue; that it is the perfection of a thing; that it is the means by which a thing performs its function well (where a thing's function is that which it alone can do, or what it does better, than anything else); that it is a mean between an excess and a defect; that it follows reason in agreement with nature, skillfully shaping impulse.

4. **Find out and memorize the specific kinds of aretē.** There are four cardinal virtues. They are practical wisdom, courage, moderation, and justice. Other virtues are related to these four. Observe your own virtues or, perhaps, what *should be* your own (related to your own functions and relationships). Practice them.

5. **Satisfy your desires by means of *aretē*** (excellence). For Homer and other early Greeks, happiness is the satisfaction of desire. Such a satisfaction comes about and is assured by means of excellence (such as battle excellence, valor, or speaking well in the assembly). Know your desires. Cultivate excellences that correspond to their satisfaction.

6. **Perform your own specific and general human functions well by means of** *aretē.* For Plato and other Greek philosophers, to do or to live well is to be well or to live happily, which is to live virtuously. Virtue is "the means by which a thing performs its function well," where a thing's function is "that which it alone can do, or what it does better, than anything else." A thing's function originates in or comes from its nature. So, it is vital to explore and be aware of human nature (including your own specific nature) in order to understand and practice virtue.

7. **Let reason skillfully shape impulse.** For the Stoics, the virtuous life is a life lived according to reason in agreement with nature. Such a life is a happy life. Though we humans have impulses (innate drives) as other animals do, nature has given us reason to skillfully shape impulse. Know your impulses. Know how they require shaping or formation (by means of education or experience). Then look to reason to perform this happy-making task.

8. **Climb the ladder to** *aretē.* Know where you are on Aristotle's ladder to virtue. If you are at bottom, move from acting on impulse (brutishness) to moral viciousness, where you mistake evil for good. Moving up to moral weakness, you know the good but are unable to pursue it consistently, given your own moral weakness. With long practice, however, you may overcome various unhealthy desires and come to a place of moral strength. Beyond this is virtue, where unhealthy desires vanish altogether, and good habit is the rule.

9. **Read and memorize sayings related to** *aretē* **and the good life.** Such sayings serve as short-cut reminders of where you are going and motivators to get you there.

10. **Live by examples. Know your heroes.** Who are your heroes?— those who have struggled to live a virtuous life? Who may serve as examples for you?—those "wise and sensible" men and women who have lived well? Learn about them and live by their example. Avoid others (warnings) who live in an opposite manner.

POINTS OF WISDOM
RELATED TO *ARETĒ*

The following points of wisdom related to aretē (excellence or virtue) are organized according to the topics given in bold. For more points of wisdom organized by these and other topics, read The Classics Cave's The Wisdom & Way of Ancient Greek Virtue or Excellence (Aretē).

The Goal of Life Is *Aretē*

The Cynics hold that the goal of life is to live according to virtue—just like the Stoics. . . . Therefore, some have said that Cynicism is a shortcut upon the path of virtue.—*Diogenes Laertius*

The human good is the activity of the soul that accords with virtue.
—*Aristotle*

Zeno [of Citium] was the first to say that the end or goal of life is to live in accord with nature, which is the same as living in accord with virtue, since nature leads us toward virtue.—*Diogenes Laertius*

God is always urging us on to virtue.—*Clement of Alexandria*

The *Aretē* Imperative

"My father sent me to Troy and insistently ordered me to always be the best and to stand out among other men and not dishonor or shame the family of my fathers who were the best in Ephyre and in wide Lydia."—*Glaucus (in Homer)*

"Old Peleus enjoined his child Achilles to always be the best and to stand out among other men."—*Nestor (in Homer)*

Seek after the means of life, and whenever you already have life, then seek after excellence.—*Phocylides*

Since evils are here in this realm, and since these evils "prowl about this realm by necessity," and since the soul wishes to flee these evils, then "we must flee from this realm." But what is the nature of this flight we must take? Plato says that it is in becoming like god—like the divinity. And this, he says, is found if one "is becoming just and holy, and in one who is beginning to live by means of practical wisdom"—which is to say the whole of virtue.—*Plotinus*

The Good of *Aretē*—Including Happiness

The only secure acquisitions are those tied to excellence.—*Sophocles*

Excellence, when it grows up with us in our hearts without alloy, is the one possession that abides with us in old age.—*Isocrates*

Plato held that the goal of life is to become god-like, and that virtue is sufficient in itself for happiness.—*Diogenes Laertius*

Nothing in the world can contribute so powerfully to material gain, to good repute, to right action, in a word, to happiness, as virtue and the qualities of virtue.—*Isocrates*

Happiness is an activity of the soul that accords with perfect virtue.—*Aristotle*

The Stoics hold that virtue is sufficient in itself for happiness. . . . *It* is the state of the soul that tends to make the whole of life harmonious.
—*Diogenes Laertius*

Virtue promises happiness and tranquility and a life that flows well.
—*Epictetus*

The virtues have become one with living pleasantly. Living pleasantly is inseparable from the virtues. . . . We say that pleasure is the beginning point and goal of living happily.—*Epicurus*

The Nature of Aretē

Virtue is in one sense the perfection of anything in general, say of a statue. Virtue may be non-intellectual, such as health, or intellectual, such as practical wisdom. — the Stoics (*Diogenes Laertius*)

It appears, then, that virtue is a kind of health and beauty and good condition of the soul. — *Socrates (Plato)*

Virtue, or excellence, is the means by which a thing performs its function well. . . . The function of a thing is that which it alone can do, or what it does better, than anything else. — *Socrates (Plato)*

Moral virtue is a habit or disposition involving deliberate choice, consisting in the observance of a mean relative to us, as determined by reason, that is, as a wise and sensible man would determine it. Virtue is a mean that falls between two vices, that which is excessive and that which is deficient. — *Aristotle*

The Four Cardinal Virtues

Of the virtues, some are primary, and some are arranged under these primary virtues. There are four primary virtues: practical wisdom, moderation, courage, and justice.

—*Diogenes Laertius (reporting the Stoic position)*

Of perfect virtue there are four kinds or forms: practical wisdom, justice, courage, and moderation. Of these, practical wisdom is the cause of right conduct, and justice is responsible for straight dealing in partnerships and commercial transactions. Courage is the cause that makes a man not give way but stand his ground in alarms and perils. Moderation causes mastery over desires, so that we are never enslaved by pleasure but live in an orderly manner.

—*Diogenes Laertius (reporting Plato's view)*

Socrates drew no distinction between wisdom and moderation. But if a man knew and practiced what is noble and good, and knew and avoided what is base and shameful, then he judged that man to be both wise and moderate. . . . He said that justice and every other virtue is wisdom. For just actions and all forms of virtuous activity are noble and good. He who knows the noble and the good will never choose anything else. . . . So it is that the wise do what is noble and good.—*Xenophon*

For of all virtue, I say, and I repeat it, the beginning is intelligence or understanding, and the fulfillment is courage.—*Demosthenes*

Nearly everyone praises and calls "divine" and "holy" such things as courage and justice and practical wisdom and, in short, every virtue.—*Dio Chrysostom*

Socrates never praised Xerxes or any other king of Persia or Lydia or Macedonia, and not even a Greek general, except for only a very few—those whom he knew to delight in virtue, and to cherish courage with moderation, and to love wisdom with justice.

—*Julian the emperor*

Doing and Getting, Training and Struggling for *Aretē*

Virtue is something you do—it is a matter of deeds. It doesn't require a stockpile of arguments or much learning.
—*Diogenes Laertius (giving the Cynic philosopher Antisthenes' position)*

Listen, Perses, you big fool. I will proclaim all this noble knowledge for you. It is easy to grab at Deficiency (Kakotēs). It is there in abundance for you. The way is smooth to her, and she dwells very near to you. But the immortal gods have put sweat in front of Excellence (Aretē). The path to her is long and steep. And so, it is rough going at first. Nevertheless, when one comes to the highest point, then the path becomes easy.—*Hesiod*

It is said that excellence dwells upon rocky peaks that are hard to climb. . . . She guards a holy place. She may not be seen by the eyes of all mortals. Only the one who experiences heart-vexing sweat from within may see her, the one who reaches the peak of manliness.

— *Simonides of Ceos*

Excellence is bought with blood. — *Aeschylus*

The excellences advance by means of hardship.

— *Euripides (the Chorus is speaking)*

"King," Demaratus said, "since you call on me by all means to speak the whole truth and to say what you will not later prove false, in Greece poverty is always widespread, but excellence is acquired as the achievement of wisdom and strong law. By constant practice of this excellence, Greece drives off poverty and defends herself against tyranny." — *Herodotus (Demaratus, a former king of Sparta, is speaking to Xerxes, the king of Persia)*

You will find on reflection that every kind of virtue named among men is increased by education and practice. — *Xenophon (Socrates is speaking to Critobulus, that is, his good friend Crito)*

I notice that as those who do not train the body cannot perform the functions proper to the body, so those who do not train the soul cannot perform the functions of the soul — for they cannot do what they ought to do or avoid what they ought not to do. For this reason, fathers try to keep their sons, even if they are sensible and wise, out of bad company — for an association with good men is a training in virtue, but an association with bad men is virtue's undoing.

— *Xenophon*

The Cynics further hold that virtue can be taught. — *Diogenes Laertius (offering the Cynic Antisthenes' and the general Cynic position)*

Virtue enters the soul by means of training — not automatically as happens with vice. — *(Pseudo) Crates of Thebes in a letter to Orion*

Moral or ethical virtue is born thanks to habit, which is to say customary behavior. . . . The [moral] virtues are engendered in us neither by nature nor yet in a way contrary to nature. Rather, nature disposes us to receive them, perfecting them by means of habit. We acquire the [moral] virtues . . . by doing them, by putting them into action, just as we do with the various arts or skills. For we learn an art or skill by doing that which we wish to do when we have learned it. We become builders by building and harpers by harping. And so, by doing just acts we become just, and by doing acts of moderation and courage we become moderate and courageous. This conclusion is attested, as well, by what occurs in city-states. Those who craft the laws make the citizens good by means of accustomization or habituation, that is, by getting used to good habits. This is the purpose of all legislators, and if they don't do this well, then they miss the mark. Indeed, this is what distinguishes a good from a bad constitution.—*Aristotle*

The first rule in aiming at the mean is that we should point ourselves away from the extreme that is more opposed to the mean. . . . The second rule is that we should look into and examine the errors that we are most likely to commit. . . . then we must drag ourselves away in the opposite direction. . . . The third rule is that we must in everything be on guard against pleasure and what is pleasant. . . . These are the things we may do that will best enable us to hit the mean.

—*Aristotle*

Socrates—the Great Exemplar of Aretē

"What would Socrates . . . do?"—*Epictetus*

All who knew what kind of man Socrates was, and all who care for virtue, all these men continue even now to miss Socrates most of all as the most helpful man in the pursuit of virtue. . . . He conferred the greatest benefits on all who dealt with him. He was . . . pious . . . self-controlled . . . wise. . . . He seemed to me the best of men, a truly happy man.

WAYS OF PRACTICE
FOLLOWING *ARETĒ*

The following ways of practice, inspired by The Classics Cave's The Wisdom & Way of Ancient Greek Virtue or Excellence (*Aretē*), *are offered with the goal of practice in mind, the application of ancient wisdom to our contemporary ways and lives. We hope they will serve, in some small measure, as a source of inspiration and motivation. Use them to contemplate your life—where you are now, where you are going, and how you can better get there. For more, pick up The Classics Cave's* Living with Virtue or Excellence (*Aretē*) Workbook & Journal. *One last note. You will likely find that the space given for responses is not enough. If so, jot your thoughts and practices down in a separate place.*

PRACTICE 1: DETERMINING MY FUNCTIONS & VIRTUES

Recall Plato's (and Socrates') key idea regarding *aretē*: that "virtue is the means by which a thing performs its function well," where the "function of a thing is that which it alone can do, or what it does better, than anything else." Take a knife. A knife cuts (its function) by means of sharpness (its virtue). Or the soul: the rational part—reason—rules (its function) by means of wisdom (its virtue); the spirited part enforces the rule of the rational part by means of courage; the desiring part nourishes and (re)produces by means of listening to and obeying the rule of the rational part (and so it goes along with the spirited part)—which is to say, by means of moderation.

In general, these three virtues apply to all of us, all human beings. But what about other virtues or excellences that apply to our individual, specific life roles or functions?

Think of yourself in terms of the roles you play (in your various relationships—with family, friends, coworkers, and others; at school, if you are in school; at work; at play; in your duty as a citizen; and so on). What are these roles (think of three)? What is the function of each? What is the corresponding *aretē* (virtue or excellence) of each? Are there any allied or subordinate virtues?

Role/function/*aretē* 1: _____

_____

_____

_____

Role/function/*aretē* 2: _____

_____

_____

_____

Role/function/*aretē* 3: _____

_____

_____

_____

Practice It ▪ Describe concrete, specific, realistic ways you can practice one of the above virtues over the course of the next week.

_____

_____

_____

Keep It Up ▪ After practicing for a week, determine how you can continue your practice. What about the other virtues—both general human virtues and ones specific to you? How can you practice? Again, be concrete, specific, realistic.

_____

_____

_____

PRACTICE 2: MY PLACE ON THE LADDER TO VIRTUE & CLIMBING UP

Where am I on the Ladder to Virtue? How can I climb up?

Virtue-Excellence • The virtuous-excellent person has proper desires and aversions. He bases himself on what is good and healthy (by the way, when you see *good* think *healthy* or *beneficial*, and *evil* or *bad* think *unhealthy* or *harmful*). How does he know what these are? By study. By deliberation. By listening to the wisdom of others. By watching the example of others. By consistently submitting to and acting upon the voice of reason.

Moral Strength • The morally strong person still has less-than-healthy or less-than-virtuous desires. The difference between him and the morally weak person, however, is that he's able to overcome the gravitational pull of these desires. He breaks free into the space of moral strength and has regular victory over pleasures and pains.

Moral Weakness • The morally weak person is the one who knows better but surrenders to the influence of various pleasures and pains anyway. As Aristotle says, "The morally weak man . . . does not think that he should, but he nevertheless pursues what he desires."

Moral Viciousness • Although the vicious person (the one who engages in vice or non-excellence) seemingly chooses and acts with what appears like reason, his reasoning is all wrong, causing him to deliberate falsely, choose foolishly, and behave in such a manner that ultimately harms himself and others.

Brutishness (Animal-likeness) • The brutish person behaves like an animal, acting directly by inspiration of the irrational, desiring part of the soul (what the Stoics call impulse), without any influence of reason or choice-will. Every feeling, judgment, and act relies on impulse rather than reason.

The Ladder in Sum • To summarize, one moves on the ladder from acting on impulse to moral viciousness, where one mistakes evil for good. Next one knows the good but is unable to pursue it consistently, given one's own moral weaknesses. With long practice, however, one is finally able to overcome various unhealthy desires, and so comes to a place of moral strength. Beyond this is virtue or excellence, where the unhealthy desires vanish altogether and good habit is the rule.

Virtue-Excellence

Moral Strength

Moral Weakness

Moral Viciousness

Brutishness

My Location ▪ Where am I on Aristotle's Ladder to Virtue?

Presently, I am on the _____ rung of the Ladder to Virtue.

For me, this means . . . _____

_____

_____

In time, I would like to be on the _____ rung of the Ladder to Virtue.

For me, this means . . . _____

_____

_____

I will climb by (specify two ways I will make the climb—as concretely as possible, ways that I can practice) . . .

Way 1 to climb & how _____

_____

_____

Way 2 to climb & how _____

_____

_____

PRACTICE 3: AIMING AT THE MEAN (PRACTICING A VIRTUE)

Recall that, according to Aristotle, "moral virtue is a mean . . . between two vices—one vice that is marked by excess and the other by defect." For instance, courage is the mean between rashness and cowardice. Moderation is the mean between immoderation or licentiousness and insensibility or a lack of feeling.

Q ▪ How can I move away from vice (the excess or defect) and aim at the mean (virtue)? Aristotle offers three rules or points of advice.

Exercise ▪ Try to apply each rule or point of advice to two virtues you would like to develop (whether a general human virtue or one specific to you and your roles). In doing so, be concrete and specific. Then practice. Repetitively do what it takes to acquire the virtue.

"The **first rule** in aiming at the mean is that we should point ourselves away from the extreme that is more opposed to the mean."

I can point myself away from the extreme by . . .

"The **second rule** is that we should look into and examine the errors that we are most likely to commit. . . . then we must drag ourselves away in the opposite direction."

The errors I will likely commit are . . . I will drag myself away by . . .

"The **third rule** is that we must in everything be on guard against pleasure and what is pleasant [relative to the virtue]."

I can be on guard against pleasure and what is pleasant by . . .

OTHER MATTERS OF INTEREST

related to *Aretē*

GLOSSARY

OF ENGLISH WORDS AND GREEK EQUIVALENTS
RELATED TO THE GREEKS ON ARETĒ—EXCELLENCE OR VIRTUE

Appetite, desire: *orexis* (ὄρεξις).

Art, skill, craft in work; for Aristotle, art or applied science or skillful knowledge: *technē* (τέχνη).

Bad, evil; bad fortune, misfortune; worthless; cowardly; a bad man or thing: *kakos* (κακός). **Failure**; badness, evil, cowardice, harm, misery: *kakotēs* (κακότης). **Vice**, moral badness: *kakia* (κακία). Also, *ponēros* (πονηρός)—bad, worthless, knavish, base.

Beautiful, fair; noble: *kalos* (καλός).

Best, most excellent; noblest, bravest: *aristos* (ἄριστος). **Best**, most excellent: *beltistos* (βέλτιστος).

Body: *sōma* (σῶμα). Bodily strength: *sōma* + *rhōmē* (or *rhōmē* alone) (ῥώμη).

Capacity; power: *dunamis* (δύναμις).

Character; a way of life, habit, custom: *tropos* (τρόπος).

Contemplation; looking at, viewing: *theōria* (θεωρία).

Courage; manliness, manhood, manly spirit: *andreia* (ἀνδρεία). **Courage**, boldness: *eutolmia* (εὐτολμία). **Courageous**; of good courage, stout of heart: *eupsuchos* (εὔψυχος). **Courage**, boldness: *tharsos* (θάρσος).

Cowardice; badness: *kakotēs* (κακότης).

Cowardly; vile, worthless; miserable, luckless, wretched, unhappy: *deilos* (δειλός).

Deficiency; want, need, lack: *endeia* (ἔνδεια).

To **delight**, enjoy, take pleasure in: *terpō* (τέρπω).

Desire, yearning, longing: *epithumia* (ἐπιθυμία). **Desire**; love: *erōs* (ἔρως).

One's **disposition**, character; habit; custom, usage, manner: *ēthos* (ἦθος). **Ethical** or **moral virtue**: *ēthikos* (ἠθικός), along with **intellectual virtue**: *noētikos* (νοητικός) or *dianoētikos* (διανοητικός).

To **do well**: *eu prassō* or *eu prattein* (εὖ πράσσω or εὖ πράττειν).

Endurance, patient endurance, perseverance: *karteria* (καρτερία).

Enjoyment, delight: *terpsis* (τέρψις). To **enjoy oneself**, take delight, take one's pleasure: *hēdomai* (ἥδομαι).

Example, model, pattern: *paradeigma* (παράδειγμα).

Excellence, virtue: *aretē* (ἀρετή). Given the context of the word, *aretē* may signify valor, manliness, nobility, merit, success, goodness, and other like terms.

Excess; a throwing beyond, overshooting: *huperbolē* (ὑπερβολή).

Exercise, practice, training: *askēsis* (ἄσκησις).

A **failure**, fault, error, sin; miss the mark: *hamartia* (ἁμαρτία).

Fate (personified); fate, portion: *Moira* or *moira* (μοῖρα).

Freedom, liberty: *eleutheria* (ἐλευθερία).

Friendship: *philia* (φιλία).

Fulfillment; completion: *teleiōsis* (τελείωσις). **Complete**, finished: *teleios* (τέλειος) (related to *telos*).

Function, work: *ergon* (ἔργον).

Glory, fame, report: *kleos* (κλέος). **Glory**: *kudos* (κῦδος).

Goal, end, target, purpose: *telos* (τέλος).

God, a god: *theos* (θεός). A **goddess**: *thea* (θεά). **Gods**: *theoi* (θεοί).

Good, noble, brave: *agathos* (ἀγαθός). **Good**, brave: *esthlos* (ἐσθλός).

Habit, an ongoing state; a possession: *hexis* (ἕξις).

Happiness, prosperity: *eudaimonia* (εὐδαιμονία). **Happy**, prosperous; blessed with a good *daimōn* or spirit: *eudaimōn* (εὐδαίμων). **Happiness**, fortune, riches: *olbos* (ὄλβος). **Happy**, blessed: *olbios* (ὄλβιος). **Happy**, prosperous, fortunate, lucky: *eutuchēs* or *eutychēs* (εὐτυχής). **Bliss**, happiness: *makariotēs* (μακαριότης). **Blessed**, happy: *makar* (μάκαρ) or *makarios* (μακάριος).

Harmony; agreement: *homologia* (ὁμολογία).

Health, soundness: *hygieia* or *hugieia* (ὑγίεια).

Holy, hallowed; allowed by divine law: *hosios* (ὅσιος). **Holiness**, piety; disposition to observe divine law: *hosiotēs* (ὁσιότης).

Honor: *timē* (τιμή).

Indifferent; things neither good nor bad: *adiaphoros* (ἀδιάφορος).

Justice, righteousness: *dikaiosunē* (δικαιοσύνη). **Justice**; custom, usage; right as dependent on custom: *dikē* (δίκη). Just, righteous; observant of custom; well-balanced: *dikaios* (δίκαιος).

Kind, fair, gentle, reasonable: *epieikēs* (ἐπιεικής).

Knowledge; scientific knowledge, science, or skillful knowledge: *epistēmē* (ἐπιστήμη).

Live well: to live (*zaō*) (ζάω) well or beautifully (*kalōs*) (καλῶς), the adverbial form of beautiful, good, fine, noble: *kalos* (καλός).

Magnanimity, greatness of soul: *megalopsuchia* (μεγαλοψυχία).

Manly virtue; bravery, the character of an *agathos* man: *andragathia* (ἀνδραγαθία).

The **mean** between two extremes; a middle or central position: *mesotēs* (μεσότης).

Mild, soft, gentle, meek: *praos* (πρᾶος).

Mind, intellect; understanding, thought; intelligence: *nous* (νοῦς) or *noos* (νόος).

Moderation: *sōphrosunē* (σωφροσύνη). Moderate: *sōphrōn* (σώφρων). **Foolish**, senseless: *aphrōn* (ἄφρων).

Nature: *physis* or *phusis* (φύσις). **Natural**: *physikos* or *phusikos* (φυσικός). **According to nature**, following nature: *kata phusis* or *physis* (κατά φύσις).

Nobleness, goodness; noble and good; the character of a noble and good person: *kalokagathia* (καλοκἀγαθία).

Outstanding, standing out; eminent, excellent: *exochos* (ἔξοχος).

Passions, feelings: *pathos* (πάθος).

Piety, reverence toward the gods: *eusebeia* (εὐσέβεια).

Pleasure, delight, enjoyment: *hēdonē* (ἡδονή). **Pleasant**, sweet: *hēdus* (ἡδύς). To **please**, delight, gratify: *handanō* (ἀνδάνω).

Practical wisdom, prudence: *phronēsis* (φρόνησις).

Practice, exercise; care, attention: *meletē* (μελέτη).

Rash, over-bold (in a bad sense); bold, spirited, courageous, confident: *thrasus* (θρασύς).

Self-control or self-governance: *enkrateia* (ἐγκράτεια). **Lack of self-control** or self-governance: *akrateia* (ἀκράτεια).

Self-sufficient; having enough; independent of others; self-supporting: *autarkēs* (αὐτάρκης).

Serious (man); excellent (man): *spoudaios* (σπουδαῖος).

Shame; a proper sense of shame; respect: *aidōs* (αἰδώς). The **shame** done one; disgrace, dishonor: *aischunē* (αἰσχύνη). **Shameful**, disgraceful; ugly: *aischros* (αἰσχρός).

Simple, frugal, thrifty; easily paid for: *euteles* (εὐτελής). **Simplicity**, frugality, thrift: *euteleia* (εὐτέλεια). **Simplicity**, plainness: *litotēs* (λιτότης).

Soul; life: *psuchē* or *psyche* (ψυχή). The **soul's three parts** as given by Plato: the **rational** part: *logistikos* (or *logistikon*) (λογιστικός); the **spirited** part: *thumos* or *thumoeidēs* (θυμός or θυμοειδής); the **desiring** (or appetitive) part: *epithumētikos* (or *epithumētikon*) (ἐπιθυμητικός).

Strength, prowess, courage, boldness: *alkē* (ἀλκή).

Strongest, mightiest; best: *kratistos* (κράτιστος).

System of education: *paideusis* (παίδευσις). Related to the rearing of a **child**: *pais* (παῖς); and to **education**, training: *paideia* (παιδεία). To **teach**, instruct: *didaskō* (διδάσκω).

To **thrive**, prosper, flourish; to be fit or proper: *aretaō* (ἀρετάω).

Training, education; a leading toward a point: *agōgē* (ἀγωγή).

Tranquility, tranquility of mind; calmness: *ataraxia* (ἀταραξία). **Not disturbed**, without confusion; tranquil; calm: *ataraktos* (ἀτάρακτος). **Trouble**, confusion, disorder, disturbance; anxiety: *tarachos* (τάραχος) or *tarachē* (ταραχή) (thus, *ataraxia* and *ataraktos* are the negation of *tarachos*).

To **turn around**; to correct, repent; for Plotinus, the act of conversion that results in virtue: *epistrephō* (ἐπιστρέφω).

Understanding, intelligence in the **art of war**: *sunesis* (σύνεσις) + *stratēgikos* (στρατηγικός)

Undisciplined, unbridled; licentious: *akolastos* (ἀκόλαστος).

Unhappiness, misfortune: *kakodaimonia* (κακοδαιμονία). **Unhappy**, miserable: *kakodaimōn* (κακοδαίμων). **Unhappy**, miserable, wretched: *dustēnos* or *dystēnos* (δύστηνος).

Vice, moral badness: *kakia* (κακία).

Virtue; excellence; goodness: *aretē* (ἀρετή). See excellence.

Wealth, riches: *ploutos* (πλοῦτος).

Wisdom; theoretical wisdom: *sophia* (σοφία). **Wise**; skilled; wise man: *sophos* (σοφός). **Love of wisdom**, philosophy: *philosophia* (φιλοσοφία).

FURTHER READING

Adkins, A.W.H. *From the Many to the One: A Study of Personality and Views of Human Nature in the Context of Ancient Greek Society, Values, and Beliefs.* Ithaca: Cornell University Press, 1970.

———. *Moral Values and Political Behavior in Ancient Greece: From Homer to the End of the Fifth Century.* New York: W.W. Norton & Company, 1972.

———. *Merit and Responsibility: A Study in Greek Values.* Chicago: The University of Chicago Press, 1975.

Aquinas, St. Thomas. *Treatise on the Virtues.* Translated by John A. Oesterle. Notre Dame: University of Notre Dame Press, 1984.

Boardman, John, Jasper Griffin, and Oswyn Murray. *The Oxford History of Greece and the Hellenistic World.* Oxford: Oxford University Press, 2001.

Bourke, Vernon J. *History of Ethics: Volume 1 Graeco-Roman to Early Modern Ethics.* Mount Jackson: Axios Press, 1968.

Copleston, Frederick. *Greece and Rome: From the Pre-Socratics to Plotinus.* Vol. 1 of *A History of Philosophy.* Westminster: Newman Press, 1946.

Dover, K.J. *Greek Popular Morality in the Time of Plato and Aristotle.* Indianapolis: Hackett Publishing Co., 1974.

Ferguson, John. *Morals and Values in Ancient Greece.* London: Bristol Classical Press, 1989.

Gottlieb, Anthony. *The Dream of Reason: A History of Western Philosophy from the Greeks to the Renaissance.* New York: W.W. Norton & Company, 2016.

Hadot, Pierre. *What Is Ancient Philosophy?* Translated by Michael Chase. Cambridge: Harvard University Press, 2002.

———. *Philosophy as a Way of Life.* Translated by Michael Chase. Malden: Blackwell Publishing, 1995.

Hall, Jonathan M. *A History of the Archaic Greek World ca. 1200-479 BCE.* Malden: Blackwell Publishing, 2007.

Kenny, Anthony. *Ancient Philosophy.* Vol. 1 of *A New History of Western Philosophy.* Oxford: Oxford University Press, 2004.

Jaeger, Werner. *Paideia: The Ideals of Greek Culture.* Translated by Gilbert Highet. 2nd ed. 3 vols. New York: Oxford University Press, 1945.

———. *Early Christianity and Greek Paideia.* Cambridge: Harvard University Press, 1961.

Kreeft, Peter. *Back to Virtue.* San Francisco: Ignatius Press, 1992.

Lesky, Albin. *A History of Greek Literature.* Translated by Cornelis de Heer and James Willes. Indianapolis: Hackett Publishing Company, 1996.

Martin, Thomas R. *Ancient Greece: From Prehistoric to Hellenistic Times.* New Haven: Yale University Press, 1996.

MacIntyre, Alasdair. *After Virtue.* 3rd ed. Notre Dame: University of Notre Dame Press, 2007.

Miller, Stephen G. *Arete: Greek Sports from Ancient Sources.* Berkeley: University of California Press, 2004.

Myer, Susan Sauvé. *Ancient Ethics: A Critical Introduction.* New York: Routledge, 2008.

Nagy, Gregory. *The Best of the Achaeans: Concepts of the Hero in Archaic Greek Poetry.* Baltimore: The Johns Hopkins University Press, 1979.

———. *The Ancient Greek Hero in 24 Hours.* Cambridge: Harvard University Press, 2013.

Pearson, Lionel. *Popular Ethics in Ancient Greece.* Stanford: Stanford University Press, 1962.

Pope Benedict XVI. *The Virtues.* Huntington: Our Sunday Visitor, 2010.

Ricks, Thomas E. *First Principles: What America's Founders Learned from the Greeks and Romans That Shaped Our Country.* New York: Harper, 2020.

Schafer-Landau, Russ. *Ethical Theory: An Anthology.* 2nd ed. Oxford: Blackwell Publishers, 2013.

The Classics Cave. *Happiness: What the Ancient Greeks Thought and Said about Happiness.* Sugar Land: The Classics Cave, 2021.

Young, Tim J. *A Hero's Wish: What Homer Believed about Happiness and the Good Life.* Sugar Land: EuZōn Media, 2015.

Will you help the Cave?

- **Talk** to friends and family about Cave books and other offerings at the Cave (www.theclassicscave.com).
- Leave a **positive review** online.
- **Write us** at contact@theclassicscave.com to let us know how you've benefited from our work.

THE CLASSICS CAVE is a small, shoestring operation, on fire to spread the wisdom and ways of ancient literature. We **rely on you**, the friend of the Cave, to let people know how you liked and benefited from what we're doing. We also **depend on you to improve our books**. Did you see something that requires editing? Something we got wrong? Something we need to add? Despite our great effort and care to get everything right, it happens. So please **let us know** by emailing us at contact@theclassicscave.com. Otherwise, **support our mission** to spread the wisdom and ways of ancient literature by reading more from the Cave and visiting our ever-growing collection of online material at www.theclassicscave.com.

Read and enjoy more from **Hesiod**!

If you benefited from *Aretē: Excellence or Virtue*, you may wish to pick up another Cave book. There are many now available and many on the way. Visit the Cave at www.theclassicscave.com.

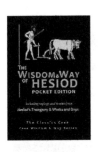

www.theclassicscave.com

Looking for the **best books** ever?

Hunting for **wisdom** and **ways** that
are time-tested and people-approved?

When you read a Cave book, an ancient classic,
you'll have a better idea about where you're
going in life and how to get there.

You'll feel smarter. Be wiser.
And if you practice what you've encountered,
you'll live a better life. Be a little happier.

Choose a book from one of **our series**. The Best of Series. The Wisdom & Way Series. The Workbook & Journal Series. The Cave Sparks (Conversation Starters) Series. And more! **You'll be glad you did!**

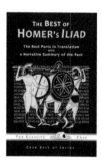
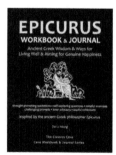
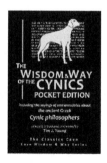

www.theclassicscave.com

Printed in Great Britain
by Amazon

25099298R00189